DECISION FOR EUROPE
The Necessity of Britain's Engagement

DECISION FOR EUROPE
The Necessity of Britain's Engagement

J. L. ZARING

The Johns Hopkins Press   Baltimore

PREFACE

This book is primarily a statement of a point of view regarding critical issues of power politics in western Europe in the late 1960s. Many of these issues have grown out of and will be decided by the outcome of intricate and often tedious disputes going on within and around the European Community. When I started, my plan was to focus mainly on the larger issues which involve neither more nor less than a contest to determine what forces will be dominant in Europe by the end of the century. However, in discussing my views with others, I found myself engaged in first trying to explain what the European Community is, what it stands for, and where it seems to be going. Without some measure of agreement on these fundamentals, the discussion would quickly degenerate into noncommunication.

I have therefore felt compelled to compromise my initial intention and provide a picture of how the community came into being, how it works, and what it has accomplished. Thus, in Parts I and II I have discussed the economic and political status of the community as it exists a decade after the Rome treaties came into effect. While the expert may find some familiar material in these sections, they will remind him of and introduce the general reader to the background necessary for my thesis regarding the critical necessity of Britain's admission to the Common Market, and they have allowed me to fortify my case with the central premise: the importance of preserving the community. The penalty of this approach is the somewhat too abbreviated final part of the book in which I have tried to put the community issues and their outcome in a European, Atlantic, and global context.

The European Community has inspired an impressive and growing volume of literature. I cannot pretend to be familiar with more than a small portion of it. Moreover, source materials are so plentiful that it is difficult to be certain who first distilled a particular insight and to give sufficient credit. To those unacknowledged ones who have become not only the bibiliography of the community, but also, in a real sense part of the community undertaking itself, I hereby acknowledge a debt.

There are several to whom I am especially indebted: Henry S. Myers, whose sharp eye for relevant materials and even sharper eye for the dubious conclusion is reflected throughout the book; Thomas W. Fina, and Victor B. Sullam, both of whom read the manuscript and were more than generous with their time, interest, and support; Robert E. Osgood, who invited me to the Washington Center of Foreign Policy Research of The Johns Hopkins University School of Advanced International Studies, thereby providing the necessary time and stimulating atmosphere; and finally, my wife, whose knowledge of and interest in Europe—and general sustenance—greatly enlarged whatever capacities I brought to this undertaking. None of these is, of course, to blame where I am wrong.

Washington, D.C.
September 5, 1968

J. L. ZARING

CONTENTS

DECISION FOR EUROPE
The Necessity of Britain's Engagement

I

THE PERSPECTIVE

For the better part of a quarter century, much of western Europe—
with the active support of the United States—has engaged itself in
a collective effort to create an effective economic and political organization from the suspected obsolescence of the European city-states.
When measured against the customary ingredients of "realistic"
policy, this inspired, if extravagant, enterprise has been doomed to
failure again and again. Massive misjudgments of the requirements
of such a union have followed one upon the other, and some of the
mistakes have been made more than once. It was accepted only belatedly and reluctantly, for example, that the agrarianization and
degradation of Germany would be an insupportable burden for any
union. And twice—with the abortive defense community and multilateral force projects—an untimely movement toward German military parity put an equally insupportable burden on European cohesion.

In large part because Britain could not agree that the essence of
unification is the acceptance of common constraints on freedom of
action, there was in the early postwar years no effective technique for
advancing toward unity, and the results were the disappointments
of the Council of Europe and other such high-minded undertakings.
When a technique was finally devised in the Schuman plan, the con-
currence was confined to the six signatories of the Treaty of Paris,
and the crises which have erupted periodically since then are only
the more dramatic manifestations of the lack of consensus even
among the Six on the objectives of union and the means to approach
it. The seemingly intransigent problems of the Common Market's

internal organization, the unresolved issues of how the community's institutions shall function and evolve, and the deadlock on whether and how the community will be extended attest to the persistence of basic differences.

Nevertheless, from the generation of effort put into the attempt to create a European union the only consequence of current significance is the European Community. As Jean Monnet foresaw when the Coal-Steel Community was being organized in 1952, the community movement was and would remain the core of the unification movement. "Europe is," he then said, "the united Europe which is about to be born, the ensemble of institutions which we are now setting up. As yet it is a small thing, but it is the only real center of European action and construction. It will be possible to enrich it with new functions and to extend it geographically, but today it is only this community and what we shall be able to do with it and through it. . . ."[1]

In January 1968, however, a few months after he had sat hopefully in the gallery of the House of Commons to hear the debate which affirmed Britain's acceptance of Europe and the community as its intended future vocation, and just a month after de Gaulle had for the second time vetoed that intention, Monnet told a moved and sympathetic audience in Saarbrücken that he was no longer optimistic for the future of Europe. Noting with regret Britain's voluntary absence for so many years from the community undertaking, but excoriating de Gaulle for having again denied Europe's most democratic people the chance to take up its European role when it had finally decided to do so, Monnet declared that France had deprived Europe of the means to achieve the very objective the Gaullists had professed to wish—a Europe capable of competing with the Soviet Union and the United States. But Monnet advised his listeners to uphold the community as the only real center of European action and construction. "A deadly blow would be struck at our community and at this work of European unification," he said, "if solutions really were to be sought in the old forms of cooperation and association."[2]

This book is about the outlook for this enterprise which has always inspired just such hope and despair. On July 1, 1968, the Common Market, which for all practical purposes *is* the community, achieved

[1] Quoted in Altiero Spinelli, *The Eurocrats* (Baltimore: The Johns Hopkins Press, 1966), p. v.
[2] *Christian Science Monitor*, January 30, 1968.

one of its prime objectives: the completion of the customs union. On the same date, a truly federal system for the regulation of agriculture and trade in nearly all agricultural products was complete and in effect, and within a matter of weeks thereafter, regulations were approved permitting a community worker to seek and accept employment anywhere in the community, substantially without restriction. The "technocrats" of Brussels, looking back over the previous decade, could also have pointed with pride to numerous other ways in which the Coal-Steel Community had become, as Monnet had hoped, an economic and political entity—sufficient, were it allowed to do so, to lead to the profound European renovation which the integration movement had as its goal.

Yet, there were few celebrants on July 1—not merely because of a new confrontation with France at the time, but because of general recognition that the community is gripped by a crisis of confidence and stagnation in which it is possible to see harbingers of an ultimate failure. As frustrations have mounted, competing objectives (national independence, hegemony, alternative allegiances or groupings) have become more attractive and threaten to divert members and candidates for membership into undertakings more "realistic" than the community. European leaders perceive "renationalization" as a prospect just when the old European system of national rivalries, shifting alliances, and temporary equilibriums seemed decisively rejected as hopelessly outmoded. We are confronted, as the London *Times* has put it, with a "desiccated" Europe[3]—an ideal of harmony through unity from which all substance has evaporated.

The faltering of momentum principally since 1966 is much more serious than any of the celebrated crises of the past. The collapse of the European Defense Community only destroyed what did not exist; the subsequent negotiations of the Western European Union seemed at the time a significant new British involvement on the continent, and it permitted the rehabilitation of Germany to proceed by other means and without disastrous repercussions on the balance of European power. However unjustified de Gaulle's first exclusion of Britain from the Common Market, a period of apparent consolidation of the market's internal organization ensued. Even though the "great crisis" of 1965–66 removed any lingering illusions that de Gaulle still accepted the community's goals, it could be taken in its origins as symp-

---

[3] *The Times* (London), February 29, 1968.

tomatic of a successful working of the community technique—and in its outcome as by no means a defeat.

The crisis of the late 1960s is of a different order, if only because there is more history behind it and more at stake. The status quo of the community cannot be sustained: It must either go forward or go back. To go forward, the members must accept new undertakings which clearly imply substantial new derogations from national sovereignty and the delegation of new powers to central institutions under democratic control. The alternative is the community's continued stagnation and eventual decline—and not necessarily into an innocuous desuetude which, from the point of view of nonmembers, might be the happier outcome, but to the use that its most powerful member or members might contrive to make of this combination of resources.

The case for the possibility that Europe may still avoid the second alternative is set forth in the chapters which follow. The argument has four main points:

(1) The European Community, which operates primarily in the economic arena, has, by extending the area of interdependence and narrowing the possibility of national action, created a vacuum which is both the imperative and the incentive to further economic and political integration.

(2) The political system envisaged by the community—combining a certain balance of power among the members with an independent representation of the common interest and the progressive introduction of majority decisions—provided an effective means by which that vacuum was being filled until the system's normal operation and further evolution were challenged by de Gaulle.

(3) Despite the growing awareness in major economic sectors and in public opinion of the community's significance to individual well-being, this indentification of interest has yet to produce the supranational political action centers on which the community can rely for sustenance. Hence its future still depends on deliberate moves by the nation-states to recreate a climate favorable to the resumption of the integration process.

(4) Since the process of integration can resume only in a community of sufficient size, diversity, and balance that the threat of withdrawal by any one member is no longer a mortal threat, the community will find the means of its survival only in its extension. The community which was founded on the premise of openness cannot

become a closed one; above all it cannot exclude Britain, becoming thereby a coalition against it.

In putting forth the opinion that Britain's European engagement is the crucial decision which Europe faces today, one is of course painfully aware of the rapidity with which Europe's circumstances can change. By mid-1967, Wilson had made remarkably well the new case for Britain's admission to the Common Market; the prescribed procedures for the handling of such applications had been initiated; and the Commission's subsequent opinion was an unequivocal call for the opening of talks. By December, however, Britain's payments crisis had become full-blown, the Elysee had seized on sterling's devaluation to declare the British candidacy unacceptable, and the long-standing campaign to unseat sterling and the dollar as reserve currencies was renewed. By May 1968, the general strike in France had revealed the grandeur of Gaullist France scarcely more substantial than the washed faces it had put on the national monuments in Paris, and the Gaullist pretension to European ascendancy looked more preposterous than ever. And by late summer, the Soviet repression in Czechoslovakia of the hopeful trend toward liberalization in eastern Europe had recreated the atmosphere on which, sadly enough, Western solidarity in the past has tended to thrive.

Thus within the space of a few months radical changes can be wrought on the face of Europe, and some further time will have to pass before it is clear what lasting impact the changes we have recently experienced will have. A weaker France need not necessarily mean the restoration of a new and healthier equilibrium in western Europe. The belated program of social expenditure to which the Gaullist government resorted to preserve its tenure will not make economic union in the community necessarily easier to achieve. One can hope but scarcely expect that a chastened de Gaulle or a Gaullist successor will look with greater respect and sympathy on the problems and aspirations of the British rival. Nor is it very clear that the renewed sense of danger will serve to put the presumed obstacles to a resumption of progress toward unity in more hopeful perspective.

If, however, we have now entered upon a period in Europe which is more fluid and less predictable than we have lately become accustomed to, the very uncertainty may reinforce the message of this book: that the only focus of European regional stability which holds any great promise for the future is the European Community system;

that history will record among the items in de Gaulle's legacy to Europe the precious time lost while he sought to undermine that system; and that, for the first time in the two decades since the British reneged on their promise to Europe, it is London which has the best possibility of keeping alive the ideal of Europe's unification.

Part I: The Economic Community

II THE COMMUNITY OF REGULATIONS

An introductory overview of the community's successes and failures in the economic sphere, as well as the political content and implication of them, must begin with a discussion of the "community of regulations." These regulations—decisions taken, policies approved, and mechanisms set up on the foundation of the Rome treaties—constitute together the community's specific achievements. They have as their object the removal of barriers to economic activity among the member states and the institution of common rules applicable to such activity. The "mission" of the resulting union, as set forth in the EEC treaty, is to promote a harmonious economic development, continuous and balanced expansion, increased stability, a more rapid improvement in standards of living, and in general, closer relations among the member states.

The community has become so vast and complex an enterprise that this review of its regulations will be at best a partial one. The development of the Coal-Steel Community will be referred to only tangentially, and major achievements in EURATOM—such as its establishment of an effective safeguards system, the operation of its nuclear materials supply agency, and its administration of a research program—will be passed over here. However, since the future of the economic community rests primarily on the organization of the internal market, our concentration on this in this chapter will permit us to assess in the following one how well the community has fulfilled its intended economic mission, and it will make it more evident why the gap between potential and realization has become so discouraging and dangerous.

THE CUSTOMS UNION

In a number of important respects, the Common Market is accomplished fact,[1] particularly where its treaty called for the achievement of specific objectives at specified times. This is notably the case with the establishment of the customs union for industrial raw materials and manufactured products. In eight decrements, two of them effected ahead of the schedule provided in the treaty, the member states have progressively reduced the tariff rates from those obtaining in 1957 when the Common Market was established. On July 1, 1968, the remaining 15 percent of the old rates was removed, and the third and final adjustment of tariffs applied to imports from nonmembers was made. Thus, free trade among the member countries and a common charge on imports from outsiders were simultaneously instituted eighteen months before the expiration of the minimum transitional period the treaty envisaged. According to community calculations, the common external tariff on industrial imports—reduced considerably by the Kennedy Round negotiations—averaged about 10.7 percent when it went into effect on July 1 and will decline to about 7.6 percent when the Kennedy Round reductions are fully in force in 1972.[2]

By July 1, 1968, other obstacles to free trade within the Common Market in industrial products had also been removed. Quantitative controls on internal trade had been virtually abolished, and considerable progress had been made toward eliminating controls or charges with effects similar to quotas or tariffs.[3] The impediments in question range from comparatively simple matters (various types of countervailing duties; packaging, marking, and testing requirements; and regulations on public health, safety, and morals) to the complex problems involved in liberalizing government procurement regulations and adjusting or eliminating state monopolies in oil, alcohol, and to-

[1] For details of the earlier developments in the community, see U. W. Kitzinger, *The Politics and Economics of European Integration* (New York: Frederick A. Praeger, 1963). See also European Economic Community Commission, *Tenth General Report on the Activities of the Community—1 April 1966–31 March 1967* (Brussels: Publishing Services of the European Communities, June 1967). (Hereafter cited as *Tenth General Report*.) For a concise but generally nonevaluative review of the community's accomplishments during 1967, see the European Commission Spokesman's Group, "Taking Stock in 1967," *Europe Agence Internationale d'Information pour la Presse* (Brussels, December 29, 1967), Europe Document No. 457. (Hereafter cited as *Agence Europe*.)

[2] See Community Press Release, "Deadline: July 1, 1968; Common Market's Customs Union Complete," *News from the European Community* (Washington, D.C.: European Community Information Service, June 14, 1968).

[3] For comment on the significance of the "emergency measures" put into effect in France at the end of June 1968, see Chapter VI.

bacco. The Commission has long sought to bring these "technical obstacles" under restraint and has been working on a program which would call for their abolition by 1970.[4] Even if this is achieved, however, the effective elimination of trade borders in a broader sense is a more distant and illusive objective.

The removal of interstate tariffs and the initiation of nominally free circulation of goods within the community has also required the community authorities to move toward the creation of a single customs jurisdiction—in fact, if not in form. In preparation for this, the Commission had, prior to July 1, 1968, proposed a number of regulations designed to minimize the need for any border formalities,[5] and eventually to permit the community importer to choose his port of entry on the basis of cost and convenience considerations alone. Some of these regulations would be based on close cooperation among the customs administrations of the various states with a provision for supervisory and adjudicating mechanisms in case of disputes. Certain common standards or rules would be instituted, for example, on valuation procedures, the definition of origin of goods, and the conditions for the admission of goods in transit or for storage or processing. Other regulations would require direct community administration— for instance, the enforcement of antidumping measures, community liberalization lists, or the management of tariff quotas either retained by some of the members or granted by the community itself in the Kennedy Round.

Measures such as these are among the basic instruments with which any modern nation controls its foreign trade, and taken together, they would constitute an essential element of the common commercial policy which the Rome treaties require the community to adopt by 1970. It is therefore understandable that the regulations have been sharply disputed and that only the more urgent ones were accepted by July 1. Some of the remaining regulations will no doubt be adopted, but the difficulties so far encountered make it all too evident that the only way to harmonize the administration of customs totally is to institute a *community* collection system.

THE AGRICULTURAL MARKET

Parallel with the introduction of internally free trade in industrial items, the community has also had since July 1968 a common agri-

---

[4] *Tenth General Report,* p. 18.
[5] *Ibid.,* pp. 16–17.

13

cultural policy (CAP), the result of ten years of tedious negotiation and violent conflict. The major agreements are the January 1962 decision on the basic plan for the agricultural market and for the market organizations for cereals, pork, eggs and poultry, fruits, vegetables and wine; the December 1963 agreements on the markets for beef and veal, dairy products, and rice, and on the establishment of the Agricultural Guidance and Guarantee Fund (FEOGA); the December 1964 compromise on how to unify grain prices throughout the community; the May and July 1966 agreements fixing the common prices of certain additional products, arranging financing for FEOGA for the remainder of the transitional period, and setting July 1, 1968 as the deadline for completing the introduction of internal free trade in the major farm products; and the May 1968 agreements on meat, milk, and dairy prices which, reached at the eleventh hour, made it possible to fulfill the July commitment.

A description of the immensely complex arrangements by which the community has succeeded in meeting the treaty obligation to extend the common market to agriculture would be tedious. Suffice it to note that the system is based on the concept of regulated prices as the controlling mechanism in the market. Target prices are established for each major product for each marketing year. The producer is assured against drastic price fluctuations by the obligation of the public authorities to purchase any amount he may offer at intervention or support prices—some 5 to 10 percent below the target prices. He is likewise protected against price competition from abroad by threshold or minimum import prices and variable import levies, which bring import prices up to the community level. There are, of course, variations in these basic arrangements by products. In some cases, quality norms and ordinary tariffs are used in conjunction with or instead of levies, and for some few products, the precise final arrangements are yet to be decided upon.

It is important to recognize the extent to which the system is in fact a community one. The national quota, licensing, tariff, and state-trading arrangements which characterized the regulation of agricultural trade in the member countries prior to the Common Market have for the most part been replaced by the CAP arrangements. In the formulation and administration of that policy, the community's powers are comparable to those disposed of by the U.S. federal government, and they are more *dirigiste* and less subject to parliamentary control. The FEOGA, the community agency which

14

sustains the entire program, has budgeted close to $2 billion for the financing of market supports, export subsidies, and structural farm improvements in the 1967–68 crop year. With the adoption in May 1968 of a margarine tax, the CAP has for the first time acquired an independent, if limited, source of revenue.[6]

THE LABOR MARKET

The Rome treaties also provided for the establishment of community-wide free movement of workers, entrepreneurs, and capital. The community's progress in these areas has also been extensive, although not as impressive as in agriculture.

Despite alarmist predictions of mass migrations of workers, steps toward the creation of a community labor market were taken as early as 1961—facilitated no doubt by the acute demand for labor at that time. The 1961 regulation provided in general for the abolition of national quota restrictions on admissions of foreign employees, made job vacancies still unfilled after a short period of time available to community applicants, gave such workers certain rights to automatic renewal of work permits, and guaranteed their families and children rights of residence and access to educational opportunities. These provisions were further liberalized in 1964. A third basic directive, approved in July 1968, calls for the elimination of work permits, the abolishment—subject only to limited *community*-administered safeguards—of any national discrimination on access to jobs, and the guarantee that migrant workers in any member country will receive social benefits and tax treatment equal to those accorded the country's nationals.[7]

Community programs have also sought actively to encourage labor mobility and to create conditions conducive to it. Among these measures are the Commission's informational and statistical reports on employment opportunities and working conditions; the attempts to improve national placement services and the establishment of clearance machinery for intracommunity job applications; efforts to encourage harmonization of national legislation or practices in the so-

[6] The U.S. Department of Agriculture's Foreign Agricultural Service has published numerous analyses of the CAP. See, for example, "The EEC's Common Agricultural Policy Is Nearly Completed," *Foreign Agriculture*, August 15, 1966, p. 7; "Financial Implications of the EEC's Common Agricultural Policy," *Foreign Agriculture*, October 31, 1966, p. 5.

[7] See *Agence Europe*, July 30, 1968, for a detailed summary of this important step toward the creation of a true community labor market.

cial field; and more recently, the increased interest in furthering scientific and technological training. Moreover, from 1960 through 1967, the European Social Fund subsidized national retraining and resettlement programs to the extent of about $60 million.

All in all, these measures have no doubt tended to improve working conditions within the community, to ease the social cost of adjustment to a larger market, and to facilitate the creation of a labor market which, in years of high economic activity such as 1966, has filled well over a half-million job vacancies with nonnational workers. Nonetheless, whether these activities add up to a farsighted community social policy is very much at issue, and what direction that policy should take in the future is one of the key issues the community must decide.

FREEDOM TO DO BUSINESS

To secure to entrepreneurs and to the professions the opportunities which a large market ought to provide has proved more difficult than the treaty had anticipated. A timetable for the removal of intracommunity obstacles to the supply of services and to the establishment of businesses was adopted in 1961, but the program has lagged since then. The problems involved are delicate ones: Professional standards vary from country to country; mutual recognition of qualifications must be obtained; there is often wide variation among national requirements for the opening of a business, and the administration of these regulations can in some cases be highly restrictive. Moreover, as the Commission noted in its *Tenth General Report* of June 1967, once agreement is reached on community standards, verification of national compliance and nondiscriminatory application is still required.[8]

Community discussion on the so-called "freedom of establishment" has since 1965 increasingly focused on the question of the need for a "European company law." The obstacles which many kinds of firms face in forming combinations, amalgamating, or in setting up subsidiaries or branches in other member states have been reduced; conventions on mutual recognition of companies, on international bankruptcy law, and on jurisdiction and execution of judgments in civil and commercial cases have been drafted; and progress is being made toward coordinating the national provisions on the incorpora-

[8] *Tenth General Report*, pp. 20–21.

tion of companies. Nevertheless, it has been widely felt that the existence of some kind of community incorporation legislation would greatly facilitate the doing of business on a community-wide basis, would permit associations and forms of company organization now hampered by national regulations and tax laws, and would in general encourage the establishment of corporations with sufficient capital and technical resources to compete effectively outside, as well as within, the Common Market.

Whether and in what form such facilities will become available—with all this would imply for the creation of a truly multinational economy—has not been decided. In 1965 the French urged that measures of this sort be put into effect through the negotiation of an ordinary convention which would oblige the member states to pass uniform *national* legislation for the incorporation of European-type companies. Paris has in consequence been cool to the *European* statute approach which the Commission has sponsored. All parties are aware that community legislation in this field would not only have important implications for existing national legislation, but would also generate further pressures for community legislation in related fields—such as taxation or social policy. Unless European incorporation is easy and advantageous, the purpose of the exercise is obviously defeated. But, without some limitations on access to this device and some harmonization of its provisions with existing corporate law, the European company might become an attractive way to avoid, or evade, national laws which, for instance, require worker co-management or ownership or the registration (for tax enforcement) of share ownership.[9]

THE CAPITAL MARKET

The removal of restrictions on the free movement of capital is similarly an area in which, after an initial surge of activity, progress has become increasingly difficult. Directives issued in 1960 and 1962 provided for unconditional liberalization of direct investments, real estate investments, movements of personal capital, short- and

---

[9] In the spring of 1966, the Commission submitted to the Council a memorandum setting forth its response to the earlier French proposals and suggesting alternatives to them. A summary of this memo is contained in *Agence Europe*, May 5, 1966. Upon receiving and studying this memo the Council thereafter appointed a working group chaired by Professor P. Sanders of the Rotterdam Faculty of Law to consider further the possibilities for a European company law. A summary of the Sanders report is contained in *Agence Europe*, May 2–3, 1967.

medium-term credits for commercial transactions involving residents, and payments for securities quoted on stock exchanges. Other capital movements, such as the issue of foreign securities, dealings in non-quoted securities, and loans not involving residents have been con-ditionally liberalized—i.e., the member states may, after consulting the Commission, reimpose restrictions in the interest of safeguarding their economic stability. Short-term financial operations, such as the purchase of foreign treasury bills and credits not involved in commer-cial transactions, have not been liberalized.

Since these early moves, the Commission has continued to press for a further easing of capital movements, proposing the abolition of all discrimination among community residents in their access to the various capital markets in the member countries. Approval of this further step has been held up, however, principally because the Dutch, Germans, and Belgians have insisted that the French econom-ics minister's retention of power to authorize any financial operation would deprive further liberalization of the necessary reciprocity. Moreover, the new exchange controls put into effect by the French in the wake of the May 1968 upheaval—although not in violation of the earlier community directives on capital movements and osten-sibly temporary—have obviously been a psychological setback.[10]

The problems which the community has had in achieving complete liberation of capital movements are illustrative of the most charac-teristic tendency of the community's development: the difficulty of resolving any particular issue or of scoring any advance in isolation. To achieve even the specific goals of the Rome treaties, such as the customs union and the mobility of labor, capital, and enterprise with-in it, has required the Common Market to move ahead more or less contemporaneously on a wide front on the basis of agreements of progressively greater depth and detail on common policy objec-tives. To reach agreement on the various common policies which the treaty calls for—social, transport, commercial, etc.—has increasingly engaged the member states and the community's institutions in the search for a broad consensus which is the rough equivalent of the public policy of any modern state. Thus, integration has been both a horizontal and vertical process. Current achievements have of

---

[10] The measures required to free capital movements and to establish a real European capital market have been examined at great length by an expert committee appointed by the Commission. Its findings are available in a report entitled *The Development of a European Capital Market*, also known as the Segré Report.

necessity required some concept—perhaps an unconscious one—of Europe's future shape and direction.

COMPETITION POLICY

The attempts to enforce the treaty restrictions on monopolies and agreements in restraint of trade is a further example of this. In December 1961 the community adopted the first regulations to implement the treaty articles which prohibit agreements restricting or distorting competition, but exempting those agreements which contribute to improvement in the production or distribution of goods or which promote economic or technical progress. These regulations reaffirmed in effect the automatic applicability of the treaty prohibitions, but, by setting up a procedure for the notification of industrial agreements, gave to the Commission and the Court of Justice a discretionary authority. With notifications pursuant to this and later regulations approaching the 40,000 mark, the Commission has been forced to resort to block exemptions for innocuous agreements. Even so, well over half the cases before it remained to be settled at the beginning of 1968.[11]

Nevertheless, Commission advisories and opinions and several Court cases are a start toward the creation of something comparable to U.S. antimonopoly jurisprudence, and in fact, Article 85—as well as Article 86 prohibiting "improper exploitation of a dominant position" in interstate commerce—are philosophically derivative from the U.S. experience. The community approach to competition, however, has always reflected two special considerations: (1) the significance of the member states and their activities as competition-restricting factors in community commerce, and (2) the recognition that legitimate combinations are one of the desirable objectives of economic union. The treaties thus take into account not only private sources of unfair competition but also public by covering the policies of public enterprises and utilities. The member states are enjoined from granting subsidies and aids which distort competition in interstate commerce; and harmonization of national legislation is envisaged to the extent required to equalize the burdens imposed or the advantages conferred on "home" industries by such legislation. Thus the decision

[11] The Commission has been especially eager to find means of encouraging company agreements which facilitate rationalization, technical cooperation, and scientific research and in mid-July issued a "communication" defining a variety of such agreements which are "legal." Other such exemptions are contemplated. A summary of the latest "communication" is available in *Agence Europe*, July 22, 1968, p. 10.

taken in February 1967 to adopt a value-added system of turnover taxes—important from a fiscal viewpoint—was also a noteworthy step toward equalizing the conditions under which community firms will in the future compete with each other.

The salient feature, however, of the community's emerging policy on competition—initially conceived as a weapon for *preventing* cartelization from defeating the purposes of the larger market—is the extent to which it has become an instrument for *attaining* those purposes. In the *Tenth General Report*, the Commission wrote: "Stated simply, the objective of the common industrial policy is to strengthen the competitive power of European industry. The maintenance and strengthening of competition within the Common Market undoubtedly play a substantial part in achieving this objective."[12] But, as the Commission made clear, fair trade practices are only one element of an effective industrial policy. It must also include the approval of the European company legislation (which would facilitate certain kinds of mergers and combinations), the creation of a European capital market (which would permit the growth of firms capable of competing in and out of the community), and the coordination of structural and regional policies (to facilitate the adaptation of specific industries or of whole areas to the larger competitive framework the EEC is trying to construct).

REGULATION OF TRANSPORTATION

The same concept of the community as a general renovating process, a concept vigorously promoted by the Commission, has also contributed an additional sense of urgency to the efforts to end the long impasse in the instituting of common transport and energy policies.

The Rome treaty provided for the abolition of any discrimination in rates or conditions of transport based on the national origin or destination of goods and for the cessation of any favorable treatment which the states may accord specific industries in transport rates or conditions. By and large, these "negative" objectives have been achieved in the transport industries to which the treaty is applicable (i.e., the road, rail, and inland waterway carriers), but surveillance must of course continue. However, the treaty also set forth certain "positive" goals: the institution within the framework of a common transport policy of "common rules applicable to international transport" and the establishment of "conditions for the admission of non-

[12] *Tenth General Report*, p. 38.

resident carriers to national transport services within the member states." For a number of reasons, this community-regulated and -organized transport market has not materialized—not least of all because of extensive state intervention (regulation, protection, subsidization, and public ownership), which has historically prevailed in the transport industry, along with fairly extensive international regulations such as that which resulted from the Mannheim Convention on the Rhine. As a result, the rights of establishment have not applied to the provision of transport services, optimum competition between means of transport and among the various carriers has not developed, and transport costs and regulations have remained an unnecessarily large obstacle to competition generally.

A detailed account of the tangled web of the transport negotiations since the early 1960s would interest only the specialist, but for those inclined to dismiss the Common Market as a mere customs union, the scope of the kind of regulation under consideration may come as a surprise. The three-part program proposed by the Commission in May 1963 called for the establishment of minimum and maximum freight rates, the opening of community quotas on haulage between states, and harmonization of the conditions of competition in the transport industry. The transport policy which was approved by the Council in June 1965 had the following key features: a more flexible rate-bracket system which would go into effect at the same time as community quotas on haulage, a timetable for the preparation of basic community regulations (e.g., on road taxation, social conditions in the industry, state aids, allocation of infrastructure costs, etc.); and provision for a market supervision committee to assist the Commission in the exercise of its jurisdiction over domestic and interstate commerce.

These two programs proved too large a chunk of federalism to be swallowed by the member states. The measures proposed for further consideration in a December 1967 agreement are considerably more modest, and due in part to the onset of the crisis in France the following May, the agreed July 1968 deadline for approval even of these could not be fully met. Even so, the seven-odd priority regulations, five of which have been approved, are significant: a system of minimum and maximum rates for interstate transport of goods by truck, a community quota for trucks authorized to do interstate hauling, regulation of working conditions in the trucking industry, rules on fair trade practices in transport, controls over state aids, abolition of double taxing in interstate trucking, and revocation of taxes on fuels in truck tanks.[13] Several additional measures being pushed by the Commission—such as capacity controls for road and water transport, sharing of infrastructure costs among road users, and harmonization of the public obligations of transport utilities—would constitute a meaningful interim program. Some of the outstanding regulations will likely be approved by 1970, but it is difficult to forecast when and if a comprehensive policy will be effected. The lengthy delays already encountered have encouraged some of the members to try to deal with their transport problems unilaterally, and in an area in which national regulation is tradition, it will not be easy to decide what precise powers a community "interstate commerce commission" should ultimately have.

THE ENERGY MARKET

The difficulty of delineating a community role in areas where public intervention is already large also accounts considerably for the prolonged stalemate in energy policy. In this instance, however, the problem has been complicated by the inadequacy of treaty provisions, the unusually severe economic and social problems to which the declining coal industry has given rise, the power and influence of the international oil companies, and the possibly exaggerated concern of the national authorities (citing military as well as economic exigencies) for security of access to supplies.

With the exception of a brief protocol and the inclusion of petroleum on the list of products on which no agreement for a common external tariff could be reached, the EEC treaty contains no special provisions on energy and sets forth no concept of a market similar to that envisaged for agriculture or transport. In consequence, the EEC has been able to function in the energy sector only by virtue of the general treaty provisions, and two energy sources—nuclear and coal—come under the purview of EURATOM and the CSC. In 1959 an Inter-Executive Committee on Energy was set up to coordinate respective jurisdictions, and in 1967 when the executives of the three communities were merged, energy was at long last placed under a single Commission directorate. But the basic defect—the absence of broad, treaty guidelines for an energy policy—cannot be remedied until the projected merger of the three treaties takes place, probably not until the 1970s.

[13] *Agence Europe*, July 19, 1968.

Nevertheless, there has been no lack of community activity in the energy sector. Customs duties on trade in oil and oil products within the community were abolished at the end of 1964, for example, but free circulation of these products is still impeded by the well-known obstacles, of which the French oil import monopoly and the self-imposed import quotas the German companies enforce are only the more notorious examples. As early as 1958 the High Authority had removed all of the usual restraints on intracommunity trade in coal and coke. But the CSC's main preoccupation in recent years has been to preserve some influence over the market in the face of the largely unanticipated glut of coal which first appeared in 1958, and, using the inadequate instruments the CSC treaty provides, to assist the coal industries to adapt to the competitive inroads of oil.

EURATOM has faced a similar situation in its power program—how to sustain an undertaking which was initiated on the basis of much too sanguine projections of nuclear energy needs and costs. The anticipated response from private industry did not materialize and the whole effort to give the development of nuclear industry on the continent a community character was consequently hurt from the beginning.

Given the basic conflict of interest between the member countries which are predominantly importers of energy and those which have substantial assets, and given the adjustments required by the spectacular changes in consumption and production patterns in the energy sector in the past few years,[14] it is conjectural what kind of energy policy will ultimately emerge. Community authorities have bravely upheld the ideal of a competitive market which "will have to lead to completely free movement of energy products." Moreover, the "Protocol of Agreement" on energy, adopted by the CSC Special Council in 1964 as a first step toward a common policy, continued to emphasize the need for cheapness of supply, freedom of choice for the

---

[14] From 1960 to 1967, production of coal in the CSC declined from 237 million tons to 184 million tons, and the number of coal miners dropped over 40 percent—from 547,000 to 322,000. Community-produced coal now accounts for no more than 30 percent of annual energy consumption. On the other hand, consumption of petroleum products has increased so substantially that these now account for nearly half of total energy requirements. However, less than 5 percent of the oil consumed by the community is produced there, and, apart from Japan, no other major economic area is so dependent on foreign imports of oil. Among the conventional fuels, only natural gas production seems likely to make sizeable gains in the community in the next decade, and according to Commission estimates, may by 1980 satisfy up to 13 percent of total energy demand. (See *Agence Europe*, May 24, 1968, p. 11, and May 28, 1968, pp. 9–10.)

consumer, and fair competition among the different energy sources. At the same time, however, the Council accepted the necessity of assuring security of supplies, of avoiding the disruption of "social and regional structures" as a result of shifting demand for particular fuels, and of safeguarding the interests of the workers in particular energy-producing enterprises.

The latter three criteria appear to have carried greater weight in community counsels than the former three, and the trend appears to be toward a highly organized and managed energy market, rather than a free one. The emergency program for coal which was approved in February 1965 has permitted the states— after community authorization—to increase their subsidies to the coal industry every year. In 1967 government aids of this sort came to about $1.4 billion.[15] In some of the member countries, government assistance to ease the burden of social charges has amounted to as much as $7 per ton. Assistance to the coal industry was further extended in 1967 when, for the first time, the community itself provided financing to subsidize the price at which community-produced coke could be made available to the iron and steel industry.

Many of the same tendencies have been evident in the slow evolution of the community's policies on the petroleum and natural gas markets. The memorandum prepared by the Commission in 1966 also makes its bow in the direction of low prices, well-diversified sources on the world market, "judicious development" of community production, and abolition of discrimination based on nationality. Nevertheless, since the memorandum was issued, there have been strong pressures from community interests to make additional support and protective devices available to encourage an "indigenous" petroleum industry, such assistance being denied the internationals by a narrow definition of what constitutes an eligible "community company." Like oil companies elsewhere, those in the community would like tax benefits, subsidies for prospecting, measures to prevent foreign take-over, etc. Thus, one must wonder whether the policies the community eventually adopts on petroleum, on top of those "temporarily" in force for coal, will in fact—as the Commission alleges—enable European consumers to enjoy advantageous prices

[15] "Information Memo" (summary of Commission of the European Communities, *First General Report on the Activities of the Communities, 1966–1967*), February 1, 1968, pp. 5–6.

and "permit establishment of a common energy market *sufficiently open* [sic] to the outside world."[16]

THE PROBLEMS OF A COMMUNITY PUBLIC POLICY

Ideally, the sectoral policies as they exist in the case, for example, of agriculture, or as they may eventually emerge in the case of industry, transport, and energy, should ultimately fit together as subordinate, coherent, and mutually supporting parts of a common economic policy. This goal is, or ought to be, the common concern of every community citizen, even as it is, or ought to be, the prime issue of public debate, discussion, and political activity in any organized society. The community's authorities fully recognize that the Common Market's future effectiveness, stability, and perhaps even its survival as an integrated undertaking depend on the development of adequate mechanisms for regulating, controlling, and directing the community economy as a whole. And they are also aware that the existing mechanisms are increasingly inadequate for the task.

The tempo of economic activity and the allocation of resources is determined by public authorities who use the same means by which any modern country directly or indirectly influences economic activity: taxation and public spending, credit and credit policy, wage and incomes policies, etc. These instruments are mainly in the hands of the member states. In signing the EEC treaty, however, the members accepted (or professed to accept) general and specific restraints on the use of these instruments. They agreed, for example, to the following: the general objectives set out in the preamble; the general purposes of the community mentioned in Article 2 (among them, to "approximate" their economic policies and promote a balanced expansion with increased stability and accelerated rises in the standard of living); the community "activities" listed in Article 3, which, in addition to the creation of the common market, include the "application of procedures which shall make it possible to coordinate the economic policies of the member states and to remedy disequilibria in their balances of payments"; and the general undertaking in Article 5 to take all measures necessary to achieve the treaty objectives.

Other such undertakings, more or less specific, are scattered

---

[16] *Tenth General Report*, p. 42. For a useful, if somewhat uncritical, review of the problems of the common energy policy, see the Spokesman of the CSC's High Authority and the European Community Information Service, *Europe and Energy* (Luxembourg, 1967).

throughout the treaty. In some instances, the member states have gone very far toward accepting *community* jurisdiction over the regulatory devices, such as in the control of foreign trade and in the regulation of agricultural markets and prices. In other instances, the *national* authority remains intact, but the members are legally obliged and to an increasing degree, practically constrained to treat their national policies as matters of community concern. The treaty requires, for example, that the national governments consider their countercyclical policies as a matter of common interest and that they consult with each other and with the Commission on the measures they propose to take. They are likewise obliged to ensure an over-all equilibrium in their balance of payments, to coordinate their economic policies, and to treat their exchange rates as a "matter of common interest."

As the creation of the customs union has proceeded, however, it has seemed more and more imperative to the community's authorities that they use these far-reaching if ambiguous commitments as the basis for the development of a concerted, community economic policy. An important step in this direction was taken in April 1964 when the Council—having seen for the first time in the Italian balance-of-payments crisis that disequilibrium in one member country can spread to the entire community—decided to institute new procedures for giving greater direction to national economic measures. To this end the Council set up several new agencies along side the existing Monetary Committee: a Committee of Central Bank Governors, a Budget Policy Committee, a Short-Term Economic Policy Committee, and a Medium-Term Economic Policy Committee. With the exception of the first, an EEC Commission member sits on each of these committees, and the Commission provides the permanent staff. Their main work is to provide on a regular basis objective data on economic trends in the community, to conduct a continuing confrontation on national economic policies, to make specific policy recommendations, and to draw up long-range policy guidelines—in effect, a "plan." When approved by the Council, Commission proposals based on the recommendations of these committees become, theoretically at least, obligations of the member states.

The work of the Medium-Term Economic Policy Committee has in particular aroused increasing attention. The Committee's first five-year program, which set forth the main lines of economic policy that should be followed and which attempted to assure the mutual consistency of these policy lines, was approved by the Council in February 1967. The program contained a summary of economic projections; it called for a vigorous incomes policy and budgetary and monetary measures to restrain demand; and it urged upon the community the desirability of various measures to increase investment, bring about structural adaptations in industry, and encourage development by regions. The Committee's second draft program, completed and submitted to the Council in March 1968, is in part a sequel to the first, but goes beyond it in evaluating existing policies and proposing new ones to encourage the modernization and rationalization of the community economy. In particular the Committee cautions against measures which would prolong the life of declining industries rather than stimulate those whose future health is more promising, sharply criticizes the overreliance on price supports in the community's farm program, and comes down hard on the need for an increased flow of investment funds as the keystone to an effective structural policy.[17]

The second draft program is therefore another, though cautious, move on the part of the Commission to confer increased authoritativeness and force on the policy recommendations of the Medium-Term Economic Policy Committee. As the Commission described it in the *Tenth General Report*, the Committee's reports should set out the broad lines of economic policy the community and the member states should follow on the basis of sophisticated community forecasting; they should put the individual sectoral policies (social, industrial, agricultural, and commercial) within this framework; and they should identify and illuminate economic problems and objectives for which policies—preferably community ones—should be devised. "Those responsible for the conduct of the community's economic policy must show sufficient imagination to cope with the novelty of the problems raised in each of our countries by the construction of the community. They must take as many liberties as prove necessary with old habits of thought and must not hesitate, should the need arise, to reject them outright: one of the aims of the medium-term policy is to prepare men's minds for the major changes—both inescapable and salutary—which sooner or later will have to be made."[18]

If the economic community is to fulfill its intended mission, there

[17] See *Agence Europe*, March 27, 1968, pp. 3–5.
[18] *Tenth General Report*, p. 31.

can be no doubt that precisely this kind of programmatic policy making is required. But, as we shall see in succeeding chapters, the European Community is unique among the great or potentially great economic powers in the late 1960s in the profusion of decision-making authorities which must approve or respond to centrally determined policies and which may ignore and render them meaningless; it is unique in the flimsiness of the centrally controlled means by which it makes the over-all policy effective; and perhaps only in the Soviet Union are those who decide on central public policy more remote from direct and effective popular control than they are who would perform this role in Brussels today.

III   AN ASSESSMENT OF THE ECONOMIC UNION

From the foregoing review it should be evident that the community of regulations, although an impressive achievement, is nonetheless far from completion and perfection. However, since these regulations are not ends in themselves but steps toward an economic and political union, it is not easy to decide how serious the shortcomings are. In a general way the relevant considerations to any such judgment would seem to be: (1) whether the specific achievements have had a unifying effect and point toward a more thoroughgoing union; (2) whether the accomplishments are sufficiently rewarding and complementary to offer reasonable assurance that the community will not break down from its internal contradictions and tensions; and (3) whether the gap between realization and potential seems likely to narrow sufficiently in the future so that the presumed advantages of pursuing the undertaking will continue to outweigh the expected costs.

THE COMMUNITY IN STATISTICS

Judging by the very rough measurements which statistical indications can provide, the distance between the European Community and a true economic union of first rate dimensions remains a challenging one.

The community's resources are exceeded only by those of the two superpowers. The Common Market has a civilian work force—some 75 million—which is almost the same as that of the United States. In 1966, the community members imported from each other and from the rest of the world twice as much as the U.S. ($53 billion compared to $25 billion) and the value of their exports (some $52 billion) exceeded the U.S. performance by nearly as large a margin. The community's gross reserves of gold and convertible currencies, which were only half as large as those of the United States ten years ago, increased from $11 billion to $21 billion during that time, while the U.S. reserves fell to $14 billion. The Common Market produces about three-fourths as much steel as the United States; production of textiles, chemicals of various kinds, motor vehicles, and housing units compares favorably with or exceeds the U.S. performance; and in 1966 the percentage of gross national product directed to investment was nearly six points above the American rate.

The Common Market began functioning in 1958, and since then, though not exclusively for that reason, the community has been an area of dynamic growth—at least, until the late 1960s. Between 1957 and 1967, the gross community product increased nearly 60 percent (against 50 percent in the United States), and the increase in industrial production—some 70 percent—was only slightly less than the American. Intracommunity trade more than tripled; total trade nearly doubled. The number of employed persons increased in every country except Italy, and the over-all rate of unemployment declined from 3.5 percent to 1.8 percent, falling in every member country except France. Wages and private consumer expenditure roughly doubled, and the community (and European) consumer made great strides in acquiring the standard appurtenances of modern industrialized societies—cars, telephones, and television sets.

Yet the gulf between third and first place is still an enormous one. The GNP of the United States in 1966 was $756 billion—of the EEC, $323 billion. The total goods and services thus available to the citizen of the richest community country were scarcely more than half those the U.S. economy produced for the average American that same year, and the citizen of the poorest community country garnered less than one-third. Total Common Market energy consumption, which is one of the measures of industrialization, is still no more than one-third that of the U.S. Whereas agricultural production accounts for about 3.7 percent of the American GNP, the range is from 5.1 percent (Germany) to 12.5 percent (Italy) in the EEC. Despite the "agricultural revolution" which has been sweeping Europe since the war, more than 10 percent of the German civilian workers, 17 percent of the French, and 24 percent of the Italians still make their living from the soil.[1]

The growing literature on the technological gap has convinced many Europeans that there is no hope of closing the gulf between the two economies. While some of the statistical disclosures are no doubt politically motivated and overly dramatic—e.g., the comparisons of the number of computers in the U.S. versus the number in Europe— such serious investigations as those undertaken by the Organization for Economic Cooperation and Development (OECD) have nevertheless confirmed that the Europeans face a serious problem in keeping abreast of the technotronic age. The United States spends six times as much on research and development as the six community countries do; there are thirteen times as many scientists, technicians, and engineers doing research-related work in the U.S. as there are in the community; the U.S. spends about 3.4 percent of its GNP on R & D programs, while no community country spends as much as 2 percent; there are some 700,000 full-time American scientists and technicians, whereas France and Germany each employ about 100,000. Furthermore, the figures exaggerate the size of the European undertaking owing to a "certain amount of overlapping . . . given the multiplicity of decision-making centers and the fragmentation of R & D programs in all sectors of the economy in Europe. . . ."[2]

Whether the community is making progress toward the replacement of fragmentation with that "combination of resources" to which the Rome treaties hopefully referred is by no means incontrovertible. Many of the earmarks of a developing single economy are readily apparent. Trade within the market accounts for increasingly large proportions of the members' total trade, ranging upward from 36 percent in the case of Germany to well over 60 percent in the case of Belgium-Luxembourg.[3] Interpenetration of markets has increased,

[1] Statistical Office of the European Community, *Basic Statistics of the Community* (Brussels, December 1967).

[2] The foregoing should not be taken as an endorsement of the simple-minded view of the extent, nature, and origin of the so-called technological gap. The OECD studies have served the useful purpose of demonstrating that the effectiveness of a nation's industry is determined not only by the size of its scientific undertaking, but by a host of other factors such as size of market, industry structure, access to foreign technology, government expenditure and procurement, attitudes of management, etc. For a useful summary of the OECD's findings see: "The Impact of Science and Technology on Social and Economic Development," *The OECD Observer*, no. 33 (April 1968), pp. 15–38.

[3] *Basic Statistics*, p. 120.

and in a number of cases, the consequences for individual "domestic" industries have been highly painful. There have been thousands of regroupings and reorganizations of businesses within the individual member states and among them as well. It is generally accepted that the establishment of a larger market is a critical factor in the determination of investment patterns (for foreign as well as community investors) and that it is a significant factor in determining the level of investment. The impact which the leveling off of economic activity in Germany in 1967 had on the whole community is further proof that none of the member countries is insulated from the business cycle trends of its partners.

However, the community economy is still far from unity. Despite growing intracommunity trade and interpenetration of markets, signs of harmonization of prices (which would result from competition) are still too few. In April 1967, the Commission conducted a survey of some 200 consumer items which indicated striking price differentials from country to country, varying from as little as 29 percent for some items (cars and gasoline) to as much as 72 percent (foodstuffs), with the differentials for most categories falling in the 45 to 55 percent range.[4] Along with the numerous regroupings of firms *within* the Common Market, many of the more important ones have been negotiated between European and American companies. Despite the hopeful moves in the direction of community-wide trade unionism, international wage contract bargaining is still in the future. Under pressure of slackening economic activity in the community in 1967, the Netherlands, Belgium, and France all reinstituted priority for their own workers over community workers. And so long as discrimination against nonresidents on issues, investments, and listing of shares on national exhanges continues, nothing like a European bond and share market can be expected to emerge.

The half-finished edifice of the community's economic regulations would thus seem to have its counterpart in the half-response of the European economy and its major factors—capital, labor, and enterprise. This is no proof that integration is ineffective; but it does mean that the community has much more work to do. It raises some doubt that the advantageous consequences of the Common Market, though obviously very great, are so substantial and manifest that the member

[4] Statistical Office of the European Community, *Statistiques Sociales, Marché Intérieur*, no. 4 (1967). Also see, "The Real Story on Consumer Prices and Purchases in Europe," *European Community*, no. 111 (April 1968), pp. 4–6.

states will in all circumstances be impelled to move ahead. Partial integration produces its own inner tensions, the logical resolution of which is another advance. But is there any reason why those tensions should necessarily propel the community ahead to a later stage of development rather than back to an earlier one?

A REVERSIBLE COMMUNITY

There is ample evidence that the assurance of the community's continued advancement will be found, if at all, not in what lies *behind* it, but in how well it copes with what lies *ahead*. The mere existence of the CSC, EURATOM, and the Common Market testifies to the creativity of the member countries, but there are no guarantees that the requisite talent and determination will always be at hand. The three communities were fortuitously established at a time of economic recovery and expansion, and how well they would weather the problems of a general decline is still to be seen. Built-in rigidities of policy are prevalent in and peculiar to the community, and its policy-making machinery is by no means a model of efficiency.

The development of the community has at no point been a steady progression, and the wreckage of European enterprises on the landscape recommends an ordinary prudence in projecting the future. Prior to its merger into the Commission in 1967, the High Authority had become a secondary influence, at best, on the organization of the coal market—in large part because of its earlier failure to persuade the Council to authorize the declaration of a "manifest crisis" in the industry. Nothing like a competitive coal market has since existed; the reorganization of the German coal sales agencies was a practical failure, and with the exception of the temporary community program for coke, the High Authority's role in the coal sector became one principally of policing the subsidies which the national governments were willing to grant.

EURATOM has likewise demonstrated that the communities are established fact only to the extent that they are constantly activated. The prominent place which was initially envisaged for the community in assuring the availability of nuclear supplies never fully materialized. France has taken the position that the treaty article establishing the Supply Agency has legally "expired," and it is far from clear under what terms the Agency's mandate will be renewed. The safeguards program organized by EURATOM was a pioneering effort in supranational inspection and control over the uses of fissionable materials. But, the 1960 nonproliferation treaty provides for international safeguards administered by the International Atomic Energy Agency (IAEA), and whether the negotiations between the IAEA and EURATOM on their respective control functions will leave a significant operation for the latter remains to be seen. Moreover, the expiration at the end of 1967 of the second five-year research program has provided the justification (or the excuse) for a complete reappraisal of EURATOM's work. It may lead to a more effective community or it may not.

Both the CSC and EURATOM are, it is true, special purpose communities, overshadowed by and destined to be "folded into" the more generalized economic community when the Treaties of Paris and Rome are combined. But since the meeting of the Council of agricultural ministers in October 1967 it has been clearly evident that even the EEC and its proudest achievement, the common agricultural policy, are by no means immune to the need for change. While the ministers did eventually succeed in fixing the community target prices for most of the major farm products for the 1968–69 marketing year, the difficulty they had was an indication that the price-fixing process is likely to be a delicate affair each year.[5] In addition to the usual pressures from the farmers for general price rises (there were riots in Brittany in October 1967), there is simply the inherent difficulty of determining the impact of any particular price-mix on the diverse interests of the member countries. For example, the Dutch and Italians, importers of corn, do not see precisely the same merit in higher corn prices as do the French, who wish to increase their corn production, discourage the output of surplus soft grains, and cut down on imports of feed grains from noncommunity sources.

The same difficulties were evident in the minicrisis of May 1968 over the support prices for milk and dairy products. On the one hand, the Council was confronted with the resistance of farm groups in France and Belgium to any reduction in prices and by admonitory demonstrations in Brussels and elsewhere against such reductions. On the other hand, it was faced with butter stocks of some 150,000 tons and the refusal of some of the member states to go beyond certain limits in funding the disposal of such surpluses. The Council chose at the last minute to compromise—but at the expense of the

[5] *Agence Europe* maintained a running commentary on the critical negotiations throughout the month of October. Also consult *Journal of Commerce*, especially October 17, 1967.

CAP itself. Given the political situation in France at the time and the necessity of meeting the July 1968 deadline for the completion of the internal market, agreement was no doubt imperative. But since some variation in support prices will be permitted from state to state, a single market for dairy products will not really exist. The surplus states, rather than the community, will have to finance part of the surplus disposal, and the total cost of the dairy program for 1968–69 (over $800 million) is likely to be one which will not readily be agreed to again.[6]

Critics of the CAP have long felt that it involved the community in an overly schematic, costly, and protectionist undertaking, and in October 1967, Commissioner Mansholt—whose tour de force the CAP is—joined those critics. He was reported by the press to have told the Council that the system of managed prices on which the CAP is based had proved insufficient. The common prices which the community establishes must be based on the "normal" farm with the average productivity. If prices are raised enough to assure a fair income to the submarginal farmer in less-developed regions or in areas remote from markets, the consumer will suffer, labor costs will rise, and the community's agricultural fund will be burdened with unacceptable expenditures for price supports and surplus disposal. While these are problems which the national governments had failed to deal with for years, Mansholt argued that, rather than accentuate them, the EEC should embark on a program to supplement the price system—to modernize, rationalize, and restructure community farming.[7]

In assessing the permanence of the community's accomplishments, one must bear in mind that the budgetary, political, and social costs of giving the CAP a new direction will also impose a major burden on community cohesion. The first real debate on a structural program for agriculture was to have taken place after the Commission had submitted its recommendations in March 1968, but the dispute over dairy prices consumed the available time and energy, and consideration was delayed. It cannot be postponed indefinitely, however, and anyone familiar with the negotiating marathons which produced the agricultural policy can anticipate the agonies which lie ahead.

[6] See *Agence Europe*, May 29, 1968, pp. 3–6.

[7] A summary of Mansholt's position is contained in the Commission of the European Communities, *First General Report on the Activities of the Communities, 1966–1967*, February 1968.

A PARTIAL COMMUNITY

In assessing the community's future prospects it is important to consider the consequences of its failure to achieve some of the specific goals established in the treaties or which have since been recognized as a more or less immediate concern. Some of these measures will no doubt be instituted as the requirements for them become more compelling—the full opening of the customs union in July 1968 made further progress toward the harmonization of customs procedures mandatory. Where pressures are less than insistent, the prospects for major advances are more remote.

So long as these gaps exist, the community does not function at its optimum, and the members are deprived of its maximum potential benefit. The Commission, whose responsibility it is to represent the community interest and whose admonitions reflect only in part its political aspirations, has frequently lectured the members that the advantages of having successfully moved in one area may be denied by a lack of movement in another, that trade and commerce will not achieve the ideal volume and pattern, and that there will be distortions of investment and regional development.

There are numerous such warnings in the *Tenth General Report*. Commenting on the *customs union*, the Commission observed: ". . . there is as yet no real common market. Intra-community trade is still subject to a number of restrictions that obstruct the movement of goods, result in hold-ups and checks at frontiers, and involve firms in useless expense. Trade between the member countries has not yet become genuinely 'domestic.' Apart from customs and quota frontiers, which will disappear on July 1, 1968, for all manufactures and nearly all farm produce, there are other 'frontiers' impeding the free movement of goods—tax frontiers, patent frontiers, monopoly frontiers, the frontiers raised by customs legislation. The opening or elimination of such frontiers is one of the main tasks for the coming years."[8]

Regarding the absence of a *common energy policy* the Commission stated: "The adverse consequences for Community industry of this division of the energy markets are self-evident. Price disparities place user industries on unequal competitive terms. Investments are influenced by these situations of inequality in such a way that they do not always meet the requirement of maximum profitability."[9] Appeal-

[8] *Tenth General Report*, p. 14.
[9] *Ibid.*, p. 41.

ing for further measures to *free capital movements* and integrate the capital markets, the Commission warned: "If the community process is not brought to this logical conclusion, there is a risk that progress already made may be prejudiced, for a European capital market will be a basic element in a competition policy designed to ensure for firms equivalent conditions as regards the cost of and access to funds; it will also be a determining factor for the establishment of monetary union within the community."[10]

The cost of a failure of community momentum may be a simple matter of waste. Under the community-authorized program, the individual governments paid out in 1967 some $1.4 billion in aids to the coal-mining industry which, socially justified though they may have been, are indicative of the price of the failure to establish real competition within a community-wide energy sector. The subsidies were, incidentally, almost precisely equal to the estimated cost of building a community isotope separation plant. Other polities, of course, also pursue wasteful policies, but the European Community is especially vulnerable to that charge. Commenting in March 1968 on the debate over the Commission's proposals to freeze the guaranteed prices for milk and to take other steps to discourage the alarming overproduction of dairy products, the *Agence Europe* wrote: "An agricultural policy founded more or less entirely on guaranteed prices is in itself an unbalanced policy. This unbalance is accentuated when the establishment of these prices takes place in a political and social context which takes much more account of short-term repercussions and local, even election, circumstances than of a coherent view of the community as a whole. . . . If this should lead to over-production, then we shall see: the national governments will move . . . when milk overflows in the roads. Thus we will be directly back to 'national policies.' . . ."[11]

THE SPECTER OF RENATIONALIZATION

Should the community, failing to strike the necessary balances of national interests or for other reasons, leave vacuums where community programs ought to exist, the member governments most vitally concerned will act to fill them. For example, in 1966 when the CSC was unimaginative and dilatory in producing remedies for the dis-

[10] *Ibid.*, p. 23.
[11] *Agence Europe*, March 14, 1968.

tressed steel industry, the German companies moved toward further cartelization, and France—despite the community-wide worries about over-capacity—launched a government-subsidized reorganization and modernization program of such dimensions that protests were still being heard two years later in the European Parliament. In 1967 the community was agitated by proposed legislation in Germany which, designed to force long-distance hauling off the highways and on to the railroads, would have obvious implications for community transport policy so long at an impasse.[12] Likewise, if there is no agreement on a EURATOM research program, the resources for such research will shift to national programs.

To avoid "renationalization," however, requires more than the elimination of national policies in conflict with common objectives; a fully effective economic union requires the *activation of community priorities* where community problems exist or opportunities arise. The existing, and essentially federal, community regulation of monopolies and cartels does not produce companies of the optimum size for a market of 183 million consumers unless combined with the necessary combination of encouragements and restraints on a broad front. In addition to community company and patent laws, adjustment and equalization of numerous national regulations applicable to business undertakings, the harmonization of tax advantages or disadvantages, and positive inducements to business expenditures for research and development may be required. Industrial rationalization and modernization on a community basis logically implies certain regional policies: the use of community resources and instruments (e.g., the funds of the European Investment Bank and the Social Fund, harmonization of social legislation, transport policy) to transcend the limitations imposed by national borders on the development of areas which, in a larger market, are natural economic regions. Without capital, community business will not be able to adapt to and take full advantage of the opportunity which has been opened by the completion of the customs union. This requires not only the lifting of the remaining exchange controls, but the adoption of fiscal

---

[12] In February 1968, the Commission advised Bonn of its "recommendation" that important features of the Leber transport legislation not be adopted. Such recommendations are not binding, and it is unclear how the German government will respond. If the legislation is passed, the Commission's views notwithstanding, and is found contrary to the Rome treaties, the Commission could still have recourse to the Court of Justice. See *Agence Europe*, February 1–2, 1968.

and monetary measures which will encourage the establishment of a real community capital market and the creation of savings which would flow into it.

EQUITY VERSUS NATIONAL AND SECTORAL INTERESTS

In addition to endangering past achievements, slackening of the community's pace and of its will to continue onward to a more perfect union will aggravate the divisive issue of equity. If it is to prosper, the community must ultimately confer roughly equal blessings on all its members and on all economic and social classes. It cannot be a community of the "interests," national or sectoral.

The maintenance of a certain parity of national advantages and burdens resulting from community participation is a political necessity. In the earlier stages of the community's development something popularly known as the "community spirit" made it possible for various governments to concede a point with regard to a given sector in expectation of receiving compensation later on, perhaps in another sector. This flexibility has become progressively more constricted, especially since January 1963 when de Gaulle first demonstrated the possibilities for national self-assertion within the community. For de Gaulle to declare bluntly that without the CAP the EEC would have no meaning for France, and for the Five to respond that without the Kennedy Round there would be no completion of the CAP, is one way of doing business perhaps, but not a particularly elevating one. Nevertheless, the increasingly frequent resort to timetables, work programs, and end-of-the-year negotiating sessions on "package deals'" merely shows that an equilibrium of national advantage is for the present at least essential to community progress. For example, for the Dutch, retention within the framework of the common transport policy of the advantageous position their aggressive transportation industry has achieved is a matter of national importance. There is unlikely to be a common energy program which does not strike some balance between competing national industries and interests, and the structural program Mansholt apparently has in mind for marginal farms will surely inspire demands for community-financed aid to other distressed industries. Nor is a technological community likely to materialize if it focuses solely—as Paris seems to desire—on those technical developments which are of special interest to France.

The question of equity among the various economic interests was recognized even in the Treaty of Paris, which included among the

CSC's missions the betterment of working conditions and improvement of standards of living, provided certain (minimal) safeguards against "abnormally low wages," and permitted the High Authority to use its financial resources to assist in the retraining and resettlement of surplus workers. The EEC treaty extended the social aspects of the community's operations, and it was thought that its general approach to integration would minimize the interest-orientation which the sectoral approach had tended to give the CSC. Moreover, in setting up the Economic and Social Committee, the treaty provided that it be "composed in such a manner as to secure adequate representation of the different categories of economic and social life."

Despite the useful work of the CSC in the social field, the High Authority—prior to its merger into the Commission in 1967—had become the object of frequent charges that it was the creature of, rather than the authority over, the coal and steel interests. Public regulatory bodies everywhere tend to identify themselves with the problems of those they regulate, all public policies tend to be compromises upon the ideal, and in its deliberations on the future of the coal industry, the High Authority could obviously not ignore the social considerations involved. It would nonetheless be difficult to hold that the broadest conception of the public interest prevailed when the High Authority decided to raise steel tariffs in 1966 or when, out of concern for the coal industry, it has contributed to the community's commitment to a high-cost energy policy.

Nor has the EEC escaped the pitfalls of too close an identification with sectoral objectives. The Economic and Social Committee has proved a disappointment; it is often ignored, and when it is not, the voice of the dominant interest involved is too often the only one heard. Contrary to the treaty's intention, community policy has tended to prolong the sectoral approach—with policies for this and that, integrated with great difficulty, if at all, into a community policy. Commercial and social policy considerations, for example, gave way before the CAP with its high food cost and protectionist bias. If the CAP is now reoriented as Mansholt has proposed, there will also be important social implications in this. Yet, the Commission has been having great difficulty in persuading the member states to increase the resources of the Social Fund and to permit it to extend its activities in the fields of occupational training, regional policy, and the provision of housing, social assistance, and training for migrant workers.

Basic differences among the member states over how the EEC

should go about "equalizing upward" living and working conditions have in fact tended to make social policy the stepchild of the community and to give to community policy generally an old-fashioned conservative flavor, along with the heavy dosage of *dirigisme*. As the European Organization of the International Confederation of Free Trade Unions (ICFTU) declared in its Fourth Activity Report at the end of 1966, the EEC has not been "generous" to the workers or to their organizations.[13] The treaty calls on the Commission "to promote close collaboration between the member states in the social field," but there is strong resistance in several quarters—Germany is one—to "community social legislation," and the French are, as usual, in the forefront of the opposition to the Commission's efforts to preserve its rights of initiative and to deal directly with the employers and unions. And even the Commission has been under fire from the trade unions for having allegedly agreed too readily in December 1967 to limit its access to industry and labor representation in drafting a number of studies which were authorized at that time and which may constitute a basis for harmonizing and upgrading social legislation.[14]

The community's problem is complex. In creating a large economic union from six smaller ones, the EEC by its very nature aims to promote adjustments which may be painful and initially, at least, far more likely to benefit the big than the small. It was to be expected that in adapting to the larger market, some economic sectors would move more quickly than others. In fact, the community-wide organizations of farmers and of some industries have already become powerful ones. The European organizations of the unions on the other hand are comparatively weak, and, despite the symbolic importance of the agreement signed in June 1968 by the community organizations of farmers and of farm employees on hours and working conditions of field hands, generalized community-wide collective bargaining by industries is still a dream.[15] Moreover, with decision-making authority

[13] *Agence Europe*, October 4, 1966.

[14] *Agence Europe*, May 10, 1968, p. 8.

[15] The agreement concluded in June between the Committee of the Agricultural Professional Organizations of the EEC (COPA) negotiating for the farmers and the ICFTU Agricultural Workers Secretariat and the Agriculture and Food Workers group of the ICFTU negotiating for the employees establishes for field workers certain standards on annual and weekly hours of work, time off, holidays, night work, etc. Although these standards, to have legal effect, will have to be renegotiated at the national level, the pressures to reach such national agreements will probably be strong as a result of the community-wide accord. Meanwhile, there are new indications that some of the international labor groups may be giving more serious consideration to the problems

still residing predominantly in the community Council, systematized representation of the *public* interest is unlikely to be the normal thing. It is understandable that ministers of agriculture, meeting in Council, think first of the farmers. Whether this is tolerable indefinitely is another question, however. As the costs of the CAP continue to skyrocket, the finance ministers are becoming more and more insistent that they should have some voice in the community's agricultural decisions.

Thus, a community excessively focused on sectoral interests faces a grave risk of ultimate irrelevance (or worse still, of negative relevance) to the interests of broad segments of its population. In the "manifesto" which it released on July 1, 1968 in celebration of the completion of the customs union, the Commission declared that one of the community's main objectives in the next five years must be to persuade the major economic, social, and intellectual forces of Europe to take a greater part in the construction of Europe. The Commission announced its intention to meet later in the year with the Economic and Social Council in order to begin a far-reaching examination of the community situation and to organize thereafter symposia for discussions with representatives of three groups: employers and labor, farmers, and youth and university people.[16] In view of the widespread impression that the community has lost the capacity to inspire either interest or enthusiasm, especially among those who are most critical of the institutions of the nation-state, even the intention to initiate such dialogues is encouraging. But the discussions will be useful only when and if they produce a response—in community policies, actions, and institutions—which is sufficiently meaningful to attract those who are disenchanted with a Europe which seems largely technocratic.

THE NECESSITY OF COMMUNITY ENCROACHMENT

The community's present viability as well as its future will remain in question so long as the gradual constriction of national prerogatives is not offset by a corresponding expansion of community power. In the area of trade, consider the example of the development of the common commercial policy. When the customs union was

---

of industrial wage disparities within and among regional groupings and may be moving to do something about them as a long-term program. See, for example, the preview report on the meeting in May 1968 of the World Auto Council, "Equal Pay Is Mission of Reuther," *The Washington Post*, May 16, 1968, p. G7.

[16] The text of the manifesto was published in *Agence Europe*, July 1, 1968, as Europe Documents No. 483.

completed on July 1, 1968 the member states eliminated all tariffs and, with the exception of the emergency measures taken by France, virtually all quotas on trade among themselves, and instituted a common level of tariff protection on their imports from abroad. The level of the common external tariff (CXT) was initially a rough average of the previously existing national tariffs. It was reset in the Kennedy Round in which the EEC participated as a unit. Therefore, the level of the CXT as well as a number of import quotas are community obligations.[17] The Commission has for some time been pressing the members to proceed with the necessary preparation for the common commercial policy—not only specific steps, such as the adoption of community antidumping and antisubsidy regulations or the replacement of the remaining national quotas with a community-administered system, but also serious planning for the harmonization and eventual transfer to the community of the bilateral or multilateral commercial commitments of the individual members. The Commission has encountered the predictable resistance: The French, for example, insisted at one point that the treaty does not provide for the "gradual" institution of a common commercial policy and that, until the transitional period ends, the members have no obligation to proceed in that direction.[18]

The member states know, however, that a customs union of any real substance or permanence must mean that the regulation of trade as a national instrument of domestic economic control is substantially weakened; and if total trade is roughly equivalent to 30 percent of gross national product and if one-third to two-thirds of each member's trade takes place within the group, the ramifications extend to general policy as well. But the logical next step, even to a common commercial policy, will also mean a further sizable and painful sacri-

---

[17] These commitments were negotiated by the Commission pursuant to Council directives (which, after 1966, could have been approved by majority vote). The relevant article, Article 111, further requires the members to "coordinate their commercial relations with non-members in such a way as to bring about, not later than the expiry of the transitional period [December 31, 1969] the conditions necessary to the implementation of a common policy in the matter of external trade." As described in subsequent articles, this posttransitional common policy shall be based on "uniform principles" regarding tariffs, liberalization, export policy, and protective measures; the community will "only proceed by way of common action" in any economic international organizations; and the Commission will conduct any "required" negotiations with third countries on the basis of policies which it will recommend and which the Council may approve by majority vote.

[18] *Agence Europe*, September 19, 1967.

fice of national sovereignty, including some further surrender of the privileges of conducting a national foreign policy.[19]

The same is true in such areas as fiscal and monetary policy. In February 1967, when the Council agreed that all of the member states should adopt a single valued-added turnover tax (TVA) no later than 1970, the Commission also transmitted to the Council a general program for fiscal harmonization. The Commission considered it important that by mid-1968 agreements be reached to do the following: extend the TVA to agriculture; eliminate discrimination based on nationality in the application of excise taxes; begin to harmonize certain excise tax rates; and adjust certain direct taxes which distort or interfere with capital movements, investment, and industrial mergers. After mid-1968, the Commission urged, the community should move still further toward the harmonization of taxation systems and administration, as well as the actual alignment of rates of all taxes which affect business.[20]

The preliminary deadlines proposed by the Commission have not been met, and it is clear that a common system of taxation is still a long way off. Nevertheless, with the the approval of the TVA, the community embarked on a course the implications of which go far beyond the immediate objective of eliminating "tax frontiers" and equalizing the conditions of competition. In the *Tenth General Report*, the Commission wrote: "About 52 percent of the total tax revenue of the member countries comes from indirect taxes, and rates sometimes differ considerably. The process of harmonization, therefore, *will necessarily involve substantial changes in the tax revenue of the member countries. . . .* These [changes] will be tolerable only if the member countries still have enough room for maneuver in tax policy to offset the effect of harmonization on their budgets without producing undesirable economic and social consequences."[21] Thus, in the Commission's view at least, a workable community would have an influential voice in the determination of the heretofore most sacredly sovereign of public policies—the raising of public revenues and their expenditure. This is not so startling as it may seem. The CSC has always had power to tax coal and steel production; the com-

[19] For an interesting statement on some of the implications of the community's common commercial policy see: Werner Feld, "External Relations of the Common Market and Group Leadership Attitudes in the Member States," *ORBIS*, no. 2 (Summer 1966), pp. 564–87.

[20] *Agence Europe*, February 27, 1967.

[21] *Tenth General Report*, p. 19. (Italics supplied.)

munity-determined expenditures on the CAP are by no means niggardly; and in May 1968, the Council approved a community tax on margarine thus giving the EEC its first independent source of revenue.[22]

If the community is to be effective, however, the process of encroachment on the nation-states has only just begun. That the fiscal, monetary, and budgetary intentions of each member is the mutual concern of all has, of course, been recognized: hence the work of the Medium-Term, Monetary, and Budget Policy Committees, and hence the repeated pleas of the Commission for "fuller coordination" of monetary and financial policies. But is *coordination* enough? Compared with the instruments available to the federal government in the United States they are woefully weak. It is one thing for the Federal Reserve Board—acting independently—to raise or lower the discount rate in order to damp inflationary trends or encourage investments; it is quite another for the community agencies to attempt to persuade the six national banks to keep their interest rate policies in equilibrium or to achieve the full advantages of manipulating them selectively so long as short-term capital movements have not been liberalized. The U.S. government, using its taxing authority and an annual budget of some $200 billion to achieve a specific countercyclical effect, is one order of things; the community, with a miniscule taxing authority and an annual budget of a little more than $2 billion, using its Budgetary Committee to urge fiscal restraint on the national authorities is another.

Moreover, the weakness of community public policy lies not only in the making of it, but in the self-imposed limitations on the content it may have. For example, since total community reserves are now in excess of $20 billion, it should have—even by conservative standards—leeway to pursue a highly flexible countercyclical course. But because those reserves are not pooled and therefore not available to bail out any member in temporary balance of payments difficulties, the members are more or less obliged in general to maintain a rigid equilibrium vis-à-vis each other, and condemned in particular to resort to massive deflationary measures (as Italy and Germany have notably done) whenever deficits begin to occur.[23] Ironically it is pre-

---

[22] The Netherlands' approval of the tax was conditioned, however, on the community's reaching an agreement on the budgetary powers of the European Parliament.

[23] The options are further circumscribed when, as in the case of France, reserves are earmarked to serve the *Grosspolitik* of the regime.

cisely the charge of too limited a policy option which the community
—reflecting on Britain's periodic financial crises—has laid at London's door.

A MONETARY ROUTE TO MORE EFFECTIVE UNION

It is for this reason that community concern with the growing complexity of state-community relationships has been increasingly focused on the ambiguous situation which inheres in the monetary sphere. Critics of the EEC treaty have often deplored the weakness of the monetary articles which failed to provide for a payments union or central reserve system, let alone a thoroughgoing monetary union. The member states are, it is true, adjured to treat their exchange rate policies as a matter of common interest, to pursue policies maintaining confidence in their currencies, and with the assistance of the consultative Monetary Committee, to coordinate their policies in monetary matters. The 1964 agreements obliged each state to consult with the other members and the community authorities before embarking on any course that might significantly affect its internal economic situation or its participation in the international monetary system.[24]

Nevertheless, while the independence of each state in the monetary sphere thus remains legally intact, the practical—as opposed to the legal—restraints on national action in monetary matters are important, real, and increasingly restrictive. This particularly applies to the limitations on exchange rate manipulation. In the May 1967 issue of *Banker*, the former EEC Commissioner, Robert Marjolin, is reported to have stated in an interview that devaluation by one member country is not unthinkable or impossible—only more and more difficult. Noting that between 1958 and 1966 intracommunity trade had increased two and one-half times, and that more than 60 percent of one of the country's exports go to its community partners, Marjolin observed that a unilateral devaluation of any great dimension would have a highly disruptive effect on the devaluator and community alike. Since July 1968, moreover, community prices—calculated on the basis of units of account of fixed gold content and value—have come into effect for all the major farm commodities. A devaluating country would accordingly have to increase its agricultural prices (and its cost of living) proportionately with the devaluation, and un-

---

[24] Will the French government bear this commitment in mind as it proceeds to implement the social reforms the Gaullists promised in the May 1968 elections?

less other compensatory measures were taken, farm incomes would soar and real wages would decline.[25]

F. Boyer de la Giroday of the Commission staff has carried this line of argument still further. In his view, once a substantial part of the national product of any country begins to come from exports and its rate of growth and full employment have accordingly become dependent upon trade, then it is no longer possible for that country to secede from an integrated market by exchange rate adjustments. As soon as the flow of goods, capital, and labor has been sufficiently freed, common prices will tend to emerge for a wide range of products, and governments will have lost control over exchange rates *except*, of course, to the extent that they resort to coordinated moves with their partners. Such an equilibrium of exchange rates will be stable so long as there is a sufficiently free circulation of capital throughout the market; a country in balance-of-payment difficulty can rely on short-term capital imports to tide it over a crisis rather than having to resort to deflation. Thus, something like a de facto monetary union will have come into being, even though the various national currencies should continue to circulate.[26]

The capacity of governments—especially authoritarian ones—to resist the powers of persuasive thinking is staggering. However, if the foregoing analysis is correct, the community is close to the feasibility threshold of an important advance. There have been no adjustments in exchange rates in the community since 1961, and with or without minor adjustments, the additional step (which Boyer de la Giroday considers psychologically important) of formally pronouncing fixed rates would not be a difficult one. (The European Parliament has even suggested that the community begin a limited coinage of "Eurofrancs.") With the community as a whole running a balance of payments surplus, there are no insoluble technical obstacles to the pooling of some portion of external reserves and providing some common management over them. The Commission has consistently pressed for the further liberalization of exchange controls and the institution of measures to facilitate creation of a community capital market. And provided they were strengthened, the mechanisms which exist could provide the coordination of budgetary, credit, and general economic policies essential to a fairly extensive monetary unification.

[25] "Interview with Robert Marjolin," *Banker*, 117, (May 1967), pp. 384–95.

[26] F. Boyer de la Giroday, "Through the Monetary Looking Glass," *Columbia Journal of World Business*, Winter 1966, pp. 53–64.

Among the many who recognize the urgency of such measures is Prime Minister Werner of Luxembourg, whose views are highly respected in the financial world. In January 1968, he proposed a specific action program for the achievement of a European financial and monetary policy. Among other things, Werner would define more clearly the monetary obligations of the member states toward each other, establish a European unit of account and formally fixed exchange rates, extend the community's authority in international monetary affairs, and set up a European Monetary Cooperation Fund to assist members in balance of payments difficulties.[27] In much the same terms, the Commission, in its July 1968 manifesto, called on the member states to get on with the monetary union, "first by harmonizing the monetary policies of [the] six member states, and then by creating among them a degree of monetary solidarity which will lead stage by stage to the copestone of the economic edifice—a common currency superseding the old national currencies."

SUMMARY

The member states have created an economic community of vast potential and still limited means. Progress made in many areas has accentuated the lack of it in others, and the closing of one gap tends to open another where the community must ultimately move. If the member states are to enjoy the full benefits of removing some of the obstacles to free commerce among themselves, they must not permit restraints of another sort to arise; policies adopted in one sector must not defeat the objectives hoped for in another, and there must be a general policy for the whole; and when the integration process narrows the policy options left to the nation-states, those options must become community prerogatives. Above all, the member states must in the end bring themselves to accept the political community which their economic union implies.

[27] The speech, delivered by Werner to EUROFORUM 1968 in Saarbrücken on January 25, is discussed in *Agence Europe* in the February 19 and 20 issues.

Part II: The Political Community

IV   THE POLITICAL COMMUNITY: THE CONCEPT

In 1957 the Common Market and EURATOM treaties were hailed as the "relaunching of Europe." The simple and widely understood meaning of this was that the new projects, by working in the economic area, would endeavor to resume the advance toward the European union which the EDC fiasco had brought to a halt. At the time there was no question that political unity was the community's ultimate purpose—whatever the skepticism that it would be quickly achieved—and it is only in subsequent years that the goal has been denigrated as a quixotic, or even an objectionable, ideal.[1]

It is perhaps understandable why this should be the case. The EEC and EURATOM have been heavily engaged in their developmental problems, and the idea that the two communities remain the effective instruments of Europe's unification has become increasingly difficult to defend. The institutions with which they were provided were weak to begin with and slow to develop, and they have been the issue of fierce controversy. As often as not in the 1960s, the six community members have been deeply divided on vital issues of foreign policy and defense, and the search for greater unity has frequently propounded institutional arrangements outside of or superimposed on

[1] "The negotiations [on the EEC treaty] were an intricate mixture of academic exercises in abstruse economic theory and poker games of political skill. To the pure economist without knowledge of the course of the negotiations, the provisions of the treaty may thus sometimes seem strange. But as its aims are political, so its methods are politically conditioned. . . . In the minds of the draftsmen of the treaty, their economic task is chiefly valued as a step toward political integration. . . ." (U. W. Kitzinger, *The Politics and Economics of European Integration* [New York: Praeger, 1963], p. 18.)

the community framework. Above all, Paris, at odds under de Gaulle with the political purposes of the Rome treaties which the Paris under others had accepted, has seen the communities alternately as the means of or as a menace to France's achieving a European position the other European powers decline to accept.

From another point of view, however, the great controversies which have agitated the Common Market might equally well be seen as symptomatic of its political development—not necessarily the withdrawal of political significance from the community, but the confirmation that it exists. Who in fact can really doubt that the balanced development of the Common Market is as much a balance of power requirement as it is an economic necessity? Can it be denied that de Gaulle's rejection of Britain's accession in 1963 had to do with its implications for the future power balance in the community and Europe? Isn't France's quarrel with Brussels centered on the locus of decision-making authority within the community? And who can dispute that the commercial policy to be adopted will of necessity be a political reconciliation of competitive national and sectoral interests, reflecting as well some conception of the political and economic role the community should play in the world?

When the six member countries opted in the Rome treaties negotiations in favor of an integrated economic community they necessarily opted at the same time in favor of a political community.[2] So long as they remain committed to the economic union, the issue is not whether there will be a political community, but of what kind, shape, and effectiveness. The crucial questions which the community of the late 1960s must decide are: the area and content of its jurisdiction and how far and how rapidly it should be extended; where and how the political decisions required to operate the community will be taken; and related to this, what kind of institutional machinery will best assure that these decisions are reached with a decent and equitable regard for the multiple interests which are affected.

[2] "Whether the community is primarily an economic or primarily a political enterprise . . . the very question is based on a fallacy—on the notion that there are two different species of questions, some called economic, others called political. There are many different problems—economic, social, moral, penal, diplomatic, strategic—and any of these may at a given moment become political. . . . Politics is not the name of another subject, but of the arena in which these subjects are thrashed out toward a communal decision. Today economic problems are among the most important of these subjects: And that is why the Economic Community is a political enterprise not least precisely *because* it is economic. (*Ibid.*, pp. 62–63.)

All of these questions are political, and the architects of the European Community had a concept of how these questions might be answered, together with a strategy to encourage evolution in the direction the concept logically required. The result was a unique political system which was sufficiently effective to produce both the community's impressive initial achievements and the inevitable counter-revolution of the Gaullists in the crisis of June 30, 1965.

DESIGN PRINCIPLES

While it might perhaps mislead to suggest that the treaty establishing the economic community is a document comparable to the constitution of the United States, it may nonetheless be useful to note that points of similarity are more numerous than is usually supposed.[3]

It may be argued that the six heads-of-state in whose names the community is created confer upon it a different legitimacy than "we, the people of the United States," but the stated purposes—with one notable exception—of both are remarkably the same. The constitution's, "In order to form a more perfect union," may be more elegant, but it is not basically different from a determination "to establish the foundations of an ever closer union among the European peoples." Nor is the intention to establish justice, insure domestic tranquillity, promote the general welfare, and secure the blessings of liberty a higher order of endeavor than "to ensure the economic and social progress of their countries," to direct their efforts to "the essential purpose of constantly improving the living and working conditions of their peoples," and to achieve the harmonious development of their economies "by reducing the differences existing between the various regions and by mitigating the backwardness of the less favored."

True, the Rome treaties do not call on the Common Market to "provide for the common defense." But it is not without relevance that the six founding members could declare—even in the backwash of the EDC disaster—their resolve "to strengthen the safeguards of peace and liberty by establishing this combination of resources and calling upon the other peoples of Europe who share their ideal to join . . . their efforts." It is also true that the bulk of the U.S. constitution

---

[3] "In political terms, the activity of the states in the economic sphere has moved far in the direction of a federal or cooperative form. The treaties of the communities are living constitutional documents, the beginnings of a European constitution." (Walter Hallstein, address on being elected president of the European Movement, *Agence Europe*, January 24, 1968, Europe Document No. 461.)

is concerned with establishing the federal institutions, setting forth their respective jurisdictions, and delimiting the federal powers—whereas the bulk of the EEC treaty is concerned in endless elaboration of the "bases" of the community and its various policies. But those who have not recently compared the two documents may be surprised by the extent to which they cover the same ground.

Of the seventeen specific powers granted the Congress in Section VIII of Article I of the constitution, eight deal in whole or in part with economic or social matters, and to some degree at least, most of the eight also fall within the purview of the community. Paragraph 18 of Section VIII grants the Congress the general authority to make the "necessary and proper" laws to carry into execution all the powers vested in it or elsewhere conferred on the federal government. The EEC treaty (principally in Article 189) likewise authorizes the Council and Commission to adopt regulations and directives and to make decisions of binding force—i.e., to legislate—in order to effectuate the treaty's objectives, and Article 235 establishes a procedure whereby actions "necessary to achieve one of the aims of the community" may be taken "in cases where [the] Treaty has not provided for the requisite powers of action." Sections IX and X of the constitution enjoin the states from taking certain actions; the EEC members are likewise circumscribed in several cases from doing the same things. Indeed, the EEC treaty contains a general provision obliging the members to take all "general and particular" measures to assure that treaty obligations are carried out, and to abstain from the contrary—a provision, the potentially profound implications of which are unfortunately still to be tested.

We could pursue these comparisons still further, but the point is a simple one: not that the community must necessarily function in a federal way (although this too may be true), but that it is bound to act in a political way. Much of a nation's business is in fact business—not, as that benign President implied, by leaving the field to the entrepreneur (although that too would be a political choice), but by determining through political action and decision the conditions in which economic activity will be carried on. The founding fathers were obviously aware of this in 1789, and so were the founding members in 1957. In neither case was there lack of awareness of the implications for greater unity of the creation of areas of economic activity in which common rules have been made to prevail.

It is not our purpose here to draw any simplistic parallels or historical precedents for the Common Market—although the influence of the American model is amply evident. The great debates which preceded and accompanied the establishment of the Common Market make it clear that the evolvement of its basic concept was a much more sophisticated process than any such parallels would suggest. The debate over the free trade area alternative with which Britain belatedly sought to entice the Six confirmed instead their earlier commitment. The FTA was rejected for many reasons, including well-founded suspicions of London's intentions, but it foundered in the main because it could not be reconciled with continental conceptions of how modern economies are operated.[4]

The British claimed that the members of a free trade area could gain the advantages of a large and stable market if they relinquished their right to impose tariffs and quota controls on trade among themselves in their domestic manufactures. The EEC countries were convinced that other measures would be necessary. Trade freed of customs duties might be subsequently restrained by private means—cartel agreements—or unfairly distorted by dumping, subsidies, exchange controls, or tax reliefs. To assure that the maximum possible advantages would be fairly shared by the members, free trade in industrial items would have to be balanced by mobility of labor, capital, and enterprise. Those countries in which trade accounts for a critical proportion of gross national product would, if in difficulty and deprived of one means of regulating trade, use other means—such as the revaluation of its money.

In short, even in a limited free trade area, the EEC countries believed, each member would acquire an interest in the economic policies of every other member, and the growing interdependence of them all would create the need for precisely those instruments of common control which the free trade area advocates sought to avoid.[5] There is no real doubt who was right in this dispute, as the EEC and European Free Trade Association (EFTA) experiences have both shown. When the Wilson government came to power in 1964 and faced the first of its serious payment crises, its first act was to im-

---

[4] See Kitzinger, *European Integration*, pp. 22, 63, and Chapter 5.

[5] "As Mr. Heath has pointed out, membership of the community is not just a matter of giving up some elements of national sovereignty, it involves sharing in the sovereignty of other countries. Mr. Wilson, speaking in Brussels recently, recalled a pithy remark he had made four years back: 'a progressive surrender of sovereignty is a mark of an advancing civilization.'" David Spanier, "How Decisions Are Taken in the Common Market," *The Times* (London), April 3, 1967, p. 1.

pose an import surcharge which wiped out all the benefits its EFTA partners had gained from six years of mutual tariff cutting—and it seemed surprised its partners were annoyed. And still today those EFTA members who from time to time cherish renewed hope of "making more of EFTA" primarily aspire to see their association move into those areas of economic cooperation, if not union, which they had earlier rejected as unnecessary or too political in the EEC.

Because they were concerned with giving direction to the total enterprise and with relative power and influence of those who would decide what that direction would be, the Rome treaties were, in a very real sense, an exercise in limited constitution-making. The makers saw the need for giving a constitutional form to certain rules of conduct, they thought creative as well as administrative institutions essential, and they tried to imbue the whole structure with a dynamic from which a more perfect union would gradually evolve.

Foremost among the political principles on which the community was based was the conviction that the formal equality of the members was a categorical imperative. The community would prosper, the participants thought, only if each of them had and continued to have a substantially equal stake in its survival. In other words, the initial balance of mutual advantage and disadvantage from community participation must be guaranteed by something like a parity of influence—without which the community could become the creature of its strongest member.

The six initial participants could proceed to erect a community based on this concept because—unlike the British who had opted out —in important respects they considered themselves to be equal: all of them defeated in the war, occupied and humiliated, disillusioned and weak in a nuclear world, faced with the actual or potential dispossession of colonial empires, and hopeful of regeneration within a European framework. In other respects, of course, they were less confident that the harmonious kingdom of the poor had emerged from the war. The "economic miracle" was running at full tide in the Federal Republic; it was widely assumed that French and Italian industry could not withstand community competition; and there was an undercurrent of fear that Germany might reappear in a dominant economic position on the continent. At a time, moreover, when French and Italian governments were regularly changing, Bonn's obvious handicaps—the continued division and occupation of the country, the burdensome legacy of its past, and the formal limitations which the London and Paris agreements had placed on German rearmament—could allay but not end the apprehensions that Germany might once again bid for ascendancy in western Europe.

But the two psychologies, the hopeful and the timorous, both served to promote the development of a community in which the assumption of equality was buttressed by a variety of practical guarantees against claims to pre-eminence. This was the genius of the original Schuman plan—that it could combine the two in a generally acceptable way. The proposals for the Coal-Steel Community were a response only in part to the failures of the Council of Europe to produce a federal authority—they were also a French reaction to Germany's economic resurgence, to the incipient erosion of the controls on Germany which the occupation had provided, and to the uncertain future of the French industries in competition with the German.[6] Rather than calling for a renewal of the discriminatory restrictions on Germany, however, Schuman proposed instead that the "whole of Franco-German coal and steel production be placed under a common higher authority"—this solidarity making war between France and Germany "not merely unthinkable, but materially impossible," laying "the real foundations for their economic unification," and constituting "the first step in the federation of Europe."

The same concept was carried over into the Rome treaties. Although the community in form is French in its inspiration, there is no hint of an intended French hegemony—nor of an intended subordination of others. In the main body of the treaties, articles placed there at the behest of and to the obvious advantage of one or the other member are nonetheless equally applicable, and with two or three exceptions—such as the articles making the treaties applicable to the overseas departments of France or safeguarding the Benelux Union—the remarkably few derogations from general applicability of the treaty are relegated to the protocols.

It is difficult to conceive of the community having begun at all except on this equalitarian basis.[7] In this sense, the idealistic "com-

[6] See Kitzinger, *European Integration*, p. 10.

[7] The postwar evolution of the egalitarian concept is an interesting one. For example, the Draft Declaration of the European Resistance Movements of July 1944 called for a Federal Union of Europe which would "allow the German people to participate in the life of Europe without being a danger for the rest," but at the same time declared that Germany must be totally disarmed and subjected to federal control. A little over two years later, Churchill, in his famous speech in Zurich, was calling for a partnership between France and Germany and declaring that the "small nations will count as

munity spirit" which made the Common Market possible and which in great part sustained its initial rapid advance was "political realism"; it was the only practicable way to proceed. In a similar sense, it was also "realistic" to postulate an equal good faith and devotion to the community's objectives, as well as the perpetuity of basic commitment. Since not all of the community's purposes could be accomplished in one moment of time, any progress at all would be contingent on the confidence of the initially less-favored ones that sooner or later they, too, would receive their just due. Nor would any member—or for the matter, any enterprise—otherwise begin to undertake the sometimes painful adjustments required by Common Market participation were it not reasonably convinced that the treaty setting up the community had been concluded, as stated, for an "unlimited period" of time.

GUARANTEES OF PRINCIPLES

It is the interweaving of devices to assure that an equality and balance among the membership would continue which gives to the community its unique design. In part these devices were of a practical nature— in the economic sphere, for example, compensation was provided the weak for the advantages which the community was expected to bring to the strong, or in other cases, greater sacrifices were asked of the stronger in return for later gains. Thus the provisions for mobility of labor and the establishment of the European Investment Bank to facilitate regional development were intended primarily to redress Italy's disadvantageous competitive position, and the inclusion of agriculture in the market, the numerous safeguard clauses, the intended equalizing of "social charges," and the association of the overseas countries and territories were primarily for the benefit of France. So, too, in order to compensate the more outward-looking commercial countries—particularly Germany and the Netherlands—for accepting the too-narrow confines of a six-nation community, provision was also made that "any European state may apply to become a member" and that the "community may conclude with a third country, a union of

---

much as large ones and gain their honor by their contribution to the common cause."
Six years later the treaty to establish the EDC specified—in Article 6—that "the present treaty shall in no way discriminate beween its member states." See U. W. Kitzinger, *The European Common Market and Community* (London: Routledge & Kegan Paul, 1967).

states, or an international organization agreements creating an association. . . ."

The assurances against national hegemony or—what might be the
same thing—national obstruction—were by no means confined to
the economic or commercial sphere, however. They were also political: in part, institutional mechanisms with built-in checks and balances,[8] and in part—as the provisions for the community's geographic
expansion would suggest—balance-of-power arrangements of a
more traditional sort. Security for the smaller members could perhaps
have been provided by either political approach: a better balance
which Britain's participation would have assured from the beginning,
or, a more far-reaching delegation of powers to a truly representative
and effective European government. As the Dutch were wont later to
say in response to de Gaulle's *Europe des Patries*, either a supranational political union or one including Britain. But, in the mid-1950s,
it was too late for the one and too early for the other, and the result
was improvisation: a six-nation but open-ended community; a certain weighting of the system in favor of the smaller and weaker
members; the creation from the beginning of an independent "community representation"; and, linked with the expectation that the advance of economic integration would make the need for central direction increasingly exigent, the provision for parallel growth of central authority.

In 1955, West Germany's GNP was roughly twice as large as Italy's
and nearly 40 percent larger than France's; its population exceeded
that of the other two, respectively, by five and ten million. Yet in the
institutions of the community, the "big three" were treated equally.
Each country was allotted, for example, thirty-six delegates to the
European Parliament and twenty-four members on the Economic and
Social Committee of the EEC; each country was made responsible in
general for 28 percent of the Common Market's financial requirements, and—limited by the treaty to no more than two of its nationals on the EEC Commission—each has in practice claimed its
maximum representation. On the EEC Council, the three larger countries are equally represented, each has the right of veto when the
treaty requires a unanimous decision, and in those cases in which

[8] For a brief, sober, and revealing account of the community's institutions and their
working, see Emile Noel, "The Working of the Institutions," reprinted in Kitzinger,
European Common Market, pp. 85–104.

only a weighted majority is required, the three have the same number of votes.

The added institutional weight the Rome treaties gave the three smaller members is even more striking. With roughly 12 and 14 percent respectively of the community's 1955 population and GNP, the Benelux countries were allotted 24 percent of the parliamentary seats, 28 percent of the membership of the Economic and Social Committee, and 33 percent (in practice) of the seats on the EEC Commission—all in return for the comparatively modest contribution of 16 percent to the Common Market's budget. With a population of 308 thousand in a community of 167 million, Luxembourg received six parliamentary delegates, seats on the Commission as well as on the Council, and like the other members, a veto which, for the protection of national interest and exchequer, it has given the impression on occasion it would use. The delay, for example, of many months in the agreement to consolidate and relocate the three community executives was attributable at least in part to Luxembourg, which insisted on compensation for the transfer of the High Authority to Brussels.[9]

The favoritism shown the smaller countries as well as the implicit discrimination against Germany may appear at odds with the ideal of an equalitarian community. However, none of the Five, and certainly neither France nor Italy, could have accepted any institutional recognition of Germany's superior material resources—to accept Bonn even as an equal in community counsels, without specific restraints or controls, was politically and psychologically an enormous step for all the Five. The Germans were well aware of the distrust in which they were held, and the principle of nondiscrimination was more important to them than the precision of its application. Moreover, in the historical context of the Low Countries' long struggle against subjection, the disproportionate weight given to them was not on the face of it so drastic a departure from the equitable.

[9] A slight rectification of the overrepresentation of the Benelux countries in the executives of the three communities is in prospect as a result of the executive fusion agreement which came into force in 1967. Under this agreement the community Commission will be reduced to nine members in 1970. Since there must be at least one member from each state, the Benelux countries will have at least one-third of the seats. In the present transitional Commission and in the old multiple executive, the Benelux countries have claimed slightly more than one-third of the seats. After 1970 when their representation on the Commission is reduced, the Belgian and Dutch governments may find it difficult to settle on a single candidate who will be acceptable, not only to the other member countries, but also to the ethnic, religious, and political interests which these governments must traditionally take into account.

In any case, since the objective of the Rome treaties was a stable political association, strictly representative institutions and delicate calculations of relative national standings in them were less relevant and reassuring than the readiness of the membership to accept the community itself as a separate, benign, and superior entity. The community, as a manifestation of a shared common interest, would be represented in the institutions in a way which would tend to compensate for any initial disproportion in national weight or representation, and which, as the community evolved, would become the authentic spokesman of the constituent "peoples."

In greater or lesser degree, *all* the institutions created (or carried over from the CSC) by the Rome treaties—the Court, the Parliament, and the Council—are "supranational" in character, in the sense that they belong to the community, are the creatures of none of its members, and assume the existence of that measure of interdependence without which the association could not function. This is true even of the Council, the most representational of the community's major agencies. As we shall see later in our discussion of the 1965–66 crisis, the six foreign ministers meeting as ministers is quite another matter from the same six officials meeting "in Council," who become thereby a college, having certain powers, rights, and duties, proceeding in accordance with prescribed rules, and engaging in a common pursuit.[10]

None of the community institutions, however, has the precise "European" character of the Commission—that extraordinary invention of the community movement. Still further removed from the states and incarnating an additional loyalty, the Commission has that special attribute of *independence* which allows it to speak for the community with legitimacy. De Gaulle's subsequent denigration of the Commission as a group of "technocrats" lacking an essential allegiance to the nation-state should not obscure the fact that the treaty drafters—the French among them—fully intended to accord and guarantee to the Commission this very quality. To begin with, the individual Commissioners, while owing their nominations to the member governments, are appointed by "common agreement" among those governments. Once nominated and appointed, the Commis-

[10] Lindberg has said that "What distinguishes the Council from an intergovernmental body is the existence of a certain corporate spirit, which is very difficult to describe." One minister told him, "We are all 'conspirators,' no matter how violently we disagree." (Leon N. Lindberg, "Decision Making and Integration in the European Community," *International Organization*, 19, no. 1 [1965], pp. 56–80.)

sioners therefore "belong" to no state, nor are they responsible for their offices to the Council. Article 157 makes even clearer the treaty's intentions: The Commission members shall be "chosen for their general competence and . . . indisputable independence," and they "shall perform their duties in the general interest of the community [and] shall not seek or accept instructions from any government or other body," and on entering upon their duties, they shall give "solemn undertaking" to respect the obligations of the office.[11]

The treaty strives to assure the Commissioners against pressures from any quarter, giving to them a kind of judicial immunity. The states undertake to "respect" the character of the Commission and are specifically enjoined from seeking to influence the members in their performance. The Commission acts by majority vote, but at the same time, it is collectively responsible for those acts. The membership as a whole may be removed only by motion of censure and two-thirds vote of the Parliament (such vote representing a majority of the parliamentarians), and even after a vote of censure, the Commission remains in office until "common agreement" is reached among the governments on replacements. While there are arrangements for provisional suspension of Commissioners charged with malfeasance, impeachment requires a Court decision in response to Council or Commission petition.

The Commission's functions serve to fortify its key role in the institutional machinery. These functions are summarized in a general way in Article 155 which states that: (1) the Commission shall ensure the application of the EEC treaty and of the measures enacted by the EEC institutions pursuant thereto; (2) formulate recommendations or opinions where the treaty so provides, or, as the Commission itself may consider necessary; (3) participate in the preparation of "the acts" of the Council and Assembly while disposing of a specific power of decision of its own; and (4) exercise the competence conferred on it by the Council in implementing the rules the latter may lay down. As we have seen, specific authority is conferred on the Commission in numerous places throughout the treaty: It is responsible for policing the operation of the customs union, it was required to "submit proposals" for the common agricultural and transport poli-

---

[11] The distinction between the obligations and the proprieties of an office is always a delicate matter—as demonstrated most recently by the decision of one of the Commissioners of French nationality to take leave of absence in order to run—as a Gaullist —in the June elections for the French National Assembly.

cies, it negotiates commercial agreements in behalf of the community, it represents the community in legal actions, etc.

The Commission's powers are both autonomous and derivative.[12] In one of its incarnations, the Commission is head of the community bureaucracy. It carries out the measures the community has approved. In this function, the Commission's powers are principally derivative, and were they entirely so, it would still be an influential role: In policy, the EEC is remarkably *dirigiste* in character; in form, the trend may well be toward a further centralization in the French manner; and in practice, the Commission has displayed a strong— some consider, a dismaying—tendency to "govern" by proliferation of regulations which, too numerous and too complex, escape either national or supranational control. But the powers of the Commission, even as head of the bureaucracy, are not solely dependent on community decision. Were this the case, then the language of Article 155, directing the Commission to "ensure the application of the provisions of [the] treaty and the provisions enacted by the institutions," would be tautological. To the contrary, the clear meaning is that the Commission acts in its own right in determining whether there is a proper implementation of the treaty.

That the Commission was intended to exercise such autonomous powers in the conduct of community affairs is also clear if one examines its relationship with the Council. In some respects that relationship is similar, in theory if not always in practice, to the interplay between executive and legislature which is characteristic of a modern presidential democracy.[13] True, the community's executive is a plural one, its main legislative body (the Council) is small and unrepresentative, and the nominal parliament has no real powers to make laws. But these are irrelevancies so far as the concept is concerned.

[12] For the character and working of the Commission, see Noel, "The Working of the Institutions"; and Lindberg, "Decision Making and Integration."

[13] Kitzinger has argued that "only a body which feels itself to be as responsible for the whole as the President of the United States, a body which is not responsible, not beholden, and not partial to any of the constituent parts as against the rest can take supranational (or 'objective') decisions for the community as such—can act, in other words, not simply as a mediator reconciling existing national policies framed, as they often are, largely to bounce the damage off onto the neighbors, but can look afresh at specific problems as they present themselves on a Community scale and can seek solutions for them at the Community level." (*European Integration*, p. 62.) See also Noel, "The Working of the Institutions" (Kitzinger, p. 96); and David Spanier, "How Decisions Are Taken in the Common Market," *The Times* (London), April 3, 1967, p. 1.

Article 145 of the EEC treaty, describing the Council, states that "with a view to *ensuring the achievement of the objectives laid down in this treaty,*" the Council shall ensure the coordination of the general economic policies of the member states and dispose of a power of decision. Article 155, describing the Commission, states that "with a view to ensuring *the functioning and development of the Common Market*" (italics supplied) the Commission shall (in addition to its administrative functions already described) formulate recommendations or opinions, dispose of a power of decision (in fact quite limited), and participate in the preparation of acts of the Council and the Parliament.

There are obvious difference between these two formulations, allowing even for the imprecision of language. The Council is in one way an instrument for continuing the negotiations among the Six beyond the stage reached when the Rome treaties were concluded. It has the principal power to decide—i.e., to legislate; and it stands between the community on the one side and the member states on the other, reconciling and providing a necessary link between them. The Commission, by contrast, stands at the community center and apart from the states; from this perspective it formulates policy issues the Council is to decide; it is the guardian of the treaty and the guide to the community's further development. In short, the Commission is—or it should be—the community's motor and its inspiration, providing in much the same way as presidential leadership does a periodic assessment of the state of the community (the General Report on the Activities of the Community), proposing a program of action and specific legislation, and working to achieve within the Council and among competing community interests that necessary consensus which is the basis of public policy.

It was precisely to this end (i.e., to bring into existence an independent community executive exercising the prerogatives of executive leadership) that the Rome treaties gave to the Commission the right of initiative and tied this in with voting arrangements in the Council which would assure a progressive decline in the possibilities of either national domination or obstruction.

In some few instances, the member states reserved to themselves an autonomous right of decision—without intervention in any way by the Commission. One of these, as we have seen, is the appointment of the Commission which, unlike the procedures provided in the Paris treaty for the High Authority, includes no arrangement for cooptation of members. While "common agreement" among the *governments* is the voting rule in this specific instance, in matters requiring no Commission proposal the Council may decide if it is unanimous in its view or—less frequently—if there is a "special majority." There are also a few issues which the Council may decide by "simple majority" (the approval of any four of the six Council members). And finally, there are some matters on which the member states have reserved a right of veto in perpetuity even though a Commission proposal is required.[14]

In the main, however, and especially since January 1966 when the community entered upon the third and final stage of the transitional period, the most important policy decisions may be taken pursuant to a Commission proposal with the approval of only a "weighted majority" of the Council. The procedural rules set forth by the treaty in such cases are clear and precise. The Council may not act or legislate except on the basis of a draft regulation, directive, or decision formulated or at least approved by the Commission. The Council may amend that proposal—as distinct from approving or rejecting it in its entirety—only if all six members agree to the amendment. However, so long as the Council has neither approved nor rejected the proposal, the Commission may change or withdraw it—especially, as the treaty specifies, in those cases requiring the opinion of Parliament.

Moreover, the formula for a qualified majority is such that the Commission's position is in effect a component of the majority, even though the Commission has no formal vote in Council.[15] When the proposal before the Council is one advanced by the Commission, there are seventeen Council votes—four each for Germany, France, and Italy; two each for Belgium and the Netherlands; and one for Luxembourg. Twelve votes constitute a majority. Thus no state, big or small, holds a veto; any one of the three largest may block a Commission proposal only if supported by either Belgium or the Netherlands; only when they are in agreement with a Commission proposal may the three largest states combined outvote the three smallest;

[14] For the most part, these are matters which involve an extension of the obligations of membership beyond those specifically called for in the treaties, such as a further financial commitment or the revision of national legislation to conform to a common standard.

[15] "This means that the Commission has a genuine negotiating power in the Council. Discussion can be joined and it is in fact joined on the ground chosen by the European body." (Noel, "The Working of the Institutions," p. 95.)

and, theoretically at least, the Commission may maintain its policy position indefinitely, being able in principle to block any other approach so long as it retains the support of at least one of the Council's members.[16]

It is therefore evident that the right of initiative is a powerful tool—especially so in conjunction with the Commission's other attributes. It gives to the Commission that necessary measure of executive-legislative authority to permit it to surmount the formidable obstacles to community policy-formulation posed on the one hand by the ostensible separation of powers in the community design, and, on the other, by the still broad reservation of sovereignty by the member states. Like any good secretariat or bureaucracy, the Commission commands the expertise and objectivity to suggest the ways in which the common objectives of an association can best be achieved. But unlike any other secretariat or bureaucracy, the Commission is unique in the independence of its decision to select from among those ways one approach which should be advanced as community policy, and unique in its capacity to resist other proposals while developing support for its favored policy.

If the Commission is to provide effective community leadership, however, the right of initiative is not enough—it must be combined with some restraint on the agency or agencies which retain the right to decide. This is the real significance of majority voting in the Council: It enlarges the scope for, and the possibility of, executive leadership. This is not to say that the six member countries, had the treaty left the absolute right of veto totally unimpaired, would inevitably and consistently have abused that right, nor is it to suggest that the Commission, denied the leverage provided by the possibility of resort to decision by majority vote, would thereby have been deprived of the powers of persuasion and conciliation which are important instruments of its leadership. But, to retain the unrestricted right of veto is to reserve the right to deter leadership as much as it is to refuse to be led. And in an association like the European Community, a

---

[16] The voting rule applicable in those few instances when the Council may act without a Commission proposal indicates the extent to which the treaty drafters were preoccupied with the need for safeguards against domination of the community by one of the bigger powers. When no Commission proposal is involved, the treaty requires, in addition to twelve votes, the affirmative vote of at least four members—i.e., the big three would need the support of at least one Benelux country in order to have a majority. In a curious way the Benelux countries thus share with the Commission the role of defender of the common interest.

liberal resort to the threat to use the veto may have the result of substituting the negative capacity for leadership of the individual member for the positive directive capacity which the community executive was intended to provide.

POLITICAL DYNAMICS

There is ample evidence in the treaty that the member states viewed the possibility of a directionless and drifting community as a more serious threat to vital national interests than the possibility of being overridden by a community majority. As the preamble makes clear, the members idealistically wanted a dynamic and developing community and expected positive advantages from it. Practically, however, they were equally aware that integration is a process in which the laminated growth of interdependence would more and more involve them in each other's economic and political life, would make individual national obstruction dangerous and ultimately intolerable, would require that community decisions become increasingly easy to reach rather than more difficult, and which would therefore necessitate the emergence of an executive leadership aware of the national particularities but responsive ultimately to the community universality.

The treaty provisions for the creation of a Common Market in three transitional stages with specific objectives and deadlines for each stage were geared to serve this political design. While such staging provided occasion to review progress and an opportunity for each member to reassess the risks of becoming more deeply involved, it was also an assurance for one member against backsliding on the part of another, and the rules for moving from one stage to another were strongly weighted in favor of progress. Thus, under the treaty, the first stage could have been automatically extended by a year in the absence of unanimous agreement in the Council that the objectives of that stage had been achieved. After two such delays, however, only a qualified majority vote in the Council would have been required to move to the second stage. Moreover, once the first stage was completed, the states were virtually deprived of the possibility of any further delays since extension of either the second or third stages would have required a Commission proposal to that effect and the unanimous support of the Council.

The effort to make the community's political system a dynamic one is even more evident in the rules applicable to the specific objective of each stage. As we have indicated earlier, the opening of each successive stage brought with it a further extension of the possibility of majority decision and a further restriction of the right of national veto. A typical example of this is in Article 54 concerning the Right of Establishment which says that "in order to implement the general program—the Council, on a proposal of the Commission and after the Economic and Social Committee and the Assembly have been consulted, shall, until the end of the first stage by means of a unanimous vote and subsequently by means of a qualified majority vote, act by issuing directives." The treaty is replete with such instances. According to one calculation, the number of decisions requiring unanimity in the Council in the first stage was reduced by about one-fifth on the opening of the second stage and by more than one-half at the opening of the third.

The logic of this is impeccable, fully in keeping with a hardheaded sense of national interest. If economic integration means that the participating states progressively lose independent control over the essential instruments of economic direction, then that direction must be provided by the use of such instruments in common. It is to the interest of all that the community be capable of acting with the maximum of ease, speed, and flexibility commensurate with optimum advancement of the majority interest and a decent regard for the minority. To claim or to readvance the claim to a national veto in such an association is (if, indeed, it is possible at all) to assert not only the right to disrupt the community and to thwart the common interest, but to subordinate to the claimant's interests the national interests of his partners. It is this which the community design sought on the one hand to achieve, and on the other, to avoid.

Naturally, there was neither purity of form nor perfection of design in the community approach; it was a compromise, and it was left incomplete as well. The intended relationship between the Commission and Council was demarcated with considerable precision, but the roles of both vis-à-vis the Parliament are ambiguous and contradictory. And beyond the precise rules for the development of the Commission as the community executive and the stated intention to convert the Parliament into a popularly elected assembly, it was left largely unstated how these institutions should further evolve.

In the tradition of western democracy it would be possible to imagine the Council's becoming a kind of upper house of a bicameral legislature, sharing with and—like a latter-day House of Lords—

perhaps ultimately relinquishing to the lower house the pre-eminent power to decide. This would be in keeping with the concept of an eventual community of transcending common interests and declining national power. Even in the community of the 1960s, such a "council of states" would be more realistic than the existing situation in which the power to decide is wielded by a Council of Ministers of ex officio members whose tenure is determined by political events principally of local significance, whose technical competence is increasingly in question in the complex world of community affairs, and who are far removed from the interests and the individuals affected by their decisions. But there is no provision for such a line of development in the Rome treaties, nor has anyone pressed a case that the Council members be made more representative, that they be chosen by the national parliaments (as U.S. senators once were chosen by the state legislatures), or even that they have no other jobs.

Nor is the future development of the Commission less ambiguous. The method of its selection, the sources of its power, and the prerogatives of its office give to the Commission attributes of presidential leadership, but it is difficult to see in what other ways the Commission could be confirmed and strengthened in that role. In the situation of Europe in the late 1960s one can scarcely conceive of an elected single executive, and a plural one might well be inclined to represent regional constituents rather than the community as a whole. To the extent that there has been serious thinking about the community's political future, it has been far more usual to see in the Commission the vestigial cabinet of some future parliamentary democracy. Indeed, the Commission, in one of its most "political" acts, sought to increase its own accountability under the treaty to the Parliament.

Justified, perhaps, as a response to the growing alarm that the Commission already disposes of impressive funds and power without any real control, moves to subordinate the Commission to Parliament nevertheless raise their questions, too. The Commissioners owe their offices to that "common agreement" among the states, but they are collectively responsible to Parliament which may remove them by vote of censure. The Parliament has never used that power, and more often than not, it has made common cause with the Commission against the Council and the member states. There are thus no precedents, but one may wonder whether a vote of censure would increase or reduce the prospects of creating a focus of community authority. What kind of executive leadership could be expected from a Commission whose office was conferrable by one agency (representing the governments in power) but withdrawable by another (representing—imperfectly—a cross-section of all the parties in the national parliaments), while the essential power to decide was vested in still a third agency (representing the majority parties)?

This, of course, only points up that ultimate of peculiarities—the European Parliament itself. In addition to the right of censure, the Parliament has the "powers of deliberation and of control." The Parliament must be consulted on all major Commission proposals; it receives and debates the General Report; it may submit recommendations to the Council on the budget; it has an annual colloquy with the Council; and it may interrogate the Commission, which it has endlessly done. In practice, the Parliament has become a useful forum for debate, a source of ideas and recommendations, and by virtue of the fact that its membership is still drawn from the national parliaments, another means of bridging the gap between the community and the national governments. Organized, moreover, on a party basis, the Parliament encourages thinking on community-wide policies which are hopefully more than mere combinations of the national ones. It remains the symbol of the hope for a European constituent assembly.

But the European Parliament is not the mother of parliaments. It makes no policies, passes no legislation, appropriates no money, brings down no governments. Nor does it even represent, as the treaty intended it should. None of the appointive delegations has thus far included a communist, even though the French and Italian communist parties have regularly polled 20 and 25 percent of the total vote. And while the Assembly some eight years ago fulfilled the obligations of Article 138 to "draw up proposals for [its] election by direct universal suffrage in accordance with a uniform procedure in all member states," the Council has never been able to determine "by means of a unanimous vote" the election provisions it would recommend to the member governments for adoption.[17] As the French have said, since the community as a whole lacks governmental powers, it would be risky to impute them to one of its agencies!

Thus, the European Community as a political system projects the same equivocal profile which we attributed to it as an economic one. A "political community" of sorts has been constructed, and it con-

---

[17] Key portions of the Parliament's draft convention are contained in Kitzinger, *European Common Market*, pp. 104–8.

tinues to exist; without a measure of effectiveness in the operation of its institutions it would be difficult to conceive how the community could have reached the level of development and cohesion it has by 1968. Vague though the ultimate design may be and uncertain its future development, there is in the community the potentiality for a political organization whose jurisdiction would extend beyond the economic sphere. But, objectively, one must also deplore the inadequacy of the community's institutions and be healthily skeptical that their full potential will soon be realized. In the next chapter we shall see how the dynamic elements of the EEC's political system precipitated the constitutional crisis of 1965–66, but we shall also see that it is unfortunately the Europeanists' task to defend the community's institutions rather than to reform them—not because they are the best, but because they are not the worst.

V   A TEST OF THE CONCEPT: THE 1965-66 CRISIS

In the early morning hours of July 1, 1965, the French Foreign Minister, M. Couve de Murville, then chairman of the Council of Ministers, abruptly ended a meeting of the EEC Council, declaring it impossible to reach agreement on the matter under consideration— the arrangements for financing the CAP over the next four years. Although exhausted by several days of technical discussions and heated controversy, the other ministers responded that they were nonetheless prepared either to continue the talks or to resume them at a later date, and the Commission offered to revise its proposals in still another effort to find a solution. But the French were adamant, the meeting broke up, and Couve—accusing the other EEC members of reneging on their promises and warning that "each government must draw the consequences"—departed for Paris.

So began the third, but not the last, of the French-inspired crises in the European community movement. Each of the three emergencies—the rejection of the EDC by the French National Assembly, de Gaulle's veto of Britain's first application for EEC accession, and the eight-month boycott which followed Couve's withdrawal from the Council—was highly disruptive and each was clearly related to the others. In important ways, however, the so-called "June 30 crisis" was the crucial one. Despite the technicality of the specific issues, the crisis was in fact brought on by a reaction against the growth and maturation of the community system, and it therefore developed into a contest between the community and the anticommunity. While the "Europeans" ultimately found in this instance the strength to rise to the challenge, their inability to get a clear-cut resolution of the issues in their favor is a prime source of the malaise from which the community must ultimately escape or perish. And no other event has so clearly illuminated the lasting antagonism between the community's political aspirations and those of de Gaulle.

THE ORIGINS OF THE CRISIS

The genesis of the crisis is, in terms of this discussion, more significant even than its denouement. There are earlier and excellent works to which the reader can refer for a more detailed account of the crisis and the subsequent events,[1] but without some knowledge of the precipitating causes, it is difficult to appreciate that the crisis was as much a proof of community potential as it was of poverty.

The dispute over agricultural financing from which the larger dispute emerged had its sources in the EEC treaty and, more particularly, in the inability of the treaty negotiators to decide definitively either the agricultural policy of the community or the revenue resources which would be allotted to the community as a whole. In both cases the broad objectives and the general line of development were stated, but the Council—with the assistance of the Commission —was told in effect to resume the negotiations which had not been completed when the Rome treaties were signed.

The rules the treaty prescribed in the two cases were not precisely symmetrical, however. The end of the transitional period was set as the deadline for the effectuation of the CAP, and after the completion of the first two stages of the transitional period (i.e., after January 1966) the Council was authorized to issue the necessary regulations by *qualified majority vote* on Commission proposals. But, in keeping with the chary attitude of the members toward commitments either of a financial sort or going beyond those undertaken in the treaty, no specific deadline was set for agreement on the community's eventual revenue sources, and while the Commission could submit proposals to the Council, the latter could decide only by *unanimous* vote what provisions it would "recommend" for adoption by the member states "in accordance with their respective constitutional rules."

Once the EEC was organized in 1958, steps to carry out the treaty's provisions regarding agriculture began almost immediately, and for the next several years, the CAP issue was in the forefront of the

---

[1] In particular, Miriam Camps, *European Unification in the Sixties* (New York: McGraw-Hill, 1966); and John Newhouse, *Collision in Brussels* (London: Faber and Faber, 1967).

community's internal interests. There were a number of weighty reasons for this superconcentration on what was, after all, only one aspect of the market's organization. Having made and accepted the point (particularly in the argument over the free trade area) that there could be no economic union which did not include agriculture, all the members felt more or less obliged to follow through—especially when the inclusion of agriculture was a part of the bargain to set up a balanced community. This general sense of obligation was heavily fortified by pressures from two quarters—the French and the Commission—which, with quite differing motivations, were equally insistent on the earliest possible institution of the agricultural market.

For Paris, the agricultural community was a question of money and influence. As the leading agricultural state but by no means the strongest industrially, France saw in the development of intracommunity trade in farm products the sine que non of economic parity within the EEC. It also saw the larger market as a way of accelerating the rationalization of France's antiquated farming methods, shifting part of the cost to the other EEC members, and releasing resources to enhance French industrial—and military?—potential. For the Commission, although certainly not indifferent to the monetary angle, the CAP was perhaps more a question of influence. Like the member governments, it saw and accepted the CAP as an essential element of the economic balance which, especially after the accession of de Gaulle, seemed an imperative necessity if France were to be kept fully "engaged" in the community. But above all the Commission detected in the treaty prescription for a "common organization of agricultural markets" the most promising opportunity to commit the member states more deeply to a supranational Common Market.

The result of these insistent pressures was the series of agricultural regulations which, beginning in January 1962, appeared, usually painfully but more or less regularly, until the breakdown over financing in mid-1965. The main characteristics of the CAP as contained in this legislation (see also Chapter II) are as follows: First, the kind of market envisaged in the CAP is an organized, stylized, and highly integrated one. The previously existing national mechanisms for the regulation of production and trade in farm products are replaced by product markets organized on a community basis, and control over the main regulatory devices, minimum prices and variable import levies, is vested in community institutions. Second, the CAP is a sectoral policy, designed intentionally for the primary benefit of the

farmers and therefore discriminatory in the advantages and disadvantages it confers on the member states. Inasmuch as the customs
union creates a larger market for industry and is advantageous to the
more industrialized members, "fairness" requires that the CAP provide an *assured* market for the farmer—or so it was held. And to the
extent that insufficient outlets are created within the community, the
industrialized members which continue to import food from outside
the EEC have an obligation to assist in the subsidized disposal on
the world market of any surplus produce the community itself cannot
absorb. Third, the CAP is virtually bound to be expensive, not only
in higher prices in individual countries, but in budgetary outlays by
the community itself. The CAP is in effect a bargain: In return for the
introduction of free trade in farm products within an organized market, the community assumes the costs of that market—price supports,
export subsidies, plus any additional measures undertaken to enable
the marginal producer to adjust to intracommunity competition.[2]

The ramifications of any far-reaching bargain are often imperfectly
understood at the time the deal is made, and in the case of the CAP,
there were intimations of future disputes almost from the start. While
the second thoughts which quickly followed the initial CAP agreement
of January 14, 1962 reflected some of the basic reservations we have
earlier cited, a main source of uneasiness was the program's financial
implications. The eventual costs of the CAP were even more specula-
tive in 1962 than in 1968, and unfortunately, the first attempt to
provide for them was bungled.

This first attempt was the famous "Regulation 25," one of the
numerous laws approved by the Council pursuant to the 1962 agreements which set up the market organizations for cereals, pork, eggs
and poultry, fruits, vegetables, and wine. Law 25 is the basic financial
regulation of the entire farm program. It established the principle of
community financial responsibility for the program and created the
Agricultural Guidance and Guarantee Fund (FEOGA) as the instrument to meet that responsibility. The guarantee section of FEOGA
helps finance internal price supports and export subsidies, while the
guidance section contributes funds to encourage structural improvements. Under the transitional rules set forth in the law, for example,

---

[2] An excellent commentary on the economic and political ramifications of the CAP,
including some prescient comments on its later difficulties, is to be found in an un-
signed article, "Agricultural Policy—An Affair of State of the First Rank," *Neue Zuer-
icher Zeitung*, September 2, 1966, p. 1.

FEOGA was required to reimburse state refunds on exports of farm produce to nonmembers according to a graduated scale (increasing at the rate of one-sixth per year from mid-1962 to mid-1965), and guidance disbursements were limited to no more than one-third of total guarantee expenditures.

FEOGA's fiscal requirements are an integral part of the community's budget, and Law 25 was intended to provide the necessary means. But it did so in an incomplete and sketchy way. Looking first toward the future when the "single market stage" would be reached, the regulation stated as follows (Article 2): "Revenue from levies charged on imports from third countries shall be the property of the Community and shall be appropriated to Community expenditure; the budget resources of the Community shall comprise such revenue together with all other revenue decided in accordance with the rules of the treaty as well as contributions of member states in accordance with Article 200 of the treaty. The Council shall in due course initiate the procedure laid down in Article 201 of the treaty so as to implement the above provisions."

Articles 200 and 201 are the revenue portions of the general financial provisions of the treaty. The first article states that the community's revenues, "apart from any other revenues," shall consist of contributions from the members according to the following scale: France, Germany, and Italy—28 percent; Belgium and the Netherlands—7.9 percent; and Luxembourg—0.2 percent. Article 201, however, requires the Commission to study the conditions under which these financial contributions "may be replaced by other resources of the Community itself, in particular by revenue accruing from the common customs tariff when the latter has been definitely introduced." As we have noted, such proposals by the Commission require the Council's unanimous approval and constitutional action by the member states. Thus, so far as the medium-term future was concerned, the effect of Law 25 was: (1) a straightforward reaffirmation of the provisions of the treaty, and (2) an apparent but indefinite acceleration of the procedures required for the community to acquire its own revenue resources.

Law 25's provisions concerning the period prior to the single market were a good deal more ambiguous. In the first place, it dealt with the revenue and expenditure arrangements for only the period through mid-1965, leaving to further negotiations what provisions should apply after that. In the second place, while providing that the contributions to the fund in the year 1962–1963 should be in accordance with the scale set forth in Article 200, Law 25 stated that in the two following years, 10 and 20 percent respectively of the contributions would be "in proportion to net imports from third countries," but it did not define the precise meaning of this criterion. (Indeed, a supplementary regulation approved by the Council in May 1962 placed ceilings on the maximum contributions any member would have to make to FEOGA; according to some interpretations, this would have had the effect of countermanding the scale of contributions which had been agreed to in the January regulation.)[3] And third, missing from the law's provisions were a number of key implementative and operative regulations, including the precise decision-making machinery.

Partly for what it decided and partly for what it avoided deciding, Law 25 thus contained the seeds of serious differences, and it is important to realize why. One of the reasons was the magnitude of the purely pecuniary considerations involved in financing the CAP and its implications for the individual member states and for the community.

In the 1962–64 period, when the implementation of Law 25 was initially under consideration, all of the following key decisions had to be made: the level of unified grain prices in the community, the kind of structural program which would accompany such unification, and the marketing arrangements for fats and oils. Moreover, it is in the nature of the CAP that its costs are comparatively unpredictable, depending in considerable part on the fluctuating ratio between EEC and world prices and on the effect of the former on community production. Nevertheless, projections had to be made. In 1963, for example, the Agricultural Committee of the European Parliament calculated a rise in FEOGA's outlays from $20 million in 1963 to $200 million in 1965 to a whopping $800 million by 1970.[4] Other opinion was inclined to put the maximum even higher—perhaps close to $1 billion per year.[5]

From the *community* point of view, this was undoubtedly an exhilarating prospect. From 1958 to 1963, the EEC's annual expendi-

---

[3] Examples of how it was thought this supplementary regulation would work are found in European Parliament, Documents de Séance, Doc. 82, October 16, 1963.

[4] European Parliament, Documents de Séance, Doc. 81, October 15, 1963.

[5] Since the dairy program alone is now expected to cost the community some $800 million during the 1968–69 crop year, these estimates were obviously much too conservative.

tures had remained below $60 million, and the costs of the CAP would, so to speak, thrust the community into the budgetary big league. But, to what extent the *individual member states* found themselves welcoming this event depended on their relative positions as potential beneficiaries of and contributors to FEOGA's expenditures.

In view of Law 25's limitation on disbursements for structural improvements, the balance of potential advantage on *the receiving end* was decidedly in favor of the major agricultural exporters (France and the Netherlands) and against the major importers (Germany and Italy)[6] which, while eligible for "guidance" funds, had much smaller claim on FEOGA for price supports and export subsidies. Illustrative of the sums involved in French anticipations, France's finance minister told the press in December 1963 that "in the absence of a common policy" the government's appropriation for agricultural supports was expected to double in the next three years—i.e., to about $600 million in 1966–67.[7] With the common policy developing along the lines set out in Law 25, roughly two-thirds of that amount would have been chargeable to the community.

On *the contributing end*, the balance of potential advantage was also on the side of the exporting members—provided they could hold the community to the policy line set forth in Law 25 and provided the interpretation of the law's ambiguities was a "favorable" one. If from 1965 to 1970 the proportion of member states' contributions based on "net imports" were progressively increased as Law 25 implied, and if the ceiling provided in the Council decision of May 1962 were eliminated, then under some interpretations of the meaning of "net imports" France and the Netherlands would be paying much less than the standard share called for under the key in Article 200, while Italy and Germany would bear a heavy financial burden. Whether after 1970 when, according to Law 25, the agricultural levies should become community property, the inequity would be redressed would depend on the agreement reached in the meantime on what other revenues should accrue to the community.

The pecuniary implications of Law 25 were therefore sufficiently far-reaching to reopen the whole question of burden sharing and of equitable balance within the community.

[6] The change in Italy's position from a net exporter to a net importer of food—while the CAP was being developed—was an important complicating factor in the subsequent dispute over the financial regulation.

[7] An interview reported in *Agence Economique et Financière*, December 27–28, 1963.

For the French, Law 25 was the keystone of the agricultural community and a guarantee that, to the extent the EEC failed by protective measures to provide an outlet for French production within the community, the community (and its importing members specifically) would pick up the tab for surplus disposal outside the EEC. It was essential to nail down this guarantee, and Paris was willing to pay the price (or so it appeared in 1962 and 1963) of an integrated market managed by community institutions with an independent source of revenue. In some respects the Netherlands had a very similar view. For the Germans, the Italians, and to some extent the BLEU countries, however, Law 25 raised the specter of a community whose budget would be largely absorbed by the requirements of the agricultural program—financed by them for the benefit primarily of others. In short, an EEC which had been conceived on the principle of fair shares (but with a solicitous regard for France's problems) might become in practice a community of, by, and for the French peasant.

The issues were not so starkly drawn, nor were they considered in so exclusively a crass perspective. Had the issues been debated solely on this basis, the six members—with their penchant for package deals or the postponement of decisions too painful to face—might well have found much earlier the "solution" they resorted to in 1966 after the crisis had run its course. But just as Law 25 impinged on major national concerns, it also involved the *vital community interest*. By deciding, only hesitantly and none too courageously, to remain the spokesman of that interest, the Commission precipitated the head-on clash between its concept of what the Common Market should become and de Gaulle's—a confrontation which, in any case inevitable, might otherwise have occurred somewhat later.

While the Commission shared with Paris a common zeal for early confirmation and implementation of the arrangements set out in Law 25, there was never an exact identity of interest or objective between them. Whereas France was principally interested in preventing any backtracking on the agricultural policy and in assuring that the necessary funds would without question be available, the Commission's considerations went beyond these to the importance of the financial regulations per se to the community and to its long-term economic and political development. Law 25, like the CAP itself, was for the Commission another device for achieving a truly integrated community.

If we recall some of the specific considerations involved, this was by no means the quixotic aspiration the later setbacks were to make it seem. The sums involved were sufficiently large to provoke serious reflection. Allowing for even limited growth in the expenditures of EURATOM, the CSC, and other EEC institutions (such as the Investment Bank, the Social Fund, and the Overseas Development Fund), the projected billion dollar per year budget for the CAP made it entirely likely that the community would within a comparatively short time account for a sizable chunk of total public outlays. On the revenue side of the ledger, the funds tentatively earmarked for community use by Article 201 and Law 25 were even more impressive. According to the estimates made in 1963 and 1964, the income from the agricultural levies, although highly contingent and difficult to predict with precision, might eventually total as much as $600 million a year. Were the proceeds from the common external tariff also to become community revenues, as suggested by Article 201, then total community income might amount to $3 billion a year.[8]

From the Commission's point of view, "the community interest" clearly required that this opportunity not be missed. An independent income of such dimensions would not only safeguard financially the area in which integration had already advanced the furthest—i.e., agriculture; it would extend that area in a way which would be economically, politically, and psychologically important. If the member states were to relinquish to the community such time-honored sources of public revenues as duties on imports this would involve a notable transfer of sovereignty—to be acquired by the EEC, as a natural consequence of its most striking accomplishments—the establishment of the customs union and the organization of the agricultural market. If, as seemed likely, such revenues were to exceed expenditures, then the community could either expand its operations or rebate the excess to the states, thus initiating the reversal of the hierarchical subordination of the community to the states which is the logical inference of a community dependent on "national contributions."

It was, of course, far easier for all concerned to draw these implications than it was to act upon them. For example, a community with an increasingly autonomous power to tax and to spend would need its own fiscal policy. This policy would be a less negligible and passive factor than theretofore in the harmonization of member's equilib-

[8] *Agence Europe*, March 8, 1965.

rium policies. Although this might look very desirable from a community point of view, it might have unequal appeal to the members. There was also the matter of equity. Since customs duties accounted for different proportions of national revenues (e.g., some 12 percent in France, but only 8 percent in Germany[9]), a simple decision to transfer this source of revenue to the community might involve unequal sacrifices and aggravate existing distortions of competition arising out of differing tax systems. Germany and the Netherlands, the great importing nations with the community's leading ports of entry, might find they were "turning over" to the community a substantial portion of its income. On the other hand, to the extent that the goods in question were destined ultimately for other EEC consumers, the country of ultimate destination might feel the country of entry had no legitimate claim in any case to retain the duties collected.

Of all the inferences to be drawn from the prospective implementation of an integrated and autonomously financed agricultural program, however, the most difficult—and from a community point of view the most important—to act upon was the *institutional* one. If the states relinquished not only the determination of agricultural policies, but also the wherewithal to finance them, then where in the community would political and financial accountability reside? The Commission, proposing what those policies should be and overseeing the disbursements of the funds allocated to them, is responsible to the European Parliament, but in so drastic a way that the accountability has only marginal significance. While the individual ministers are answerable to their respective governments (less immediately, perhaps, than is sometimes supposed), the Council, which legislates the program and appropriates the necessary monies, is responsible as a whole to no one. Therefore, in the view of those who were increasingly uneasy about the insulation of the community from the public interest, the absence of democratic control in an organization controlling funds running into the billions—and potentially far exceeding the requirements of the community as it had so far been agreed upon—was an alarming prospect.

It is not to the Commission's credit that it was slow at the beginning to champion the cause of democracy as opposed to the extension of the common sovereignty as such. The draft regulations to give effect to Law 25, which were proposed by the Commission in

[9] *Ibid.*

March 1963, contained no reference to the European Parliament's role. One of the parliamentary committees accordingly proposed to amend these regulations to require the Commission to submit proposals within a year to establish the European Parliament's right to approve appropriations which no longer came under the control of the national parliaments. Moreover, the Parliament as a whole *unanimously* approved a proposal to require that its views on the draft budget be accepted unless the Council by unanimous vote should reject them.[10] In fairness to the Commission, it was of course evident to all that the European parliamentarians did not speak for the member governments. Only the Dutch were determinedly insistent on "democratization," declaring that parliamentary control was a necessary condition for Netherlands' approval of any financial regulation. Even so, in December 1963, at Dutch behest, the Council did agree to insert in the minutes of its meeting a statement to the effect that it attached "great importance . . . to the problem of reinforcement of the budgetary powers of the Parliament."[11]

Within a matter of months after the approval of Law 25, therefore, all of the elements of the subsequent crisis were not only present but known, and only a few more acts were required to bring the drama to its climax. Nevertheless, it was slow to evolve. During the negotiations in the latter part of 1962 on Britain's first application for EEC membership, the French and the Commission both tried to obtain more difinitive commitments regarding the community's financial future, its revenue sources and expenditures, but the Germans and Dutch—as well as the British—declined to go beyond the unimplemented, open-ended, and ambiguous arrangements set out in Law 25. French fear that even those arrangements might come undone was almost certainly a contributory factor in de Gaulle's decision to block the British application the following January. The crisis which followed the veto was a lamentably short one, but the atmosphere was scarcely conducive to a settlement of fundamental issues, and the financial decisions taken by the Council in December 1963, while important, were the easier ones. They provided for the organization of the FEOGA, a supervisory mechanism over it, and the general rules for its operation; and at long last, the meaning of "net imports" was defined. But the Council did not determine how rapidly FEOGA would assume full responsibility for financing the CAP or how it

[10] European Parliament, Documents de Séance, Doc. 82, October 16, 1963.
[11] Commission Press Release, July 2, 1965.

would obtain the necessary funds to do this from 1965 to the end of the transition period in 1970.

Nevertheless, the agricultural policy had brought the community to the point that the further elaboration achieved in the marathon Council meetings in December 1964 would make it impossible for the governments to delay acting much longer on even the difficult implications of Law 25. On the one hand, the period for which the regulation had provided interim financing had all but run out; on the other, the new agreements had the effect of confirming the permanence of the community's commitment to the CAP while sharply increasing the size and urgency of the financial obligation involved. These agreements were: (1) the formula for the unification by July 1, 1967 of grain prices which the Germans, bowing to three months of fierce intimidation by the French, reluctantly accepted—thus clearing away the largest single obstacle remaining to the opening of a single market in grains and derivative farm products; (2) a decision that the FEOGA should assume full financial responsibility for price supports and export subsidies for the various commodities as soon as common prices for those commodities were instituted—some of these prices already decided and others projected; (3) a decision to bring fruits and vegetables within the framework of the support policy applicable to other farm products—thus increasing the potential financial requirements still further; and (4) a request to the Commission that by April 1, 1965 it submit proposals for financing the CAP from 1965 to 1970, and in addition thereto, "proposals on the conditions for implementing Article 2 of Law 25 as from the entry into force of common prices for the various agricultural products"— thus formally initiating and accelerating the procedures foreseen in that law and in Article 201 for the community to acquire its own revenue sources.

A CRISIS OF CONSTITUTION-MAKING

It is this background, that long and tedious development of the CAP from the first major breakthrough in January 1962 to the confirmatory one in December 1964, which gives meaning to the crisis which erupted with such shattering effect the following July. Eight years before in Rome—having agreed to accept certain principles, to abide by certain rules, and to create certain facilitating institutions—the six community countries undertook to launch a *process* which would culminate in the establishment of an autonomous and centralized authority over their common interests. During the ensuing eight years, this process of constitution-making—of demarcating and extending the uncertain and comparatively restricted scope of the European jurisdiction set forth in the Rome and Paris treaties—had its most significant development in the elaboration of the community's agricultural program. When Couve walked out of the Council meeting on July 1, however, he in effect declared France's intention to bring to a stop *this* process of European constitution-making—and challenged the other members to continue it in the face of the opposing will of France.

This was the meaning of the crisis of 1965–66. The reader may again refer to the cited sources[12] for a blow-by-blow account of how the community survived the critical months of the French boycott, but the comments which follow may illuminate why the crisis should be understood as the inconclusive confrontation which it was between conflicting visions of the future European order.

The Logical Imperatives of the CAP. The Commission's economic and political proposals of April 1, 1965 were in keeping with the instructions received from the Council; their content was largely foreshadowed by decisions previously taken, and they were impeccably in accord with the underlying logic of the Rome treaties—that economic-political union is the ineluctable consequence of economic integration. If in some respects they went further than some had expected or wished, the Commission was, after all, the community's designated custodian and obliged by that role to advocate optimum solutions—on their merits or whenever ambiguity of law or division of opinion should leave a choice.

The opportunities of this sort provided by Law 25 were, as we have seen, extended by the December 1964 decisions. Law 25 had said that the community should have its own financial sources at the "single market stage," but it did not define this. The December agreements therefore called for the implementation of this provision "as from the entry into force of common prices for the various agricultural products." Since the Council had already decided that common prices for grains and derivative products should go into effect on July 1, 1967, the Commission considered it not only desirable but

---

[12] Consult in particular Miriam Camps on whom I have relied for a good deal of the factual data which follows. She is a bit hard on the Commission, in my view, and I have some reservations about her conclusion, qualified though it is, that the Five "handled the crisis . . . very well." (Camps, *European Unification*, p. 124.)

proper that this should become the effective date of the "single market" as a whole and that at this time the common prices for *all* farm products should be introduced, together with complete community financing of the respective marketing organizations. Moreover, in the Commission view, it was desirable that the opening of the free market in agriculture be accompanied by the completion of the customs union for industrial products.

These recommendations were perfectly sensible. To establish a subsidized single market for some farm products but not for all would, the Commission believed, alter production patterns and benefit some producers and countries at the expense of others. Similarly, if the customs union lagged behind the agricultural market, then the whole balance of benefits within the community might be disturbed. Naturally, in the Commission's reasoning, good logic combined with good tactics—or what seemed to be, before the event. The French had argued the previous December that the "single market stage" should coincide with the introduction of common prices, and under the Commission's proposals, Paris would get its way. But, if the single market included all farm produce and were linked with completion of the customs union, then the accelerated timetable would have more generalized advantages and would command the broader support it required.

In any case, the timetable was a key element in the logic of the Commission's specific proposals for the new financial regulation itself. For the two years remaining prior to the single market stage (the crop years 1965–66 and 1966–67) the Commission asked for a mere extension of the arrangements already in effect—i.e., national contributions of an agreed amount, with the community assuming further step increases in its responsibility for paying for the CAP. But, having effectively argued the case for advancing the single market stage and the customs union by some two and a half years, the Commission was able to call on the Council simply to fill in the details of long-existing agreements. As provided by Law 25, the agricultural levies should belong in toto to the community as of July 1, 1967, and the procedures set forth in Article 201 should be put in motion so that the customs duties would begin to accrue to the community at the same time and become entirely its property by 1972. If revenues exceeded the expenditures, the Commission added, the excess would be returned to the states.

Finally, in a veritable monument to logic, the Commission tied into these financial proposals some recommendations regarding the budgetary powers of the Parliament. If the community were to obtain its own sources of financing and thereby escape from financial dependence on the national parliaments, then it was imperative that the control function begin to reappear in a representative community agency. To that end the Commission proposed several amendments to the Rome treaties. One would permit the Assembly by majority vote to propose changes in the community budget which, if approved by the Commission, could be rejected by the Council only if opposed by five of the six members.[13] Another change, to become effective only after the Parliament had been popularly elected, would permit the Council to adopt by a qualified majority vote any other Commission proposal for financing the community if that proposal had been endorsed by two-thirds of Parliament.[14]

Taken together, the Commission's recommendations would, if approved, have significantly strengthened the community at the center while beginning the much-needed process of bringing its excessive bureaucratization under democratic control. But, in the context of the community's development at the time (and certainly in the light of its future needs), the proposals were individually modest, each was the culmination of several years of development, and none of them occasioned much surprise. A possible exception to this was the Commission's suggestion that export subsidies be financed by the community only if within the framework of agreements of a "community nature." This was a frank and open bid to the members to get on with the agreement on a common commercial policy which was lagging in the face of French resistance. But, even in this case, there was ample justification for accelerating the commercial policy in the proposed early establishment of the customs union—as there was also in the growing uneasiness that the community might be called on to subsidize France's new efforts to curry favor in the East.

The Commission as Catalyst. Given the evolutionary character of the Commission's approach, the charges leveled at it—of arrogance on the one side and naïveté on the other—are debatable to say the least. De Gaulle sought to portray the Commission as an "embryonic

[13] If the Commission were opposed to the Assembly's changes, the Council could adopt the budget recommendations originally submitted by the Commission if only four of the six members approved it. The French were quick to charge that these arrangements cast the Commission in the role of "intermediary."

[14] Until the Parliament enjoyed a popular mandate, the Council would have to be unanimous in approving new sources of revenue.

technocracy" bent on usurping French sovereignty and denying to France its "freedom of action." In the first few months of the crisis, echoes of these charges were heard in surprising quarters. At the other extreme, however, some of the more ardent Europeanists have criticized the Commission, not for having political objectives, but for having reached for them in so inept a way. In his book, *The Eurocrats,* Altiero Spinelli found it nearly incredible that the Commission failed to mobilize political support for its actions, a priori. "If the facts were not spread out so clearly," he writes, "one could not easily credit the insipience of projecting a true institutional revolution without basing it on some kind of political strategy."[15]

The Gaullist position we may dismiss as self-serving, and the more widely accepted view that the April proposals marked a new and radical departure from the Commission's previous strategy for "handling" the French seems to stem in part at least from the desire for a scapegoat. The Commission, it is true, had traditionally sought to proceed when possible in association with French interests, to base itself unchallengeably on the treaty, and to link each step in logical sequence to a foregoing one. But the Commission had never concealed since its inception that the community was a political undertaking which involved for the nation-states a political price.[16] If there was any change from this in the April proposals, it was primarily one of degree and only marginally of kind. The specific advantages for the French (the accelerated introduction of the CAP with assured financing) were perhaps the largest ever—and the more difficult to reject for having been previously endorsed by Paris so clearly. Nor was the previous approach to supranationalism by slow accretion abandoned. At most, the projected advance was perhaps a more visible acceleration—and easier to oppose because it required changes in the treaties.[17]

As for the charge that the Commission, in a fit of euphoria, raised its aspirations too high, it is true that after the grain price agreement there was respectable opinion as well as injudicious boasting that the community had arrived at a point where any member of a mind

[15] Spinelli, *The Eurocrats*, p. 209.

[16] However, Mrs. Camps and others have speculated that some French ministers "conspired" to keep from de Gaulle some of the political implications of the community's advancing integration.

[17] Implementation of Article 201 required in any case a cranking up of the constitutional machinery—as did the agreement on the fusion of the community executives approved in the spring of 1965.

to withdraw would encounter almost prohibitive costs. While such a prognosis may have figured in the Commission's decision to advance its optimum proposals and to bargain hard for their approval, there is ample reason to believe that it was prepared to settle for less or to entertain a certain delay. The proposed treaty amendments which required parliamentary ratification could not, in any case, have been quickly achieved. When Couve adjourned the Council on July 1, the Commission had indicated its desire to submit new proposals, and in the bargaining which preceded that adjournment, there was evident the basis for a compromise—had the French an intention to agree.

The accusation that the Commission was guilty even more of negligence than of hubris is also a disputable one. As Mrs. Camps has pointed out, the Commission (to the annoyance of the French) took early steps to win over the European Parliament, and it had the support of the Economic and Social Committee as well. Outside the community organization, the Netherlands and Italian parliaments, individual parliamentary groups, the community representation of the socialist parties, and the only private group of real significance— the Monnet Committee—had all endorsed the Commission's proposals even before the serious negotiations began. Even granting the possibility that the Commission might have shown more initiative in this respect, it is doubtful this would have counted for more, given de Gaulle's intractable opposition to the political community and the unwillingness of the Five to submerge their individual reservations about the April proposals and to rally to their cause. Thus, the opportunity for mobilizing political action—at the governmental level in the Five and at the grass-roots level in France—arose only after de Gaulle had made it clear that the dispute no longer focused on the more or less inscrutable issues of the financial regulations, but on the future of the community itself.[18]

---

[18] Newhouse's lively and entertaining book, *Collision in Brussels*, documents very well the difficulty of evaluating the crisis and the respective roles in it of de Gaulle and the Commission. He appears to share some of the criticisms which have been leveled at the Commission's procedure in drafting the financial regulation, at its neglect of government opinion, and at Hallstein's individual foibles. (See Chapters III and IV.) If, however, "the Commission proposals were more the occasion than the cause of the crisis" (p. 21) and if "the timing and the nature and the resolution of the crisis were in larger part traceable to a hardening of Gaullist diplomacy vis-à-vis his partners and Allies, particularly Germany," (pp. 23–24) then the tactical failures of the Commission were surely not decisive nor would a more modest approach on its part (pp. 73–77) necessarily have served the community better. If de Gaulle had

De Gaulle's Objectives. Because the Five were not as determined at the beginning to defend the community as de Gaulle was to destroy it, Paris may have expected to win this larger issue by default rather than by force. According to Mrs. Camps, it was possible until the moment of Couve's walkout to see in the French position on the Commission's projosals a chance, not for compromise, but for another arrangement which would satisfy the immediate requirements of the CAP but delay the political reckoning. The French themselves had pointed to such a possibility in May by dropping their earlier support for instituting the single market in 1967. This was a reversal which undercut the rationale which had enabled the Commission to recommend that the customs union also be brought forward and that an early decision be taken on the community's own resources and on the budgetary powers of the Parliament. Naturally this did not mean that de Gaulle was prepared to delay the substance of the agricultural market (as opposed to its formality) or to accept another interim financing arrangement of limited duration. It did seem to mean he would be willing to delay the happy day when the greater share of the cost of the CAP would be definitively shifted to others.

Any hopes inspired by the relatively low profile the French presented in the earlier debates on the Commission's proposals were bound to be illusory. It is always tricky to iron out the details of a compromise which is patently one-sided and to put a proper face on it. In this case, while numerous formulations were tried, there was no way to conceal the fact that de Gaulle was unwilling to make any political concessions—he was unwilling even to set a date when he *might* make concessions. To have expected otherwise of him was to misinterpret the whole record of France's relations with the community after the Gaullist accession and to misread the intimations of preparations for a showdown which were clearly evident for several months before the crisis finally occurred.

---

decided by June 18 that he wanted the crisis (p. 121) which he later termed inevitable, it is not altogther persuasive to chide the Commission with having abandoned its initiative and mediatory functions in declining to amend its proposals until the climactic meeting on June 30. Every great crisis is inevitably accompanied by its contradictions, but it seems to me that they are fewer in this instance if one accepts that there was in fact no way for the community to avoid becoming "trapped in a political struggle" since its future was one of the key issues to be resolved. The community system—evolving out of such landmarks as Law 25—had simply become in de Gaulle's view a dangerous restraint on France's national self-assertion, and he was determined to overthrow that system.

Those who apologize for the General claim that, prior to the crisis, he kept his promise to abide by France's treaty commitments. If this is true—and it is debatable—it is in any case meaningless when applied to the Common Market where the commitment to the spirit is as important perhaps as the letter of the law. What is true is that for seven years there was a modus vivendi between Paris and Brussels which was profitable to both. But this relationship involved no conversions, as de Gaulle's tireless inveighing against the foreign "Areopagus" and his advocacy of superimposing institutions had made amply clear. And having failed since 1960 to achieve the alternative confederation based on Paris, a prospective strengthening and confirmation of the political community based on Brussels was something he was sure to react against.

Might the crisis have occurred at another time? Perhaps so, but it is difficult to attach much relevance to that possibility, given the evolution of the community, on the one hand, and the unfolding of de Gaulle's European policies, on the other. In October 1964, long before the fact of the crisis, de Gaulle was already threatening to "cease to participate" in the community if the grain price decision were further delayed. At the same time, there was the growing estrangement with Bonn over the MLF, the enthusiastic launching of the eastern overtures, and an increasing intensity to de Gaulle's attachment to the importance of "independence." In Mrs. Camps' view, even the procedural innovation announced by the French cabinet in April 1965, designed to assure that France's delegates to international organizations were properly instructed, had its ominous ring.[19] And after the fact of the crisis, we have had, not the attenuation of the main lines of Gaullist policy, but their apotheosis.

After the French withdrawal from the Council and the institution of the boycott, it should have been perfectly clear that de Gaulle was no longer interested in compromise and that, regardless of the obligations of Article 5 of the treaty, he intended to hold the operation of the community in ransom until he got his way. Nonetheless many were disposed to accuse the Commission of blundering, and strong pressures were exerted on it to bring forth new financial proposals— as though these remained the issue. It should, moreover, have been evident that the boycott was designed to prove once more that supranational institutions are impotent when vital national interests are at

---

[19] Also see Newhouse, *Collision in Europe*, pp. 65–66.

stake.[20] But even such Europeanists as Foreign Minister Spaak, who thought of himself as the father of the Rome treaties, seem oblivious to the dangers of his eagerness to reestablish direct contacts with de Gaulle and to negotiate a compromise in the intergovernmental framework which Paris had long sought to impose on Brussels.[21]

True, this and other such "conciliatory moves" and the lack of French response to them had a clarifying effect, but as no one destroys illusions so effectively as he who fosters them, it remained to de Gaulle himself to define the issue. This he did in the September 9, 1965 press conference in which he stated unmistakably and emphatically that the question between him and the Five was whether the institutions on which the community was based should even continue, let alone grow and develop, or whether they should be turned back and replaced with something else. The following excerpts give de Gaulle's views on the key issues:

On the origins of the crisis:

What happened in Brussels on June 30, *in connection with* the agricultural financing regulation, highlighted not only the persistent reluctance of the majority of our partners to bring agriculture within the scope of the Common Market, but also *certain mistakes or ambiguities* in the Treaties setting up the economic union of the Six. *That is why the crisis was, sooner or later, inevitable.* . . . [These treaties] each set up an executive structure in the form of a commission independent of the member states . . . and a legislative structure. . . . This embryonic technocracy, for the most part foreign, was certain to encroach upon French democracy, in dealing with problems *which determine the very existence of our country, and it obviously could not be allowed to conduct our affairs once we had decided to take our destiny into our own hands.*

On majority voting:

In light of this event [the Commission's financial proposals, 'which would literally have made it a great independent financial power'] we have been more clearly able to assess in what position our country risks finding itself

[20] De Gaulle has often cited the failure of the High Authority in 1958 to obtain a mandate to declare a manifest crisis in the coal industry as an example of supranational inpotence.

[21] Spaak was not alone in this proclivity. His later claim that the meeting of the Six in Luxembourg was the "Spaak formula" overlooks the extent to which his formula was "sanitized:"

if some of the provisions initially laid down in the Rome Treaty were actually enforced. It is on the basis of this text that from January 1 next the decisions in the Council of Ministers would be decided by majority vote; in other words, France would be exposed to the possibility of being overruled in any economic matter, whatsoever, and therefore in social *and sometimes political matters*, and that, in particular, all that has been achieved by French agriculture could be threatened at any moment, without France's let or leave.

On the Commission's independence and initiative:

Moreover, after this same date, the proposals made by the Commission in Brussels would have to be accepted or rejected in their entirety by the Council of Ministers, without the states being able to change anything, unless by some extraordinary chance, the six states were unanimous in formulating an amendment. We know that the members of the Commission, although appointed by agreement among the governments, are no longer responsible to them, and that, even on the conclusion of their terms of office, they can only be replaced by the unanimous agreement of the Six, which, in effect, renders them immovable. *One can see where such a subordinate position could lead us. . . .*

And on the route to a solution:

There is no doubt that it is conceivable and desirable that the great undertaking that is the Community should one day be got under way again. But that can take place, probably, only after a period of time the length of which no one can foresee. Who knows, in fact, if, when and how the policies of *each one of our partners, after some electoral or parliamentary development*, will not finally come round to facing the facts which have once more come to the fore. . . . France for her part is ready to join in all exchanges of views on this subject *which are proposed by other governments.* Should the occasion arise, she envisages the reopening of negotiations at Brussels *as soon as* agriculture is brought fully within the scope of the Common Market, and *as soon as* people are ready to have done with the pretensions which ill-founded utopian myths raise up against common sense and reality.[22]

The Denouement. The French position had its obvious ironies. Allowing for a certain exaggeration, de Gaulle's statement on the independence of the Commission and on the significance of the relationship between its right of initiative and majority voting in the Council was as orthodox as the most rabid communitarian could wish —the pristine theory as opposed to the practice. Moreover, in one important respect the French position had come full circle. Whereas

[22] Kitzinger, *European Common Market*, Document 14, p. 123. (Italics supplied.)

Couve had held in May that the political questions raised by the Commission were not germane to the financial regulations, Paris was now insistent that the prior settlement of these very questions was the necessary condition of France's return to the community fold.

In consequence, when the way was found to resume the dialogues in January (after more indecisive sparring and, more significantly, after Senator Lecanuet, the pro-European candidate, had run so well in the presidential elections in France), the Five were compelled to face the issues which they had so studiously endeavored to avoid since the previous July. With the treaty clearly under attack, they had no real choice but to defend it, and only then did they find the courage and unity to do so. Moreover, since de Gaulle had also made it clear that the price for France's return to Brussels was not a monetary one, the success of his whole maneuver would be certain to be judged by the change or lack of change it effected in the community's method of operation.

On the question of venue, raised so bluntly by the boycott itself and by the sibylline efforts of Paris thereafter to lure the Five into intergovernmental *liaisons*, there is little doubt that de Gaulle was disappointed. It is true that in the seven months the French were absent from the Council and other community agencies, no major decision was taken. But, at the same time, no decision affecting the community was taken *outside* the proper framework; the established machinery remained intact; the Council, Parliament, and the Commission carried on their business as normally as possible, and several issues of lesser importance were voted. It is likewise true that, as a gesture to French "face," the Five did not insist in the end on convening the "truce negotiations" in Brussels. But, the six ministers met in Luxembourg, the alternate seat of the Council, they met "in Council," and no issue was decided for which the Commission had treaty responsibility. Two principles were thus strengthened: (1) that, until amended by mutual consent, the Rome and Paris treaties created the only organization competent for community affairs, and (2) that no member may sabotage the community by deliberate non-participation in that organization.

The Commission, too, emerged from the Luxembourg negotiations intact, though not unscathed. After the boycott, the de Gaulle government began a strong campaign against the Commission as a whole, and the virtual vendetta against Hallstein and Mansholt created the impression that Paris hoped these two in particular could be purged.

It clearly expected as well to trim the Commission's powers, with or without a change in the treaty. Couve, in his statement to the Assembly in October, for example, referred to the need for a "general revision . . . in order to define the correct conditions for cooperation among the Six." He thereafter defined the proper role of the Commission as "before all else, to look for ways of bringing the [national] points of view closer together," which is scarcely the prescription for a vigorous executive.

On his arrival in Luxembourg, Couve had proposals for achieving both objectives—including the famous "ten commandments," a list of shalts and shalt nots to be issued by the Council to the Commission as a directive. According to the proposed directive, the Commission should adopt no important proposals without consulting the governments, nor publicize them or submit them to any other community agency before their submission to the Council; nor should such proposals be drafted in a manner to extend the Commission's discretion in their execution or to narrow the supervisory authority of the Council; nor should foreign diplomatic missions be accredited to the Commission; nor should the Commission have so free a hand in running the information service; nor, individually, should they take positions on European issues in public so much. Had these measures been accepted they would have all but deprived the Commission of the power of initiative.

The Five agreed to negotiate on these demands, but what emerged was scarcely the peremptory decalogue that Couve wanted. Several of the original points were dropped entirely; the others were recast in a far less objectionable form, and the Commission's right to submit the proposals on which Council decisions are based was specifically reaffirmed. Moreover, the directives which the French would have had the Council issue became in effect "suggestions" to be discussed between and agreed upon by the two agencies—as the treaty specifically requires. So far as is known, only one of these suggestions was subsequently discussed; they remain therefore in general without legal effect, and it would be difficult in practice to trace any specific consequence to them in the Commission's subsequent behavior, whatever chastening effect the crisis as such may have had.[23]

[23] The decalogue—subsequently referred to as the heptalogue after three of the original injunctions had been dropped—was the subject of a revealing exchange in the European Parliament on July 4, 1968 between a socialist member of the Parliament, Mr. Vredeling, and President Rey, speaking for the Commission. As reported in

Couve's second proposal—by which he hoped to achieve quite literally the decapitation of the Commission—was the high priority he insisted be given to ratification of the 1965 agreement to fuse the three community executives. Since the new executive would be named by "common agreement," France could be assured that the objectionable members of the old commission would not be reappointed to the new. Throughout 1966 and the first half of 1967, however, the guillotine was denied Hallstein and Mansholt, principally because the Dutch steadfastly refused to ratify the fusion agreement until the personnel of the new commission had been agreed upon. (By law, the old executives continue in office until they are replaced.) In the multilateral talks in the spring of 1967, the Dutch again put forward Mansholt's candidacy for the new commission and successfully insisted he be accepted. In a subsequent "arrangement" with the French, however, the Kiesinger government agreed to nominate Hallstein for only a six-month term as the Commission's president, and Hallstein decided to retire in dignity.[24] He thus became the second Commissioner to be purged by de Gaulle—the first one so honored, Etienne Hirsch, at least was French.

If an agreement is often difficult enough to evaluate, a nonagreement parading as an accord inevitably becomes the province of the jurists and the historians. Little more can be said of the "decision" taken on majority voting which on the face of it was no more than a statement on the record of the two points of view. All six agreed that when "very important issues" are at stake, "the Council will try, within a reasonable time, to reach solutions which can be adopted by all the members." The French declared, however, that they considered in such cases that "the discussion must be continued until

---

Agence Europe no. 129, July 4, 1968, Vredeling accused the Commission of not defending its prerogatives, of "back-sliding" into acceptance of the Luxembourg compromise, and in particular, of having agreed to new procedures imposed by the Council for the accreditation of foreign ambassadors. Rey conceded that the Commission had instituted new procedures on accreditation, but only after lengthy negotiation with the Council, and this was the only one of the seven points which the Commission had accepted. *Agence Europe* recorded Rey as having added in effect that the Commission "neither agreed to nor accepted the Luxembourg agreements and the famous heptalogue. . . . This was an unfortunate document belonging to the past which is now over and done with and better forgotten."

[24] In his letter of withdrawal, Hallstein stated that the proposed arrangements were both juridically and politically unacceptable. The fusion treaty established a two-year term for the presidency, and in his view, it was unthinkable that the provisions of a treaty could be changed by private agreement between but two of its parties.

unanimous agreement is reached." But in a concluding observation, all six "note" that "there is a divergence of views on what should be done in the event of a failure to reach complete agreement," and this divergence need not preclude the community from resuming its work in accordance with the "normal procedures."

According to one interpretation, which may be the French one, the effect of this nonagreement was to expunge from the treaty the provision most objectionable to de Gaulle—and to do so without resort to the amending process. Couve was permitted to record in a formal Council document France's future nonacceptance of majority voting, and in the supporting arguments he advanced, he made it perfectly clear that, whereas France would not be bound by a majority decision taken against her, she would also seek to assure other members against that fate by withholding her support from any majority. Therefore, according to this view, de Gaulle succeeded not only in preventing the scheduled extension of majority voting on January 1, 1966, but he initiated a rolling-back process as well. Because the treaty is very specific on those issues which *might* be settled by majority vote, while the proposed exemption of issues which are "very important" is a general prescription, de Gaulle may anticipate that each member, determining unilaterally what is important to it, will together exclude all decisions from the majority rule.

According to another view, however, the Luxembourg formula on majority voting was juridically meaningless but politically important. The mere recording of the French position was without legal significance so long as the Council did not accept it nor recognize the right of one of its members to usurp the prerogatives of the Court to interpret the treaty. The Five fully reserved their rights under the treaty, including the right to resort to a majority vote if no agreement were reached after a "reasonable time" and to seek the remedies the treaty provides in the event such a legally-taken decision were not applied. Therefore, from a legal standpoint, the "decision" on majority voting did no more than reaffirm the fully acknowledged existence of a constitutional issue which would be brought to a head only when the necessary circumstance—including the political will —existed. While it was perfectly obvious that the stomach for so fateful a confrontation did not then (and might not soon) exist among the Five, the fortitude to do so had likewise deserted de Gaulle. Thus, the "certain mistakes or ambiguities" de Gaulle referred to in September 1965 as the source of an inevitable crisis were translated on the record in February 1966 as "divergences of view" which need not cause the crisis longer to continue, and France could return to Brussels (as it did in March) before the financial regulation had been settled—and before the people had done with the pretensions which Utopia had raised up.[25]

[25] A new financing agreement was not reached, in fact, until the following July, and the effect of this was to defer once more the difficult issues raised by Article 201 and Law 25.

VI

VI   A FURTHER TESTING: JULY 1968

The community's operations since February 1966 have given no reason to revise the view that the Luxembourg agreements were neither a settlement nor a compromise of the community's constitutional crisis, but at best an uneasy truce, and at worst, a debilitating one. The Five blunted and turned back a massive assault on the community system at a cost, and their unexpected victory was neither definitive nor complete. Instead of a sword there fell on the political community within the Common Market a *main morte*.

During this time, the EEC and EURATOM have had, along with some notable failures, some impressive successes: the Kennedy Round above all, but also the completion and the institution of the CAP, the establishment of the customs union, a measure of cooperation in international monetary policy, and perhaps a start toward a common policy on international nuclear safeguards. The Kennedy Round agreement has been generally credited to the effective leadership of the Commission which many believe is stronger in its organization, personnel, and over-all direction than the one it replaced.

Nevertheless, it would be grossly illusory to pretend that the institutional development of the community is a healthy one. The Gaullist war of attrition against the Commission has seldom abated, and there is the constant and sometimes successful campaign to shift the power of initiative to the national delegations in Brussels. The impact of these pressures is evident in the gingerly approach which the Commission characteristically takes to any issue which arises with Paris. In the state of affairs of the community in the late 1960s, it is difficult to conceive of the Council overriding a recalcitrant mem-

98

ber by majority vote. Many ardent Europeanists are of a mind to discount the utility of this device even as theory. The pressing political issues of 1965—the budgetary powers of Parliament and controls over the community bureaucracy—have become even more pressing but are no closer to solution.

The question of institutional adequacy is in any case a relative one. In the absence of an effective institutional structure, the possibility of the community's future advance into those areas where a common European effort is the crying need (technology and science, defense procurement and conventional forces, and ultimately, a common defense and foreign policy) must seem a very small one. Even the tasks the EEC must take up before 1970—the recasting of the CAP, the next steps toward a monetary union, the conduct of a sound fiscal and monetary policy—become overwhelming ones in the continued absence of strong *community* leadership, true debate in a more representative assembly, and the possibility, after debate, of moving ahead according to the wishes of a majority of the community.

Nothing since the Luxembourg truce, however, has so illuminated the resulting parlous uncertainty of public authority in the Common Market and the attendant risks than the community response to the political and economic upheaval in France in May and June 1968. The crisis, which was accompanied by virtual paralysis of France's production, the disruption of trade, and the drainage of national reserves, was the worst to hit any member of the community since it began. Although it did not prevent the completion of the customs union on July 1 (a benchmark of the Common Market's achievement which under other circumstances might have been an occasion for general satisfaction), the crisis might also have provided an opportunity for a demonstration of community solidarity, the benefits of membership, and the effectiveness of the common institutions.

Instead, it was the occasion for Paris to attempt yet another unilateral derogation from its obligations under the Rome treaties which left the community and its other members shaken and embittered. Instead, the institutions were at first passive and then vacillating, and the kind of assistance the community was able to render the French was, to say the most, supplementary. And, instead, the members were unprepared to seize the opportunity provided by these unprecedented circumstances as an occasion for a resumption of community constitution-building, and the ambiguous precedents which were established inspire no great confidence in the outcome of the real test which will surely follow.

THE INGREDIENTS OF THE NEW CRISIS

On June 26, after a meeting of its Council of Ministers, the de Gaulle government announced that it had "decided" to implement all its engagements under the Rome treaties and the GATT but had "judged necessary" certain measures of safeguard which it had brought to the knowledge of the community and to the other member states. This in effect confronted the community with the most serious threat which may rise to a developing economic union: that a member state in extremis, responding to internal political pressures arising spontaneously or perhaps out of its participation in the union, will act to recapture instruments of regulation and control which may have been relinquished in the course of the union's formation and development. The member state will be tempted to recoup these instruments provided, of course, it can do so without provoking consequences or reprisals which are more painful than the difficulties it is seeking to resolve.

We have argued heretofore that the development of the Common Market has significantly narrowed the range of effectiveness of national public authority. It does not necessarily follow, however, that the risk of reprisal against moves to reassert that authority necessarily increases correspondingly. As the French well know, how free each member of the Common Market remains to act in its own way depends both on the extent to which community public authority has been made effective as national authority declines, and on the relative extent of commitment to and dependence on the common enterprise of each of the member states. Those least bound are not only the freest to act unilaterally, but they are the least likely to be restrained by the reaction of their partners.

The nature of the threat of reassertion of national prerogatives is well established in the literature about the Common Market; it has become a fixation with the Commission, and even prior to the French moves on June 26, there was European experience in the reality of the risk. During its balance-of-payments crisis which began in 1963, Italy supplemented a strongly deflationary policy with a variety of restrictions on imports which were equivalent in effect to tariffs or quotas, and it was largely in response to the Italian experience that the community agreed in 1964 to set up the various institutions we

100

have earlier described to harmonize the economic policies of the member countries. In 1964, as we have also seen, the British government followed a similar route and eventually resorted—without benefit of consultation with its EFTA partners—to an import surcharge which nearly doubled its average tariffs. Commenting on these episodes some years later, James Leontiades suggested that such temporary trade restrictions were not only the classic response of members of trade groups encountering balance-of-payments difficulties, but also the more acceptable one—more acceptable, for example, than devaluation. Such temporary withdrawals from the customs union or trade bloc would remain the "path of least resistance," Leontiades predicted, so long as trade within the group is "foreign trade," balance-of-payments positions are still calculated on a national basis, and each member is still obliged—in the absence of more complete integration—to defend the value of its currency with its "separate stock of gold and foreign exchange reserves."[1]

The drafters of the Rome treaties were aware of the possible need for emergency interruptions of free trade; they saw the ultimate solution in the more thoroughgoing union which Leontiades referred to; and they were much more aware than their colleagues in the Stockholm Convention of the disruptive effects which uncoordinated emergency measures could have. While they therefore recognized the necessity for precautions, for rules and restraints on unilateral action, and for the intervention of community authority, the Rome treaties were unfortunately drafted after the federalist movement had passed its zenith, and these rules are not clearly stated. Their meaning and intention are nevertheless unmistakable, and like the provisions of Article 201 from which the great controversies over the community's "own resources" have sprung, the elaboration of these rules into a set of effective and unifying procedures would not defy human ingenuity—provided all members continued to accept the common objective of effective unity. The Gaullist government, however, reacting to the pressures of the *patronat* at the end of June 1968, provided new grounds for believing that its commitment to that objective was less than complete. And instead of establishing an unequivocal modus operandi which would greatly have strengthened the community, the resulting confrontation produced once more an indecisive result. In consequence, the effect of the minicrisis of

[1] James Leontiades, "Is a Common Market a Single Market?," *Columbia Journal of World Business*, 2, no. 4 (July–August 1967), pp. 23-29.

July was to raise more insistently than ever the fundamental question whether even the *existing* economic union can survive a prolonged delay in the clarification of the prerogatives of the main sources of community public authority. And once more the answer will depend on whether the member countries can find the will to erect a procedural structure which is politically meaningful.

The applicable provisions of the treaty are largely contained in Article 226 and in Chapter 2 of Title II on Economic Policy—Articles 104 to 109. Article 226, the general escape clause included at French behest, provides that in the event a member state encounters "serious difficulties" which are likely to persist or which may seriously impair the economic situation of any region, that state may apply to the Commission for authorization to take safeguard measures "to restore the situation and adapt that sector concerned" to the Common Market. The Commission shall respond expeditiously, "determining" the measures it considers necessary, "specifying" the conditions and particulars of application, and giving priority to measures least disruptive to the community. The provisions of Article 226 are thus unambiguous: The initiative rests with the state, the decision is confided in the Commission, and the article is operative only during the transitional period (until 1970). It was clearly designed for the benefit of specific industries or regions hurt by community competition, and it has been invoked several times by the member states.

More relevant to the French crisis, but somewhat less clear in their implications, are the treaty articles in the chapter on balance of payments. The first of these, Article 104, imposes on each state the obligation to pursue the economic policies necessary to assure a balance-of-payments equilibrium and a stable exchange rate, together with high employment and price stability. The three succeeding articles provide in a general way for the coordination of economic policies among the members in order to facilitate the achievement of these objectives. They have provided the basis in part for the medium-term economic policy, the gradual removal of currency controls, and the 1964 agreement making exchange rate adjustments a matter for consultation. Finally, Articles 108 and 109 deal specifically with crisis situations ("where a member state is in difficulties or seriously threatened with difficulties in its balance of payments . . . and where such difficulties are likely . . . to prejudice the functioning of the Common Market"). They attempt to delimit the respective areas of authority of the states and the community's institutions.

It is clear that Article 108 with its strong emphasis on *Commission* initiative was intended to be the preferred and usual procedure; Article 109, with its allowance for emergency action by the *states*, was the intended exception. Article 108 provides that the Commission, in the event of difficulties in a member state, shall examine the situation and the measures which the state may have taken in order to meet its obligations under Article 104, and, in the first instance, shall recommend to the state what measures it should adopt. Should such action "not prove sufficient," then the Commission, after consulting the Monetary Committee, shall recommend to the Council the granting of "mutual assistance." Acting by qualified majority vote, the Council shall approve such assistance, including credits, common action in international forums, measures to prevent trade diversion, etc. Should the Council decline to approve mutual assistance or should that assistance prove insufficient, the Commission may specify additional measures which the state may take. However, the Council, again acting by majority vote, may revoke such special authorization or amend its terms.

The effect of Article 108 is thus truly to establish the Commission —in its role as guardian of the community interest—as the arbiter of emergency measures for a state in disequilibrium. Moreover, the Commission's preeminence is not diluted by the special provisions of Article 109. Should a "sudden crisis" in balance of payments arise and an immediate decision on mutual aid not be taken, the member state may "provisionally" take limited safeguard measures. Both the Commission and the member states are to be notified of such measures, and the Commission may then recommend mutual assistance. Moreover, *on the basis of a Commission opinion*, and after consultation with the Monetary Committee, the Council may, by majority vote, amend, suspend, or abolish the measures taken by the state in difficulty. The limited objective of Article 109 is therefore readily apparent: to reserve to the member states the possibility of emergency action until, but only until, the Commission has activated the community machinery.

THE SLOW AWAKENING

When faced with the virtual paralysis of the economic life of one of its key members, how did the community machinery respond? In the initial stages at least, it was aware of and anguished over the potentially disastrous consequences for the community's functioning.

However, while this awareness probably facilitated the May 29 agreement on the delicate problem of how to fund the dairy surpluses, it is difficult to find any evidence that the community otherwise moved to cope with the real threats the French situation was posing—until it was challenged by unilateral proclamations in Paris at the end of June.

On May 20, 1968, the influential and usually well-informed *Agence Europe* was already editorializing that what was happening in France concerned not only Frenchmen, but "first and foremost," France's partners in the Common Market; "this is the logical consequence of belonging to a community." Two days later, the paper again wrote of the surprising failure of anyone in the community to have recalled publicly that interdependence and solidarity meant not only a sharing of difficulties, but also the proffering of assistance. "It must be stated and proclaimed that the community mechanisms are there to fulfil their tasks, to help changes when they are socially and economically justified and to lessen the shock. The working classes, in France and elsewhere, must know that it would not be right to make the existence of the Common Market and the opening of the frontiers a pretext for a more or less masked refusal to entertain their legitimate demands."[2]

The Commission was reported by the *Agence Europe* on May 24 to have given "careful and lengthy attention" to the French situation, but merely to have affirmed that the decision to complete the customs union on July 1 "remained valid" and was unlikely to be questioned.[3] When at the end of May the French notified the Monetary Committee and the Commission that it had imposed new exchange controls —citing Article 109 as justification and protesting their preventive and temporary nature, the Commission seems simply to have taken note of the new measures.[4] Despite widespread speculation regarding still other measures to which the French might have to resort (adjustment of the bank rate, import controls, and even devaluation), the Commission did not move to invoke Article 108. In fact, on June 12 the Commission felt impelled to issue a formal statement denying that it had taken a stand on any measures which might be taken by France. "It is convinced," the statement read, "that France, with the help of the community institutions, can overcome its present

[2] See editorials, *Agence Europe*, May 20 and 22, 1968.
[3] *Ibid.*, May 24, 1968.
[4] *Ibid.*, June 6, 1968.

difficulties through the dynamism of its economy and its strong monetary position."[5]

The Commission's stand was not lacking in merit from a substantive point of view. Many independent observers considered France's huge monetary reserves a more than ample cushion against even several months of serious deficits, and any suggestion to the contrary might have been taken by the government as an excuse to introduce temporary protective measures which might have jeopardized the completion of the customs union and, by reducing the flow of goods, have aggravated France's most serious problem, the threat of inflation. On substantive grounds it is also possible to justify a continuation of the Commission's "wait and see" attitude even after it had received (within hours after issuing the above statement) the first formal request from Paris for authorization to apply certain selective emergency measures. The French requests were of two sorts: a renewal of its request of the previous November for authorization under Article 226 to impose quotas on imports of electrical household appliances and paper panels, and a plea for authorization to continue and to increase after July 1 certain export incentives which the Commission had previously directed be removed—an export risk insurance scheme, privileged discount rates for credits to finance exports, and certain exchange-rate risk guarantees.[6]

Both requests raised a number of questions and problems. In particular, by limiting the proposed new quotas to two sectors for which it had long and unsuccessfully solicited special protection, Paris seemed to be exploiting its adversity rather than to be seeking justifiable remedies. Moreover, because it was apparent from the broad hints emanating from Paris that other and more serious measures were under consideration, the Commission decided to give only an interim reply, requesting further information regarding the quota measures the French had proposed on June 12, suspending until further consultation its previous prohibition on the export incentives, assuring the French of the Commission's "decision to implement the means offered by the treaties to remedy as effectively as possible [France's] difficulties, particularly in the field of employment," and apparently making certain preliminary recommendations regarding France's export problems both in particular and in general.[7]

[5] Ibid., June 12, 1968.
[6] Ibid., June 13, 1968.
[7] Ibid., June 17, 1968.

From a tactical and political point of view, however, the Commission's methodical pace was perhaps more questionable. By failing to assert its prerogatives earlier, the Commission put itself in the position of having first to respond to French proposals, and though it reacted vigorously to France's subsequent announcement of the further measures it had "decided" to introduce on July 1, the Commission's posture would remain thereafter a defensive and apologetic one.

There were three sorts of additional "safeguards" announced by the French: (1) import restrictions, effective for four to six months, and designed to limit French purchases of specific items (motor cars and industrial vehicles, electrical appliances, certain textiles, and steel products) to levels ranging from the 1967 volume to 7 to 15 percent above it; (2) administrative surveillance of an additional large category of products in order to permit intervention in the event of an abnormal growth in imports; and (3) export incentives or subsidies—in addition to those proposed on June 12—justified as a "temporary compensation" for the recent wage increases, and amounting initially to 6 percent but later declining to 3 percent of the wage charges incorporated into exported products.[8] The last measure was an extraordinary one. Except in the context of a complete breakdown in the productive machinery of a country, which the French were quick to claim was the case, the idea that any nation should claim a right to compensate for a rise in wage costs (why not raw materials costs?) with subsidies is one which, if put forth generally, would lead ultimately to the breakdown of free trade.

Nevertheless, it was not so much what the French proposed to do which aroused the community (and Paris had carefully primed the other members to expect much worse), but the manner in which it was done. In defense of the French procedure, it can perhaps be said that Paris duly notified the community authorities of its intentions two days before they were announced as a decision by the French Council of Ministers on June 26. And, the notification, transmitted by the French ambassador to President Rey on June 24 did apparently propose that a special session of the community Council be convened "next month," i.e., after the measures had gone into effect.

Otherwise the French move had all the earmarks of a carefully

[8] *Ibid.*, June 25 and 26, 1968.

contrived fait accompli. In his statement of explanation to the European Parliament on July 3,[9] President Rey made it clear that the French notification had come as a surprise to the Commission and without prior consultation, even though the Commission had a week earlier assured Paris that the resources of the treaty would be put into effect "to help France surmount a difficult period in its economic history." The new request on June 24 replaced the former, Rey said, "by covering it completely." Yet, unlike the earlier one, this new request referred to no article in particular of the treaty, but to unspecified provisions which allegedly permit a member state to take precautionary action in the event of unforeseen difficulties or serious disturbances. Only subsequently did the French authorities claim Articles 104, 108, and 109 as the basis of their action. But, as we have seen, the first of these articles is a prelude to a requirement (in Article 105) that the members coordinate their economic policies; Article 108 depends on Commission initiative, and Article 109 allows only provisional safeguards in the event of sudden crisis—hardly a program of export subsidies. Moreover, the projected quotas on steel were in clear violation of the CSC treaty.

With so clear a challenge to its authority before it, the Commission, surprisingly lethargic in its earlier response to the French crisis seems to have been stung into a reaction which also surprised its critics. The Commission's line of thought, reported to the Parliament by President Rey, is a revealing one. According to Rey, the Commission examined the French "document" from three points of view: *economic*—i.e., whether the projected measures were limited to the indispensable; *legal*—i.e., whether the French "technique" in apparently invoking Article 109 and community acceptance of this would constitute a good or bad precedent; and *political*—i.e., whether a member government should decide on its own on the safeguard measures provided for in the treaty. To the first question, the Commission had reached the conclusion, Rey said, that the French had made such an effort to limit the bad effects of their measures that the Commission had felt obliged to express its gratitude. The unilateral character of these measures, however, had caused the Commission "many worries," specifically whether the French government "had actually stayed within its sphere of action." If the Commission

[9] A partial account of Rey's statement, the succeeding debate, and the full text of the Commission's reply to the French of June 28 is contained in *Agence Europe*, July 3, 1968.

had reached the conclusion that Paris had exceeded its authority, Rey continued, the Commission would have been duty bound to direct that the measures be abolished and to bring suit in the community Court if they were not. However, the Commission had thought it preferable to emphasize the political aspects of the problem, rather than the legal ones, and it had therefore decided to have recourse to Article 108 as the means to such a "political solution."

AVOIDING THE HORNS OF DILEMMA

Leaving aside for the moment whether the invocation of Article 108 was a "political solution" or not, the recourse to it was a shrewd maneuver in the Commission's view. In a letter to the French ambassador on June 28 the Commission simply stated that it "seriously doubted" that the measures announced by the French fell within the limits permitted a member when "sudden difficulties" arise, and since these measures could in any case be instituted only provisionally, the Commission considered that "appropriate community procedures should be put into operation without delay." Before pronouncing definitively on these measures, however, the Commission stated that it felt obliged to follow the procedures set out in Articles 108, and to that end, it had begun the necessary consultations preparatory to recommending to the Council the approval of mutual assistance. Finally, while again assuring the French of its desire to do all possible to remedy France's difficulties, the Commission observed—with a certain acerbity: "The French government will understand, however, that the Commission will be particularly attentive regarding the community procedures, in the present case as in any situation which could arise in the future within the community, since this respect for community procedures constitutes for all member states a guarantee of the normal functioning of the community."

Although Rey told the Parliament that the Commission's expression of "serious doubts" was the "most moderate and politically the wisest" choice of words it could have made, the Commission's letter was an exceptionally forthright one.[10] It instituted the procedures to which the Commission attached such importance. In two respects this was a fairly simple matter. Paris simply agreed to withhold the imposition of steel quotas—so clearly beyond its authority under the Treaty of Paris—until the Commission, having hastily convened

[10] See, for example, H. Peter Dreyer, "EEC Review of French Steps to Take a While," *Journal of Commerce*, June 30, 1968.

the Council for its opinion and contacted the Consultative Committee, had duly authorized them, imposed a deadline for their removal, and reserved the right to revise or withdraw them in the event the French situation improved or the other member countries were seriously hurt. Moreover, in response to complaints that the "surveillance" of imports instituted by the French involved border checks which were impeding trade generally, the Commission succeeded in bringing about procedural changes which apparently resolved this particular problem rather quickly.

In other respects the Commission's problems in substituting community action under the Rome treaty for unilateral action by France were a good deal more complicated. Having invoked Article 108, the first task of the Commission was to "examine the situation" in France and the action so far taken and "to indicate the measures which it recommends" Paris should adopt. These "recommendations" were addressed to the French on July 5;[11] they were the Commission's analysis of France's economic problems, and on the whole, it was a good one. Judging the French economy to be structurally sound, the Commission foresaw inflation and a downturn in productive investment as the main problems, and recommended a policy of expansion and international competition as the most promising remedy. While the Commission seemed to feel that the exchange controls and export aids put into effect by the French were, as temporary measures, compatible with an expansionist approach, it frankly considered the import quotas to be ill-advised. Finally, the Commission urged upon the French the desirability of looking into ways of increasing investment incentives, bringing down unemployment, and encouraging domestic savings.

In translating these eminently sensible views into a community action program, however, the Commission faced some agonizing dilemmas, substantive as well as procedural. Since the Rome treaty clearly intended that Article 108 should be the normal way of dealing with abnormal situations and since the whole emphasis of the article is on community and Commission authority and responsibility, it was obviously to the Commission's interest to move quickly from its initial "recommendations" into the development of a mutual-aid package. If this package were adopted, then the community would be nominally in control of the situation once more; if it were rejected

[11] Summarized in *Agence Europe*, July 9, 1968.

or proved "insufficient" to remedy the French difficulties, then, under Paragraph 3 of Article 108, the Commission would remain in position to determine what measures the French could legally take. But to move into the application of the mutual-aid provisions of Article 108, the Commission would first have to decide what to do about the safeguard measures which the French had already put into effect on July 1. If it decided to accept these as provisional safeguard measures allowable under Article 109, not only would it seem to contradict the "serious doubts" it had earlier raised regarding their legality, but it might also find itself involved in an attempt by the Council to rule (as provided in Paragraph 3 of Article 109) whether these measures should be amended, suspended, or abolished.

The commission resolved these dilemmas in three ways. Swallowing hard and emphasizing the provisional and emergency character of the measures the French had instituted, the Commission accepted de facto their applicability until such time as they were replaced by community measures taken under Article 108.[12] Moreover, the Commission paved the way for the continuation of the French measures—reissued in large part as Commission-authorized measures—by insisting that the mutual aid adopted by the community was of such character that immediately beneficial effects on the French economy could not be expected. And finally, in order to head off any move on the part of the Council to deal with the specifics, the Commission agreed to take into account the views of the individual members on how the Commission should adjust the French measures once the Council had approved mutual aid. In fact, the initial ardor of some of the Council members to assume responsibility for specifying the nature of those adjustments rapidly cooled, and, despite expressions of indignation and outrage, they were in the end relieved to "leave it to the Commission."[13]

The upshot of all this maneuvering was the Council meeting of July 20, which approved the mutual-aid package largely as it had been proposed by the Commission, and the Commission meeting of July 22 from which there emerged "directives" amending the

[12] It appears, however, that the Commission contrived to avoid any de jure acceptance of the measures under Article 109. The mutual aid directive approved by the Council on July 20 refers only to Article 104.

[13] See *Agence Europe* of July 16 and 17, 1968 for an account of the complicated maneuverings which preceded the July 20 Council meeting. A report on the Council meeting is given by the same press service on July 22, and the mutual-aid directive is published the same date as Europe Document No. 485.

French measures of July 1. The aid package, the first in the community's history, is an interesting one. Adopted as a directive, the package requires the member states other than France to "adopt all measures necessary" to achieve high growth rates (if necessary, by the introduction of an expansionary policy); to pursue policies favoring interest-rate stabilization; to permit insofar as possible French borrowers to float loans in their capital markets; and, within the framework of community decisions, to take a common attitude in discussions of France's situation in other international forums. An earlier Commission proposal calling for the "completion of the mechanisms" of monetary cooperation within the community was not acted upon by the Council, but referred—as procedure required—to the Monetary Committee.

Mutual assistance has thus proved to be an equivocal thing. Even allowing for the Commission's earlier decision to use the Social Fund to facilitate retraining and reemployment of French workers, the community assistance obviously falls considerably short of a decisive intervention on France's behalf. Yet as a first attempt to set about creating external conditions favorable to the economic recovery of one member, the program has more than symbolical importance. For example, according to Commission estimates, a higher expansion rate in some of the member countries might result in French export gains by as much as 12–13 percent.

A similar equivocation may also enter into one's judgment of the adjustments which, two days after the approval of mutual aid, the Commission directed be made in the measures which France had put into effect three weeks before. The export aids, including the controversial wage-cost subsidy, were considered appropriate by the Commission and authorized. Changes were directed in the import restrictions, however, which have been variously described as "minor" to "very considerable," depending on the standard of measurement. Since the community authorities had never considered these restrictions particularly advantageous to France nor excessively burdensome to its partners, the amendments required by the Commission can perhaps be considered by this standard to have been somewhere in-between. By changing the reference period for the quotas on electrical appliances, the Commission considerably eased the impact on Italian producers who bore the brunt of this particular restriction. The restrictions on textiles which, in view of the very low wages in the French industry and the problems which manufacturers everywhere in the community were encountering, had seemed the least justified were also eased, and in the case of one product, were eliminated entirely. The Commission also fixed a definite time limit for all the quotas and reserved the right to review France's economic situation again within three months.

SOLIDARITY—AT WHAT COST?

In any event, the Commission, acting largely alone, assured that the minicrisis of July 1 did not become at that crucial moment in the community's development the full-blown crisis which many feared. But was the worst merely averted and at too high a price, or did the Commission, in opting for the possible, retrieve more than the situation seemed likely initially to allow?

The former view is surely the prevailing one. In the early stages of the crisis, European and American press services freely predicted that the Commission, not wishing to "stick its neck out," would try either to drop the new issue into the lap of the Council or would itself seek some bilateral accommodation with the French. When the Commission did neither of these but assumed its responsibilities under Article 108 and called on the French to return to community procedures, it was clear that the Commission had, at the least, accomplished an act of self-preservation. However, the Commission's critics still interpreted its maneuvers as an attempt to find a way to bestow legality, or to pin a "community label," on the steps taken unilaterally by the French. Far from crediting the Commission with having managed a tour de force by bringing back to the community framework what the French had done outside it, the critics seemed to feel the Commission was at fault because the issues had escaped that framework in the first place. As one prominent British journal put it, "After fiddling around with community procedures and the equivocations of the Rome treaty, the Commission seems happy to have kept at least the appearance of making the final decision."

Given the political atmosphere which prevails in the community in 1968 and the possibility that the worst of France's problems may be ahead, it would indeed be a brave soul who finds other than profoundly negative auguries in the manner in which the crisis was avoided. But at the least, the Commission helped to clarify once more the meaning of the community and its unhappy situation, and it helped to pose a choice for the members.

The Implications of Interdependence. The member states were forcefully reminded once more that economic integration has reached a stage where national boundaries have become in the Common Market but flimsy barriers to the consequences of economic developments anywhere within the community. The problems faced by the French confronted the other members with prospective changes in France's economic indicators of so great a magnitude that it was inescapable that the effects would not be confined to France. It was also perfectly clear that the size of those effects and their nature would depend on what policy package was selected from among the available options. At the outer range of possibility, should France be forced to default on its commitments to complete the customs union or resort to devaluation, the impact on the other members would obviously be more severe. But as the Commission memorandum to the French made so clear, even within the narrower range of possibility, there were some solutions which from a community viewpoint were much to be preferred: expansion rather than deflation, export aids rather than import restrictions, investment incentives for productive industries rather than subsidies or protection for marginal ones, etc.

The Confines of National Policy. It may also be considered a "gain" that from the averted crisis emerged wider recognition that the options available to the nation-states have narrowed so much, or, if still open, are not ones which are readily exercised any longer by choice. Since the source of the crisis was a new assertion of French "unilateralism," it is ironical that a clear recognition of these limitations should have come from France. In his address to the National Assembly on July 18 after becoming prime minister, Couve de Murville vigorously declared that the "only imaginable" economic policy for France was one of "dynamism and growth." He went on to explain that France was in the Common Market, would maintain its full participation, and would therefore "do nothing to resurrect demons of Malthusianism and protectionism which are just other forms of facile solutions." Referring to monetary problems, Couve continued: "We must understand that they cannot be considered in other than an international context. This is true because of the European Community and also true on account of the role which the so-called reserve currencies—the dollar and the pound—play."[14] Though per-

---

[14] See *Le Monde*, July 19, 1968.

haps with the hint of a threat, Foreign Minister Debre took a simi-lar line in the subsequent meeting of the community Council, holding that France by rejecting the temptation either to postpone the cus-toms union or to induce severe internal deflation had taken the "most community" solution. Obviously one would prefer to have seen some manifestation of French acceptance of "togetherness" on June 26, but it is refreshing to be reminded that it is a *Gaullist* dilemma to reconcile absolute independence with the recognition of external con-straints.

The Empty Community Arsenal. It is also advantageous in terms of community development that the crisis clarified the very narrow range in which the community itself may work. The mutual-aid package put together by the Commission, though not insignificant, was surely limited, and the essentially noncommunity character of the measures called for must be fully recognized. The assistance to be rendered the French required measures to be taken by the *other states.* The obligation to put these measures into effect is a binding one, but the Council directive which makes it binding is nevertheless hortatory in a sense. More important, even if these measures are fully and fairly implemented, they scarcely qualify as *community* aid. The community has no organized capital market for which it could set the terms of access; the community has no central banking system whose manipulations of the rediscount rate would influence the community economy in the direction of expan-sion or contraction; the community has neither revenues nor ex-penditures which would make its fiscal policies a significant counter-cyclical factor; and its influence over the fiscal policies of the mem-ber states falls far short of real control. In short, mutual aid will remain a poor substitute for community aid until such time as the member states agree to move much further toward economic and monetary union, a pooling of reserves, and all this would imply for national sovereignty. Until then, the members, having to rely princi-pally on their own resources and reserves, and doomed ultimately to policies of fairly rigid equilibrium vis-à-vis each other, and it remains to be seen whether the community's expedients and France's huge reserve will allow Paris to escape in the end from the more extreme measures it claims to have rejected.

The Centralize or Not to Centralize. On the one hand, one might therefore hope that the Commission's "fiddling around with commu-nity procedure" will have had the effect of revealing once more to

114

the member states the choice they must sooner or later make: for or against an effective economic and political union. The intentions of the chapter in the Rome treaty on "balance of payments" are unequivocal, and, as a result of this first experience in the application of its provisions, these intentions have now been spelled out in procedures which could be set in motion whenever any member faces the prospect of crisis. It was the meaning of the French decision announced on June 26 that any member state in economic difficulty may determine for itself what remedies it will choose, including the easiest one of temporary withdrawal from the market. It was the meaning of the Commission's response in its letter of June 28 that there is an overriding community interest; that unilateral measures could at the most be exceptional, strictly limited, and provisional; and that the community interest is best served by community action, the determination of which the Commission should play the guiding role set out for it in Article 108. With the exception perhaps of the last, these views were endorsed by the Council at its July 20 meeting. In one way or another, all the ministers made clear their recognition that the problems of one community country are the problems of them all; all indicated to the French their distaste for the substance and the manner of the restrictions the French had imposed; and the Italian minister, the most distressed of all, echoed the Commission in declaring that integration depends on the Rome treaties, a "constitutional charter" from which no derogation can be allowed since it is the only "guarantee" for all.

The Constitutional Impasse Prolonged. On the other hand, only the utterly sanguine will assume that the Commission has succeeded in replacing a derogation from the treaty with an abiding procedural precedent which has become, so to speak, part of the common law. The crisis which was averted, like the crisis that materialized in 1965, is symptomatic of too serious a malaise to permit such confidence.

After the Council meeting of July 20, the Belgian foreign minister, Pierre Harmel, commented to the press that the running of the community left much to be desired, not only from a material point of view, but from a legal and political standpoint as well.[15] Few communitarians require such accents on the obvious. By the third week of May when it was apparent that France's economic situation might

[15] *Agence Europe*, July 22, 1968.

become so desperate that the equilibrium of the community might itself be jeopardized, the Commission—ideally—could have moved to institute the procedures of Article 108. When the French moved instead to tell the community what it proposed to do and left the community no choice but to accept, the search for a community imprimatur ought not to have taken a month. And when one was found, the solution was scarcely the "political" one which President Rey claimed. As the *Agence Europe* wrote, the Commission's reaction "highlights the limitations of European power . . . even when it is a question of seeking in the folds of the treaty the crumbs of power to which [the community] institutions can lay claim, it is more an exercise in 'political science' than a real political action. . . ."[16]

If it is true that a people gets the government it deserves, so is it true that the community's equivocations are an accurate reflection of its members' ambivalence toward their own creation. All of the members are perfectly aware that the community has created a gray area in which the exercise of public authority in the future is ominously uncertain. Yet rather than bring themselves to accept and to confirm this as an area of community authority, they will tolerate and endorse ad hoc appropriations of that authority by any member state which feels itself strong enough to do so without reprisals. The French government with one breath acknowledges an "international context" in which it must approach its domestic problems, but it could not bring itself with another to ask for advance "international" authorization for what it proposed to do. When the a posteriori debate on these measures momentarily threatened the choice which France had made, its minister served notice that the measures adopted had not been chosen "with a view to bargaining." Nor when faced with such usurpations of power can the members quite bring themselves to see that the rectification of the imbalance of power which makes such incursions possible is much more urgent than the exercise of their individual prerogatives—exercised perhaps with the view to retaining the right of usurpation themselves. How else does one explain the eagerness of some of the members to retain for the Council the right to pass on the French restrictions under Article 109 rather than permit the Commission to do so under Article 108, which would thereby confirm the Commission's pre-eminence when balance-of-payments crises arise?

---

[16] *Agence Europe*, July 16, 1968.

Thus, this crisis, like the earlier ones, has confirmed the profound political contradictions which afflict the community today. The Commission, which aspires to inherit the political significance of economic unification seems to feel required by its assessment of its circumstances to answer a political challenge to its authority with a technical, administrative, and legalistic response. That response was by no means a meaningless one, but it was scarcely commensurate with the threat. The threat was the assurance of chaos should the precedent be established that any member of the union which becomes ill acts first to quarantine itself from its partners. To permit that member to determine for itself what "measures of safeguard" it will take is to permit it to dictate some portion of the economic policies its partners must follow; either they accept, abjectly or under protest, or they resort to protective measures of their own and retaliation.

Nor is it so clear, as Brussels apparently thought, that the political situation either in France or in the community was one from which only the former might profit. De Gaulle, having emerged with *grandeur* once more from another near catastrophe, was undoubtedly in no mood at the end of June to appeal to his community partners for aid; it is not his character. But was he prepared to risk another great crisis and the measures of economic retrenchment his government claimed to have rejected had his partners sought more binding assurances of France's commitment to the community in the future?

VII THE RETREAT FROM THE COMMUNITY

When the community project was launched in 1950, no time limit was set for the realization of "an ever closer union among European peoples." Commission President Rey reminded the European Parliament of this in his inaugural speech in September 1967. "Our American friends," he said, "adopted their Declaration of Independence in 1776. . . . A quarter of a century later, the violent dispute between the Jeffersonians and the Federalists broke out. . . . The Federalists [claimed] the union would never be anything if the general interests which it embodies cannot prevail over the particular interests of the member states, however worthy, however legitimate these may be. . . ." Rey continued, "You can see how our community policies are gaining ground, and how—despite the perfectly understandable national resistance of large countries that were for so long opposed to one another in their traditions, their economies, and their history—these policies are taking shape and gaining substance with remarkable speed."[1]

In the perspective of nearly two hundred years of American constitutional development (and an evolution in the past forty years as rapid as in any previous period of American history), one perhaps may share President Rey's confidence. By the critical first half of the 1960s, only a decade after the community's beginning, the Common Market had already demonstrated that effective economic and political unity need not necessarily be the undertaking of a century or so. The problems with which the community is attempting to cope are the problems which have stunned even the established superpowers

[1] Secretariat of the Commission of the European Communities SEC(67)3710, September 20, 1967.

—a revolution in agriculture, a radical shift in the sources and availabilities of basic energy, rapid technological innovation generally, and the strains which high-consumption societies put on national income policies. But, while integration has advanced far enough that the community is confronted with the problems associated with a modern economy of first-rank proportions, the anti-integration forces, the rigidities of the European political and social structure, and the sluggish evolution of the new political Europe have denied the community equivalent means to assure adequate solutions to these problems. And the vacuum at the community's vital center seems to imperil what has already been achieved.

DE GAULLE AND THE ANTICOMMUNITY

That the postwar movement toward a political and economic union of Europe is today enervated is due in the first instance to de Gaulle. Although the French president pledged when he came to power in 1958 to abide by the Rome treaties which the Fourth Republic had done so much to design, the manner in which the Fifth Republic in fact accepted them was a denial of that pledge. That intended and purposeful denial was announced by de Gaulle long before his press conference in September 1965. In 1959 de Gaulle wrote of his thoughts in 1945: "Considering, in fact, that Germany's collapse, Europe's laceration, and Anglo-American friction offered a miraculously saved France exceptional opportunities, it seemed likely that the new period would permit me to achieve the great plan I had conceived for my country. I intended to assure France [security] in western Europe by preventing the rise of a new Reich that might again threaten its safety; to cooperate with East and West and, if need be, contract the necessary alliances on one side or the other without ever accepting any kind of dependency; to transform the French Union into a free association in order to avoid the as yet unspecified dangers of upheaval; to persuade the states along the Rhine, the Alps, and the Pyrenees to form a political, economic, and strategic bloc; to establish this organization as one of the three world powers and, should it become necessary, as the arbiter between the Soviet and Anglo-American camps. Since 1940, my every word and act had been dedicated to establishing these possibilities. . . ."[2]

[2] Charles de Gaulle, *The Complete War Memoirs*, Vol. 3: *Salvation* (New York: Simon and Schuster, 1964), pp. 872–73. It should be noted that the word "security" in the passage quoted has been translated in the English text as "primacy." While this may perhaps be justified by the context, the French word is nonetheless *sécurité*.

Thus, the treaties which five of the community members put into effect on January 1, 1958 were a different undertaking from that put into effect by the sixth. The Rome treaties aimed at a union of *equal* peoples, confirmed "the solidarity which binds Europe and overseas countries," provided for the representation of a community personality, and contained accession clauses drafted with an Anglo-Saxon power specifically in mind. The Europeans looked on the Common Market as the last chance to move toward a more rational economic and political order which would restore to Europe some portion of its historic influence in a more orderly world. Judging by his 1945 concept, however, de Gaulle saw the community as a serving up of that "bloc" in which France would retain a special position of independence and supremacy and from which it would derive the means for a radical restructuring of the repugnant balance of world power resulting from the war. And the community would quickly lose its utility for de Gaulle when, taking on a life of its own, it became a restraint on the aggressive maneuvers and shifting commitments which are the essential instruments of the Gaullist design.

The unfolding of the "great plan" which de Gaulle "conceived" is all too familiar. The first obstacles to its initiation were France's weakness at home and its overextension abroad—thus, the currency reform, the crushing of the regime of parties, the institution of the presidential system, and the military withdrawal from Africa. With these limitations on France's self-assertion eliminated or substantially attenuated in the first two years of the presidency, de Gaulle could then proceed to activate the plan in the international realm: to act "independently" and to disengage France from the network of multilateral commitments which posed any restraints on such action; to assure itself against any challenge to its European position from a reemerging and potentially more powerful Germany; to prevent Britain from re-engaging itself in Europe; and to disrupt the "two hegemonies" when they appeared on the verge of wider agreement, mediate between them when they were in dispute, and always to maintain a certain balance between the two. Hence, the kaleidoscope of Gaullist foreign policy: the recognition of Peking, the South American tour, the Canadian intervention; the concentration of France's military resources on the *force de frappe* and the military withdrawal from NATO; the first and second vetoes of Britain's applications for Common Market membership; the alternate cajoling and menacing of Bonn and the attempt to establish Paris as the arbiter of

German reunification; and hence, the Eastern policy and the increasing virulence of the anti-American campaign as American supremacy has gained.

In this context, in which the means have increasingly become an obstacle to and then a substitute for the end itself, there is no real ambiguity in de Gaulle's policies toward the Common Market—policies which have variously led him to pose as its greatest defender, precipitate its greatest crises, and, thus far at least, stop short of a complete withdrawal. While de Gaulle correctly saw in the *Memoirs* that France, by itself, would count for too little in the postwar world of giants, the community's ties could provide the means by which France, unrestrained like the other members by parliamentary regimes, and led by a charismatic figure of unequalled European stature, could acquire a voice in their internal affairs and ultimately, by threats to disrupt a going concern, leverage over their foreign policies as well. But the community could be so manipulated to serve the Gaullist objectives of France only so long as Paris remained less committed and less bound than any of the others.[3] This accounted for France's attempts, beginning in 1960, to superimpose on the community the institutions envisaged in the Fouchet plan, which would have permitted France, without abrogating the EEC treaty, to disengage itself from its political consequences. It was also the cause for de Gaulle's assault on the Commission in the September 1965 press conference: "This embryonic technocracy, for the most part foreign, was certain to encroach upon French democracy in dealing with problems which determine the very existence of our country, and it obviously could not be allowed to conduct our affairs once we had decided to take our destiny into our own hands."

The opposition between de Gaulle and the community extends from methods to objectives. There is no possible reconciliation between them, and the crisis of stagnation will continue so long as this fundamental conflict is unresolved. The community's aim is an *equal* restraint on the freedom of action of all its members to the extent necessary to achieve their *common* purposes. Those purposes and subsequent undertakings are to be freely negotiated among equals, not dictated by one member which has asserted a claim to "primacy," and the assumption is that all will abide by joint agreements. These

[3] See Leon Lindberg, "Integration as a Source of Stress on the European Community System," *International Organization*, 20, no. 2 (Spring 1966), pp. 233–65.

are not the rules by which the Gaullists, by their own admission, proceed. As the former French Premier, Michel Debre, stated in September 1965: "France can only succeed by threatening to bolt the Common Market as a whole. In this Fear lies the beginning of Wisdom."[4]

BONN IN TOW

A strategy of terror works, however, only against those who are foolish, fearful, or who have inordinate expectations of ultimate gain, and if the French have repeatedly laid claim to community hegemony, the Five have, all too often, offered little or no resistance to that demand. The fault for this must be laid principally at the feet of Bonn which—perhaps for all three reasons—has been willing to abdicate its responsibilities in the construction of Europe and to tolerate and even to support the pretensions of France.

Every postwar German government has been dedicated to the proposition that a permanent Franco-German reconciliation is the essential condition of European unity, and there is an obvious sense in which this is perfectly true. For a century and a half the hegemonial aspirations of one power or the other was the basic cause of every major European conflict, the last two—the civil wars of 1914 and 1939—destroying the fabric of the old Europe. The historic lesson of these conflicts was that Europe would accept the domination of neither one. With the postwar bisection of Europe, the two countries became geographically the European heartland and the major part of its real estate. Industrially, as Schuman fully appreciated, the triangle based on the Rhine and northern France constitutes a natural region and the logical basis of any larger economic union. Moreover, as a problem in practical politics, it is difficult to imagine how any voluntaristic European construction could get under way which did not proceed initially from the common consent of its two most powerful members.

But the opposite proposition—that European unity is the essential condition of French-German reconciliation—is also true and far more relevant. Bipolar arrangements especially between former rivals, are notoriously susceptible to assertions of supremacy by one pole or the other, either because of sudden divergences of basic interests or of shifts in the balance of strength between them. When there are more than two players, the temptation to press unilateral

[4] *Ibid.*, quoted from *La Nation*, September 15, 1968.

interests may be less, and the difficulties of doing so are likely to be greater. Other interests may also be at issue, and the shifting of patterns of support within the larger grouping may act to restore the original equilibrium or provide the necessary mediation. Nor do the condominiums of the past inspire much confidence in either the tranquillity or the durability of such arrangements. The prospective Franco-German condominium is no less unsettling to Europe than the dominion of France. Why was it easier to effect the limited rearmament of Germany in the larger Atlantic context than in the European one? Why was it possible to undertake the economic and political reconstruction of Germany only in a multilateral framework? How is it possible to imagine German reunification except in the environment of a wider European concert? In short, the French-German rapprochement is not one which, by itself, can support, bear, and absorb *any* radical adjustment of the basic facts of the relationship between them.

In this sense, the Franco-German pact which Adenauer so joyfully concluded with de Gaulle in January 1963 and which became the basis for the subordination of Bonn to Paris was also a denial of Europe. There is no way to reconcile it with the path toward unification on which the six community countries had embarked. Its immediate impact was to assure de Gaulle that there would be no effective response from the community to his veto of Britain's entry— a coup de force which guaranteed France against any new rival within the community and, for nearly three more years, disarmed the coalition of the Five. But the pact denied not only the principle of the open community; it hit at the other bases of the community as well. How could a community based on a delicate balance of power among three large and three small countries and the evolutionary development of a central respresentation of their common interests continue to thrive when one of the largest powers had committed itself to work in combination with another? How could the central institutions really develop if the two most powerful countries concerted their views in advance and held enough votes to assure—if they wished—that no decision would be taken against them or that the majority rule applied? And how could the communitarians maintain the posture that the community was the accepted route to an ever closer European union when Adenauer defended his acceptance of the pact as a start toward the kind of union envisaged in the Fouchet proposals which had foundered the previous year?

123

When the French-German alliance has been operative, it has served primarily the French interest, and since the cost, real and potential, to the community has been so high, the German motive has often seemed obscure. In fact, despite the devotion of individual Germans and the contributions of the country as a whole to the cause of European unity, there has rarely been operative in Bonn an unequivocal concept of European policy. Whatever the considerations which activated Adenauer—Rhenish separatism, a parochial view of the communist "threat," an abiding distrust of Britain, and suspicions of the Kennedy administration as well—he was an easy target for de Gaulle. Erhard, whose skepticism of Paris was always healthier, was a tireless advocate of the free trade area, and he was never reconciled to the *dirigiste* implications of the Common Market. He seemed rarely to understand the implications of the Fouchet proposals for either the community or for Germany. The balancing act of the Kiesinger government has bordered on nonpolicy. Its exaggerated hopes and fears of how France might influence the prospects of German reunification have had the effect of neutralizing Bonn as an essential component of the coalition of the Five.[5] And within the German political spectrum are the neonationalists who find in Gaullism a suitable formula and who believe a truly binding community no more in the German national interest than in the French.

The great movement toward European unity had as its prime objective the pacification of the Continent's principal antagonists, but it has thus tended to founder on the relations between the two and on their disavowal of the community as the arbiter of those relations. What the one has sought openly to suborn to its own aspirations, the other has not seen fit to defend as the best antidote to those aspirations, and the blame for the resulting stalemate is in the first instance theirs.

A NONCOMMUNITY POLICY

There is, however, sufficient blame to rub off on the other four members,[6] the Commission, the European movement and the political

---

[5] After Bonn has done little or nothing to defend the integrity of the community and its institutions against the latest Gaullist assault, it can be relied upon—invariably—to call for a European summit meeting to consider how to recharge the batteries of the unification movement!

[6] The complex motivations which entered into the national positions taken during the 1965–66 crisis, for example, are set out in some detail by Newhouse, *Collision*

parties, and on Britain—which was attracted to the community only when the risks of staying out became greater than the risks of entering.

Rome's European policies have lacked a clear direction. The Italians have been more peninsular than continental in their conception of the Italian interest, and they usually have been excessively modest in their appreciation of Italy's potentially influential role in community affairs. It has often been said that the Italians have never been certain whether they were the largest of the small powers in the community or the smallest of the big. To this basic ambivalence is attributable perhaps the absence of a clear alignment between Rome and the institutions in Brussels, an exaggerated and sometimes inconvenient tendency to mediate and seek compromises, and, along with the distrust of the Bonn-Paris "axis," an occasional affinity for directorates and exclusive arrangements—so long as they are tripartite in character. The four Italian votes, therefore, have not counted for as much as the four French or German; the delays, for domestic political reasons, in reconstituting the Italian delegation in the European Parliament has made it more difficult for that body to claim to speak for "European" opinion; and the former Secretary-General of the Italian Foreign Ministry, Attilio Cattani, who became chairman of the Fouchet Committee, has as recently as 1967 blamed the breakdown in 1962 of the negotiations on the Fouchet plan on a combination of British maneuvering, Dutch and Belgian "animosity" toward the "big'" powers (among whom he included the Italians). Had those talks been successful, he declared, "many of the adverse developments which have taken place between then and now would have turned out differently."[7] Indeed they would have.

If on balance it would have been preferable that Rome had found its European vocation in consistent association with the smaller countries in building defenses against domination by the big, it cannot in fairness be said that even the smaller countries have dedicated themselves to that end. The Benelux countries together wield five votes in the Council, and in certain instances, the favorable vote of at least

---

in Brussels, especially pp. 62–77. Professor Hallstein, in his address on assuming the leadership of the European Movement last January, charged that "the peoples of Europe have suffered their politicians to promise unification in non-committal addresses delivered on festive occasions and to forget their promise in their day-to-day policies. The peoples of Europe have tolerated a Europe of ulterior motives." (Agence Europe, January 24, 1968, Europe Document No. 461.)

[7] Europe Document No. 424, Agence Europe, April 27, 1967.

one of them is necessary for a majority. Yet, not until 1968 did the Benelux move to constitute themselves as a reliable voting bloc, and even on critical issues—during the June 30 crisis, for example— they have on occasion been divided. Whereas the Belgians, for understandable economic and ethnic reasons, are unpredictable in their capacity to resist the French, the Netherlands, with its external interests and its ties to Britain, has often seemed to have a basic reservation regarding the community as a whole.

If none of the individual governments has been willing to provide a consistent leadership to the European movement—by making the community the constant center of its national endeavor—from what other quarters might such leadership have come?

In his book, *The Eurocrats*, Spinelli accuses the Commission of not commiting itself to this essentially political role. The community came into being, in his view, because a great innovating idea was accepted by a relatively few who seized favorable opportunities to translate their vision into political action and institutions, and in consequence, ". . . the creation of a united Europe has no longer depended solely upon the rhapsodic initiative of European-oriented national political leaders, but also upon the daily accomplishments of a European Community bureaucracy and the interdependent relations which it has succeeded in creating and developing."[8] But if "the permanent adversary . . . the habit of regarding laws, customs, unity, interests and political activities as being within the traditional and well-known domain of the nation-state"[9] is to be overcome, then the community must consolidate its institutions, find its own political alternatives expressed in political language, and organize political parties which can effectively engage in the struggle to determine *at what level* the common problems of Europe will be resolved.

Spinelli believes the Commission has contributed far less than it should have. Conceiving of its task largely in functionalist terms, the Commission's prime objective has been the establishment of the community bureaucracy—"the quiet construction of a Europe of offices which would move forward in agreement with the offices of the member states."[10] To do this it has worked primarily with the national bureaucracies and created European-wide organizations of professional groups which for the most part have become lobbies for

---

[8] Spinelli, *The Eurocrats*, p. 8.
[9] *Ibid.*, p. 8.
[10] *Ibid.*, p. 71.

their own particular interests. It has avoided risky identification with the European movements, and it has held the European Parliament at arms length and remained aloof from the struggle to achieve the parliament's popular election—an achievement which would produce precisely the kind of European-wide political base on which the community must ultimately rely. The result is that the "united European authority of the Commission . . . rests primarily on the fragile base of its power to set in motion the decision mechanisms of the community with proposals for progressive economic integration."[11] While the bulk of that authority is retained by the nation-states, rival methods for its exercise are proposed, or it is wielded in fact by the hegemonial power.

Nevertheless, the Commission is a reflection of the political pusillanimity which produced it. Had the member countries been ready to accept the Commission as a European political authority, they would have added to the treaty-guarantees of its independence a less ambiguous and more clearly European arrangement for its selection. On the contrary, even the co-option provisions adopted in 1951 for the appointment of the High Authority were dropped when the Rome treaties were negotiated. Even though the EEC treaty was weak with regard to the selection of the Commission there was nothing to prevent some of the member governments from nominating candidates who were *political* figures of European stature. The first EURATOM and EEC Commissioners were in general of high caliber—but most of them were competent technicians. From among them there emerged no politicians of the first rank, even though it was Hallstein's tendency to consider himself a prime minister which caused some of his later difficulties—and even though, in the dubious alliance between Commissioner Mansholt and de Gaulle which produced the CAP (that "strange admixture of audacious innovations and rural corporativism" which ultimately confronted the community with a choice between federalism or confederalism), it was Mansholt who was looking the furthest ahead.[12]

In any case, if the Commission has had to proceed by stealth, it is due in no small part to the failure of the pro-Europeans to produce a political organization on which the Commission could rely. The European Movement has been fragmented for years, divided along ideological lines, and the main camps themselves divided. Not since

[11] *Ibid.*, p. 67.
[12] *Ibid.*, pp. 204–5.

the launching of the Council of Europe has the movement been a significant factor on any undertaking which has come to fruition. The European Federalist Movement was instrumental in establishing the ad hoc assembly which drafted the charter for the European Political Community that collapsed along with the EDC, and since that time, a portion of the federalists have drifted off into such ineffectual activities as the attempt to launch a constituent assembly through the sponsorship of unofficial popular referendums. Only the Monnet Committee, by acting through the party and trade unions represented on it, can be said to have found a formula for political action—by tapping and seeking to activate national centers of influence.[13]

Given the great emotional fervor which it inspired in its earlier days, it is on the whole astonishing that the movement toward European unity spawned no European-wide party organization. In the early postwar period, the parties of Catholic persuasion on the Continent carried the burden of organizing political support for European integration, their devotion to the objective—at least in the first flush of optimism—was impressive if not always unequivocal, and, in a fraternal kind of way, these parties supported each other. But these were parties of a traditional sort, organized in a traditional way. Despite the great personalities who lent their names to the European cause, no leader with a political base extending beyond national confines emerged. As Spinelli has pointed out, European unity did not become, even for the Europeanists, the keystone of national domestic policy; it was and remains today a "foreign" policy. Today, the Catholic parties are decimated in France and lack any clear European concept elsewhere.

If there has been any hopeful evolution of partisan support of European unity, Spinelli believes, it is primarily within the demo-

---

[13] *Ibid.*, pp. 190–201. Since Spinelli blames the Commission in large part for the failures of the European movement, it will be interesting to observe whether the arch-Eurocrat, Professor Hallstein, will reemerge as Europe's arch-politician now that he has assumed the presidency of the European Movement. In his inaugural address, Hallstein declared: "The European Movement is a political movement. As such it has, since its foundation, assumed two tasks: the task of taking the initiative and providing drive, and the task of exercising a watching brief. For it aims at nothing less than being . . . the conscience of the European nation. . . ." Yet, aside from calling for increased militancy on the part of a rejuvenated Movement, Hallstein seems to rely principally on the existing communities—not direct political action—for the "driving force" to realize the "grand concept" of a political community.

cratic left,[14] and here, too, optimism must be tempered with skepticism. Initially confined to the Low Countries, socialist support for Europeanism made dramatic gains in West Germany, Italy, and France after the Common Market became a going concern. The apparent conversion in 1966 of that most parochial and suspicious of parties, the British Labor Party, is the most remarkable achievement of all. But, the socialist party in Germany, sharing the responsibility of the national government for the first time in the postwar period, has been far more beguiled with the possibilities of inspiring new movement toward German reunification than in achieving new breakthroughs in the community; the pressures which the Italian socialists have been able to exert on the European policies of the Rome government have been fitful; and the Federation of the Left in France—mindful that the views of its communist allies toward the community are, by Italian communist standards for example, antediluvian—has yet to champion the cause of a democratic European construction as the alternative of the future to a Gaullist Europe. Above all, the notorious inability of the socialist parties on the two sides of the Channel to identify with each other has prevented the continental parties from mobilizing support for Britain's entry—even when they have realized that the Labor Party alone offers any reasonable hope of tipping the scales in the direction of a more social-minded community.

Scarcely less astonishing than the weakness of the community's party base is the failure of the economic and social organizations to become truly effective instruments of community-wide political action. There are well over two hundred professional groups of a community-wide scope; some of them—notably the industrial and agricultural groups—are powerful spokesmen for the interests they represent; and some of them have established their presence in the community institutions, particularly the Economic and Social Committee, but also in Parliament. These groups have sharply increased public awareness of a supranational interdependence of certain economic interests, of the community's significance to everyday life,

[14] *Ibid.*, p. 188. While one may take some encouragement from the positive evolution of socialist thinking toward the communities, it has nonetheless been painfully slow and often lacking in practical significance—not only because the socialists lack a community-wide base, but also because their national positions lack strength. The present outlook for the noncommunist French left is obviously not a cheering one, nor is it at all clear that the German and Italian socialists will emerge strengthened from their periods of collaboration in coalition governments.

and of the need, therefore, for the creation of ways and means of exercising an influence on the community's decision-making mechanism. While these groups have on occasion been conservative road-blocks to community action, they have on other occasions provided the impetus for action or resistance to retreat, and in either case, they reflect a political response to the community's existence.

On the whole, however, that response has been far less than one might have hoped for. It has been uneven, and the consequent result therefore unbalanced. Industry and agriculture realized the possibility and the need for organized action on a community level far more quickly than labor did. The divisions within the trade union movements in several of the member countries and the rigid rejection of the community by most of the communist-affiliated unions have made it difficult to organize an effective labor representation in Brussels. There have been hopeful signs in the late 1960s, however, that the unions might be moving toward operational methods more suitable to the advance toward a community economy.

Even when sectoral interests have effectively organized themselves, they have rarely appreciated either the opportunities provided or the responsibilities required for political action at the community level, nor have they acknowledged that the opportunity or responsibility extends beyond their own particular interests. The Commission has sought both to encourage the formation of community-wide interest groups and to stimulate these groups to formulate common positions as the basis for community policies. But, as Leon Lindberg has shown, common positions readily emerge only when common interests closely coincide, and when there is a substantial divergence of interests, the concerted positions tend to reflect the lowest common denominator, "with the final agreement rarely exceeding what the least cooperative participant is willing to grant."[15] Perhaps for this reason, Werner Feld has found that *national* economic interest groups do not as yet look to their community affiliates as the best way to influence community policy, preferring instead to route their demands through the national governments. The effect of this is to preserve the national civil servant in the exercise of his prerogatives by, so to speak, the popular demand of his customers.[16] On the one hand,

[15] Leon Lindberg, *The Political Dynamics of European Economic Integration* (Stanford: Stanford University Press, 1963), p. 99.

[16] Werner Feld, "National Economic Interest Groups and Policy Formation in the EEC," *Political Science Quarterly*, September 1966.

this may serve to delay the transfer of decision-making powers to the community. On the other hand, when decision-making powers have been effectively transferred, there is a growing gap between the power to make decisions and the democratic power to influence them.

If the community is to produce its own clientele (a partisan base, an effective organization of interests, and a popular commitment which goes beyond sentiment to productive political action), an identification of interest with European union in general and with the community in particular must occur in every member country which is sufficient to require national power centers to give a European content to their policies. The most anticommunity of political leaders has invariably wrapped himself in the European mantle, and even in France, the December 1965 presidential elections showed how quickly and how effectively the more or less inchoate attachment to the only significant European construction can be mobilized. Is it any wonder that those who most determinedly defend the sanctity of the state also most determinedly oppose a popular election of the European Parliament, which would give some concrete reality to Europe?

But in the meantime, it would be unwise to exaggerate the extent to which the community can rely for its sustenance on the existence of a political base which is not yet there. The Rome treaties created a set of institutions and an operational system to facilitate agreements on how the common advantages should be shared and the problems resolved. Ultimately, it was intended, these agreements would be bargains, reflecting the direct representation of the "community peoples" in these institutions and the balance of influence of their organized interests. However, the *effective* line of communication between Brussels and the community peoples and the *effective* exercise of organized influence is still through the nation-states. And because in varying degrees the member states are apostate—by conviction or default—the critical element in community decisions is all too often not the effective working of the community system, but the distortion of the balance of power with which the community began.

So long as this basic condition prevails, the community will have to be content with Luxembourg "settlements" and the procedural victories which the Commission can contrive, and the other members will have to accept the indignities which are the fallout of de Gaulle's games of realpolitik. If the members of the community are convinced

131

—objectively or subjectively—that the sine qua non of a community is the ordination of one of them, then the bargaining position of that pivotal member is strong, whether its actual situation happens at any particular moment to be strong or weak. When it is strong, that country simply claims the advantages which accrue to the member which enters any enterprise with the smallest commitment and the capacity, therefore, to run the greatest risk if its bluff is called. When it is weak, it fortifies its claims by pointing to the alternatives which it has diligently endeavored to show would be palpably worse: domestic chaos and/or the ascendancy of another and less acceptable power.

The defenses to be built against such hegemonial proclivities are the community's urgent task. The problem may suggest the means. The community will be shaped, not only by the outcome of its great crises, but by the minor confrontations which occur and by the decisions which are made every day. Until such time as the power centers of the new Europe develop, it is therefore essential that the European-minded countries pursue a carefully measured and consistent policy of assuring that every decision taken achieves not merely its specific end, but contributes to—or at least, does not detract from—the construction of a more effective community. However, such a determined procommunity policy will require a stamina and a commitment from the Five which has so far been lacking. Moreover, it was the manifest weakness of the coalition which emerged against France in the June 30, 1965 crisis that its five members could not convincingly demonstrate their ability to sustain the community effort in the long haul in the event there should be no agreement with France. Therefore, if the prerequisite for a resumption of progress toward a viable political community is a new equilibrium among its members, does not this imply a community of sufficient size and balance that the threat of defection by one of its members provokes a yawn instead of a fever?

Part III: The Importance of Britain

VIII   BRITAIN AND THE MARKET

Twice within the space of a half-decade, de Gaulle has proclaimed that the Common Market is closed—closed at least to Britain. On each occasion he has declared it technically impossible to bring the British economy within the confines of the economic union, and in November 1967 he seemed to feel that Britain's payments crisis was the badge of a permanent disability. He sought on both occasions to impugn the sincerity of Britain's motives and presumed to judge—negatively—whether London could or would abide by the treaty commitments involved. On both occasions, he clothed himself in European—even community—garments, claimed that only a different and weaker set of rules and procedures could accomodate Britain's admission, and strongly implied that, should the other members attempt to build this other Europe, which would fall to an American hegemony, they would so build without the participation of France.[1]

The will of the One has prevailed over the views of the many. No community member was prepared in January 1963 to fight for the continuation of negotiations with London even though many of the problems of its admission had been resolved and though, in the opinion of the Commission at least, the remaining ones were soluble.[2]

---

[1] While this paragraph is a fair summary of the main themes of de Gaulle's statements on the British question in his press conferences of January 14, 1963 and November 27, 1967, the reader may wish to consult the complete text. The two statements are remarkably similar and one will look in vain for any signs that his hostility to British membership has abated.

[2] "What was needed for a solution was in some cases mainly a move from the British government, but . . . there were also cases in which the issue turned upon proposals to be drawn up by the six themselves. . . . The problem was one of reconciling with

There were those who clearly saw that Britain's application and the manner of its rejection posed an issue going far beyond the technical problems dealt with in the nearly two years of negotiation. "Great Britain has been excluded," Spaak then eloquently told the Council, "without valid reason in the opinion of five. . . . When we made the Rome treaty we proclaimed without cease the community we were forming was an open community. . . . Today . . . we are *forced,* some of us against our wishes, against our will, against our hopes, not to respect the policy we laid down. . . . On January 14 we were faced with a spectacular reversal of French policy *demanding* a spectacular reversal of our own policy, without being forewarned by any diplomatic means at the disposal of our countries, and without even being permitted to discuss the reasons leading up to this event. . . . As soon as one member of the community wishes to *compel* all the others to take decisions which are of capital importance for its life, the community spirit ceases to exist."[3]

In September 1967, it was the Commission's advice to the Council that the best way to determine whether arrangements could be found by which an "indispensable cohesion and dynamism" could be maintained in an enlarged community was to open talks with the British.[4] But the response to the second veto, as to the first, was a remarkable admission of helplessness set forth so clearly in the Council's statement of December 19, 1967: "Five member states agreed with the Commission's point of view. They expressed their desire for the immediate opening of negotiations . . . in parallel with the reestablishment of Great Britain's economic situation. One member state considered that the reestablishment of the British economy must be completed before Great Britain's request can be reconsidered. . . . The request for accession presented by the United Kingdom, Ireland,

---

Community arrangements the action taken to adjust the British system whilst paying due heed both to Great Britain's vital interest and to a Community system which itself lay largely in the future." European Economic Community Commission, *Report to the European Parliament on the State of the Negotiations with the United Kingdom* (Brussels: Publishing Services of the European Communities, February 26, 1963), pp. 110–11. (Hereafter cited as Commission *Report.*)

[3] Quoted in Miriam Camps, *Britain and the European Community, 1955–1963* (Princeton: Princeton University Press, 1964). (Italics supplied.)

[4] Commission of the European Communities, *Opinion on the Applications for Membership Received from the United Kingdom, Ireland, Denmark and Norway,* Brussels, September 29, 1967, English Version-Advance Dissemination, p. 108. (Hereafter cited as Commission *Opinion.*)

Denmark and Norway, and also the letter from the Swedish Government, remain on the Council's agenda."[5]

In 1968 it is perhaps clearer still that the "British question" is not really concerned with the future of Britain—important though this may be. Nor does it concern the specific modalities of its admission or judgments on its economic resilience either before or after its accession. The real issue is the community itself—the community of rules and procedures which de Gaulle professes to wish be strengthened, but which in practice must apparently do his bidding regardless of the rules. The acceptance of the diktat of 1963 was the assurance of the constitutional crisis of 1965, and the indecisive outcome of that confrontation inevitably brought in train the second veto of 1967 and the renewed flaunting of rules and procedures in 1968. The result is the community of stagnation we have described, the economic union which is delayed by its political implications, and the threat of disintegration which will come when the member states can no longer find a guarantee of their vital interests in the Rome treaties.

It is in this perspective that the issue of Britain's entry must now be faced. It will not be easy to extend to ten members an economic and political system which is still in process of formulation and which in its present state is less than adequate for six. But it is possible. The British applicant of the late 1960s is not the Britain which in 1963 was still occupied with the remaining obligations of Commonwealth and empire. It is instead a country preparing itself for a European engagement which it has accepted as a political, more than an economic, imperative. Far from requiring "so monumental an exception," Britain's incorporation could be accomplished without change in community objectives or risk to its major features and methods. And rather than "weakening everything," Britain's entry would impel the community to resolve issues long at impasse and to tighten the very rules which de Gaulle disdains.

[5] As a statement on the record of the disagreement between France and the Five, the Council decision is remarkably similar in form to its decision on majority voting in February 1966. This raises a question: Since some authoritative opinion holds that the *opening* of negotiations with an applicant could be decided by majority vote, are the Five not obliged by the position they took in Luxembourg to proceed after a "reasonable time" to take a vote? On the other hand, by virtue of the position they took in Luxembourg, are not the French obliged to continue the discussion until unanimous agreement is reached?

BRITAIN'S COMMITMENT

Many of the problems which Britain and its fellow applicants raise for the community were scrutinized in the earlier round of negotiations, and the Commission's report to Parliament cited above is an even-handed record of the results it achieved. Since then there has been no lack of further inquiry into the issues, and once again, the Commission's opinion—in the formal report of September 1967 and the oral supplement in December[6]—is an impartial statement of how the majority view has evolved. The Five have endorsed that view; the British, while professing to find the negative accented, have not challenged its main lines; and even the French have used it to buttress their opposing views.

The Commission's judgment of the difficulty of admitting Britain and of the implications thereof is as follows: Because Britain's accession could not be effected apart from that of the other three applicants for membership or without regard for the interests of those seeking some form of association, the problems raised are in effect conterminous with those of effecting a viable economic and political organization of the larger part of Europe. The issues thus extend beyond those connected with the provisions of the Rome and Paris treaties and with the policies which the members have adopted and which the applicants would have to accept. Despite the enormous scope and importance of the undertaking, however, solutions could be found to all the specific problems—provided the negotiations were launched with a will to agree, provided members and applicants alike accepted the aims and objectives of the treaties, and provided all parties agreed that the community remains a dynamic, not a static, enterprise. If these conditions were met, then the community's enlargement would have distinct advantages and would constitute no less than a "decisive step forward towards completion of the work of European unification which has been going on since the end of World War II."[7]

While its report after the 1963 disaster lacked a forthright endorsement of the *desirability* of Britain's accession, the Commission's assessment of the *feasibility* of effecting it—i.e., of satisfying the necessary conditions—appears to have undergone no substantial change since the first application. Those conditions, however, are

[6] See *Agence Europe*, December 13, 1967.
[7] Commission *Opinion*, p. 14.

138

no longer precisely the same. Neither the community nor Britain has stood still in the interim. Some of the enduring issues are seen in a different light, many of the problems which loomed largest in 1962 and which then occupied the greater part of the negotiations are no longer serious obstacles, and the two or three issues which are now the focus of attention were then scarcely considered at all.

These changes are partly due to the altered nature and extent of the British commitment to membership. On August 3, 1961, the House of Commons approved a motion which authorized the Macmillan government "to make formal application under Article 237 of the Treaty of Rome in order to initiate negotiations *to see if satisfactory arrangements can be made to meet the special interests* of the United Kingdom, of the Commonwealth, and of the European Free Trade Association. . . ."[8] Among the "special interests" were the difficulties which an acceptance of the EEC's policies would pose for Britain's domestic agriculture and a generally prevailing anxiety that membership might involve unacceptable derogations of sovereignty. London's application closely followed the Common's authorization, and the same themes were stressed by the government's chief negotiator, Edward Heath, in the first formal presentation of Britain's case on October 10 in Brussels.[9] While Heath declared that London accepted the aims, objectives, and institutions of the treaties and would require at the most protocols rather than amendments to them, the bulk of his statement was a detailing of Britain's major problems and the solutions to them which London envisaged.[10]

Even though the Heath presentation was in response to a community invitation and was regarded at the time as a forthcoming one, it is now generally accepted that the request of the Macmillan government for negotiations on the terms for accession—rather than on accession itself—was a mistake. The substance of the negotiations might in either case have covered much the same ground, but the emphasis would have been different. As it was, the British approach seemed to imply that the commitment was less than wholehearted and that actual entry might be conditional on still other negotiations yet to come; it tended to identify as purely "British" a number of

[8] Text of motion contained in Commission *Report*, p. 11. (Italics supplied.)

[9] For an authoritative account of the previous round of negotiations see Camps, *Britain and the European Community*.

[10] The bulk of the Heath statement is reprinted in Kitzinger, *European Common Market*, Document 18, pp. 151–65.

problems which were in reality the community's or which belonged jointly to the two parties; and, it seemed to increase the likelihood that, London's protestations to the contrary, the end effect of the negotiations might be substantial changes in the treaty. "However grave and important the problems facing the United Kingdom may be," the Commission cautioned Heath, "they need to be settled without exceptions becoming the rule and vice versa. Exceptions made must not be of such scope and duration as to call into question the rules themselves or impair the possibilities of applying these rules within the Community."[11]

British entry has again become an issue in the late 1960s, in good part because of Wilson's avoidance of some of the pitfalls of approach which plagued the earlier one. In informing Commons on November 10, 1966 that his government had decided to try again, Wilson stated that a new high-level approach would be made to see whether conditions existed for "fruitful" negotiations with the Common Market and on what basis these might take place. If it appeared likely that essential British and Commonwealth interests could be safeguarded in the event "Britain were to accept the Treaty of Rome," then a decision would be taken to "activate the arrangements for negotiating for entry."[12] The announcement was followed not by a formal application, but by the visits to the six EEC capitals and to the Commission which Wilson and Foreign Secretary Brown undertook in the first three months of 1967. These discussions were in the character of "pre-negotiations," and while they dealt with Britain's problems, they also permitted the British leaders to put their case in the best possible light without the premature commitments of formal negotiations.

Given the long record of Wilson's personal opposition to the Common Market and the prevailing opinion on the continent that the "fresh approach" was really a stale one, this period of preparation was no doubt politically essential on both sides of the Channel. Its main consequence was to permit a major shift in the British stance— from one of suppliant seeking special dispensation, to an applicant eager for entry on terms neither more advantageous nor more exceptional than those the original members had accorded each other. Some problems stressed earlier by Wilson himself could be ostentatiously dismissed later as of no consequence (regional policy was

[11] Commission *Report*, p. 15.
[12] *Agence Europe*, November 15, 1966, Europe Document No. 400.

one); others could be placed in the community context (agricultural financing); and still others could be treated as potential advantages for the community as well as for Britain (the international role of sterling). Thereafter, Wilson could advise the Commons that he had found during his European odyssey no insuperable obstacles to Britain's entry, that all but three or four problems could be settled after its admission, and that Britain's principal requirement would be transitional arrangements.[13] Finally, when the new application was submitted on May 10, 1967, it could be a simple statement that "the United Kingdom hereby applies to become a member of the European Economic Community under the terms of Article 237 of the treaty establishing [that] community."

In the aftermath of France's second veto, it has been too easy to dismiss the significance of Britain's new posture, which is as near to an offer to "sign the treaties" as anyone might reasonably expect. True, this has made Britain no more attractive to de Gaulle—and perhaps even less so. He has continued to argue the basic "incompatibility" between Britain and the market, insisted that "everything depends on fact, not on negotiations," and inquired—disingenuously: "Britain, with a truly extraordinary insistence and haste—and the recent monetary events have shed some light on its reasons—proposed that negotiations between it and the six . . . be opened without delay. At the same time, it declared that it accepted all the dispositions which rule the community. . . . This seems to be in slight contradiction to the request for negotiations, for why should one negotiate clauses that have been fully accepted in advance?"[14]

But de Gaulle's question has caused less mischief than he perhaps had hoped. Wilson's conversion to Europe may have been stimulated by desperation—as others besides de Gaulle have suspected—and it may have been less wholehearted than one would wish. There is no way that any late arrival to the community can escape the position of *demandeur*, and until the veto is lifted or circumvented and negotiations started, both the community and Britain are prevented from consolidating the advantage which Labor's volte-face implies. Nevertheless, the terms in which Britain's candidacy is now couched minimize the disadvantages of the applicant. Where London has accepted, it is Brussels which has had to question; the argument turns

[13] See, in addition to the Prime Minister's statements to Commons on May 2 and 8, his speech to the Parliamentary Labor Party of April 27, 1967 released by the party's Overseas Department.
[14] The November 27, 1967 press conference.

less on Britain's eligibility than on its capability; and to an important degree, it is the community, not Britain, which is on the defensive.

This has meant that the community has had to think more seriously of the precise meaning and implications of its insistence that applicants are obliged to accept, in addition to the treaties of Rome and Paris, the "decisions" which have been taken pursuant to them. If this implies that the community's policy commitments are, so to speak, immutable and that adjustments in them incidental to the enlargement of the community are ruled out, then clearly this is a requirement which no applicant could meet. None of the present members is committed in perpetuity to policies which, while workable in the past might not prove so in the future, nor would any candidate for membership forswear a right to participate in the progressive reformulation of community policy as the need might arise. De Gaulle may consider the community "frozen," but this is not what the Commission had in mind when it reiterated in its September opinion that it would be impossible and illusory to call into question "these decisions [which] are the fruit of an often hard-won compromise between the six [and which] . . . have also established an incontestable de facto solidarity between them."[15]

To accept the community's treaties and its decisions can only have, for the community and applicant alike, a meaning much less simplistic than de Gaulle would give it. Community decisions are community laws, some of them more basic than others. The distinction between ordinary and constitutional law may be a useful analogy. Britain would naturally be obliged to recognize the *past* validity of the undertakings which the Six had entered into among themselves and with respect to others. Moreover, from a legal point of view, such legislation would remain valid for the enlarged community— until such time as it was changed in accordance with the constitutional procedures provided. Unless they were revised in the course of the accession negotiations, these procedures would be the various rules set out in the Rome and Paris treaties for the taking of decisions —i.e., unanimity, majority vote on a Commission proposal, etc. Some of the member states would no doubt like to protect existing policy commitments from the "threat" of future change by making these rules more restrictive; but others are fully convinced that the effective operation of a larger community would require even fewer

[15] Commission *Opinion*, p. 5.

restraints on community action. But there could not be one set of rules for the old members and another for the new: Once the British had accepted and been accepted into the community that exists, they would have the same privileges of influencing its course as anyone else.

Naturally, from a political and pragmatic point of view, there might be initial restraints on the exercise of those privileges. Any country belatedly acceding to the community would be obliged to consider the special sanctity of some of the decisions which had gone before it, especially those of a constitutional character. In various ways such sensitivity could be assured without discrimination. To the extent that the community was generous in according transitional periods in which the applicants could adapt to existing community policies, this would obviate the need for early changes in those policies, or, certain limited changes could be effected during the accession negotiations. Moreover, agreements could be reached between members and applicants on certain common objectives to be achieved in the medium-term future. These agreements would in effect be covenants of the entire membership which, much like the EEC treaty provisions respecting agriculture, would be binding with respect to the goals, but the means would be determined by the normal operation of the community's institutions.[16]

In any case, it is clear that London's agreement in effect "to sign" the Rome and Paris treaties—thereby calling the community's bluff —is a gain of lasting consequence. It has made it more evident that such an undertaking cannot be a unilateral one on London's part, but must, instead, inevitably involve reciprocal obligations. In return for Britain's acceptance of the community's major policies, the community is obliged—if it wishes to retain those policies—to accept whatever adjustments are required to assure their continued workability in a new context with new data. Either the community must propose those adjustments and negotiate them with Britain prior to its accession, or it must guarantee to Britain a full voice in effecting the necessary changes after its accession, using the institutional machinery provided. If Britain's acceptance of the treaties is in good faith, then in turn its derogations must be minimal, and after entry, it must so conduct itself that it constitutes no unusual burden on the community's normal functioning.

It is also a distinct "gain" that time and the Wilson strategy have

[16] See Commission *Opinion*, pp. 5–7.

served to demonstrate that Britain could in fact accept on the same basis as did the original members a substantial part of the community as it now exists without major qualification or adjustment. In doing so it would, of course, require a transitional period and access to the safeguard measures and adaptation facilities which the Six set up with due regard for the problems of adjustment which *they* anticipated and which were not dissimilar to those Britain would face. In one area—the existing arrangements for financing the CAP—a simple extension of community policy would create a major problem and London would clearly require some relief. And finally, in saying that Britain could accept the existing community as a policy commitment, London and Brussels alike have entered a general reservation that under present conditions the application of those policies in full might be beyond the capabilities of the British economy.

THE DIMINISHING PROBLEMS
Before discussing the problem of incorporating Britain into the community system, it may be useful to recall the extent to which the community is or is about to become accomplished fact. In addition to the basic structure of the agricultural market, there is the customs union for industrial products and raw materials; the operations of such organizations as the European Investment Bank, the Social Fund, and EURATOM's safeguards agency; the coordinative work of such institutions as the Monetary Committee and the Medium-Term Economic Policy Committee; and the various measures which have been taken to free capital movements, limit restrictions on labor mobility, harmonize tax structures, establish free entrepreneurship, and control activities in restraint of trade. None of these activities is accomplished in the sense that it is "over," but only in the sense that each of them represents a certain achievement.

It would not be possible to incorporate Britain and the other applicants into the framework of these achievements without certain adjustments of consequence for their future operation within the context of the enlarged community. Britain's participation in the EIB and the Social Fund, the application of EURATOM's safeguards to Britain's peaceful nuclear activities, the role in and competitive implications for the CSC of the British Steel Corporation and the National Coal Board, the equalization of British and community social charges, and the implications for community labor mobility of the Nordic Labor Market and the Commonwealth Immigrants Act all

144

pose problems. However, the adjustments required would not be of a magnitude to disrupt or deflect the community from its present line of development, nor is it conceivable that negotiating issues could arise with respect to them which could bar British membership. The candidates accept the objectives, they are reconciled to the chosen means, and the problems are mainly those of ingestion of new data into the community system.

Common External Tariff. Of a different order of importance, however, is Britain's evident willingness now to accept the community's common external tariff and to apply it without significant exception or adjustment. It is in fact in this area—with all its implications for Britain's relations with the Commonwealth and its EFTA partners— that one sees the most substantial improvement in the outlook for a successful negotiation.

In 1961 Heath declared that the U.K. would accept the "structure" of the CXT as the basis for the tariff of the enlarged community. He argued in favor, however, of a "necessary lowering" of those tariffs by a flat 20 percent (a position which reflected on the legality under the GATT of the CXT), and for some twenty-six specific items (which accounted for about 16 percent of Britain's industrial imports), he requested zero tariffs. Although the latter request seemed close to settlement when the accession negotiations were suspended in January 1963, it was one of the most time-consuming and divisive issues in the entire round of bargaining. The proposed linear reduction request was never resolved—the EEC insisting that any such concession on its part would have to be reciprocated by its major trading partners.

No similar problem is likely to arise in the future. In prenegotiation talks in 1967, London dropped all reference to its previous request for zero duties on specific items, and it has stated that it will accept the CXT as it emerged from the Kennedy Round. The Kennedy Round reduction in the CXT was in the vicinity of 35 percent, and when it is fully in place, the resulting EEC tariffs will be considerably below those presently in force in Britain.[17] Thus the problems Britain would face in putting the new rates into effect would be primarily those of adapting to it. This would be one of the primary purposes of a transitional period, but the British could also resort in extremis to the escape clauses and mutual assistance provisions

[17] See Maxwell Stamp Associates, *The Free Trade Area Option: Opportunity for Britain,* The Atlantic Trade Study (London, 1968), p. 40.

which are available to all members. Whether, of course, these devices would provide sufficient relief would depend ultimately on the state of the British economy and what cyclical or structural remedies London and Brussels may have jointly devised to deal with Britain's general disequilibrium.

The Commonwealth. Britain's willingness to accept the CXT is accompanied by its new attitudes toward the application of the CXT to the Commonwealth, and here too it is clear that the problems are of much lesser scale than in 1961. Indicative of the changed outlook, the Commission's 1963 report set forth for nearly forty pages the elaborate arrangements then considered necessary for the Commonwealth, but the September opinion deals with the subject in two brief sections under the relations of an "enlarged community with non-member countries." In 1961, Heath declared that trade was one of the strongest elements in maintaining the Commonwealth association and insisted that it would be a "tragedy" if Britain's entry forced the other members of the association to "change their whole pattern of trade and consequently perhaps their political orientation" as well. In 1968, these words have a peculiarly archaic ring. Whatever it is that still preserves the Commonwealth, beyond the crumbling cement of sentiment, it is not trade. Some 43 percent of Britain's imports had their origin in the sterling area in 1954 compared with only 30 percent in 1968. Even those Commonwealth countries which were most heavily dependent on the British market are rapidly directing their trade to other outlets, and this trend will be accelerated by the impact of the Kennedy Round on Commonwealth preferences.

London has referred to the possible usefulness of the 1961–62 agreements in any future consideration of Commonwealth problems, and the Commission has conceded this possibility. Nevertheless, it is difficult to imagine that these accords—to the extent that they had in fact been accepted—could be taken over in any general way. For the less-developed areas of the Commonwealth, the previous offer of association might be renewed. But this would depend on whether and how the community renews the existing association agreement (the Yaoundé convention) which expires in 1968 and which is being scrutinized in light of the changing relationship between all the industrialized countries and the LDC's—including the moves in UNCTAD to institute a generalized system of preferences. For the developed Commonwealth countries, it is, in light of the Kennedy Round, likewise difficult to conceive of the EEC's conceding

146

more than some very temporary delay in the elimination of Commonwealth preferences. The main exceptions to this are New Zealand exports of butter—some 85 percent of which still find their market in Britain—and British imports of sugar—some two-thirds of which are governed by the terms of the Commonwealth Sugar Agreement. All parties consider these problems sui generis and in view of the increasingly burdensome surpluses with which the community is already struggling, no magic solution is readily in sight.

EFTA. It is also perfectly evident that Britain's future relations with the other EFTA countries are seen in a different light in the late 1960s. In 1961 and 1962 Denmark and Norway followed Britain in applying for membership, and the remaining EFTA members requested negotiations either for association or for some other form of cooperation. When the negotiations with Britain were aborted in January 1963, none of these applications, with the exception of Denmark's, had advanced beyond the stage of acknowledgment. Nevertheless, Macmillan had pledged not to enter the EEC unless the special interests of the other EFTA countries had been met. It was explicitly stated in the so-called London Agreement that EFTA would remain in effect "until satisfactory arrangements have been worked out . . . to meet the various legitimate interests of all members of EFTA, and thus enable them all to participate from the same date in an integrated market."[18] Although it was never made precisely clear what these commitments might mean in practice, they appeared to involve several disagreeable possibilities: that Britain as an EEC member might not apply the CXT to the other EFTA members so long as they remained "outside," that the accession negotiations would not be completed until all applications had been handled, and/or that accession would remain in abeyance until the EEC had wrestled with and resolved all the complicated problems involved in the community's associative relationships generally.

The Wilson government, however, wisely did not renew the commitment made by Macmillan. London is bound only to "consult" with its EFTA partners, and "should it be necessary," to seek to provide them "sufficient transitional periods" before Britain participates in full in the Common Market.[19] As a practical matter, this is perhaps as meaningful a promise as the earlier one. It also releases British accession from bondage to the possible intransigence of the

[18] See Par. 59 of the Heath statement.
[19] Communiqué issued after April 28, 1967 EFTA Council meeting.

broad range of issues to be settled before *all* the EFTA members have achieved a "satisfactory arrangement" with the EEC—or, for that matter, from bondage to the intransigence of one interested party or another who might have seen in the earlier commitment a way of delaying Britain's entry indefinitely. Macmillan's decision to apply for EEC membership could be regarded in some EFTA quarters as desertion of the one organization and capitulation to the other; the second attempt has not been the occasion of the same degree of indignant surprise. Moreover, while there has been a moderate increase in commercial interdependence among the EFTA members between 1963 and 1968, Britain's application of the CXT to any one of them would be less painful in light of the expected reduction of tariffs generally and could be further softened by any transitional period the EEC might grant.[20]

It is indicative of the peculiar reversal of roles that it is the community—not Britain—which is still seized with the problem of policy toward proliferating associative ties. In its September 1967 opinion, the Commission took the position that the community could not make "an *a priori* selection" among those applicants whose economic development is comparable to that of the present members, whose institutions are "free," and who accept without reservation "the aims of the six in regard to political union." For these countries, the Commission therefore advocated full membership, and it saw great advantage in the community's processing their applications simultaneously, establishing a single accession date, and granting a common transitional period. Not only would this minimize the disruption of trade, but it would greatly ease the institutional adjustments required by the admission of new members. But the Commission has been much less bold when considering those countries which are applying for special arrangements and which, for political or economic reasons, are unlikely to qualify for membership. For these coun-

[20] The Wilson government's endeavors to remain disengaged from the embarrassment of Macmillan's over-commitment to the other EFTA countries appears to be holding up well despite the hopes of the EFTA neutrals that Britain will be lured into accepting trading arrangements with the EEC as an alternative to full membership. For example, the communiqué issued after the meeting of the EFTA Council in May 1968 seemed to leave Britain's hands basically untied: "All the EFTA countries should have the opportunity of taking part right from the start in all negotiaions for a trade arrangement which could follow without, however, giving up the political aims of their respective governments: either to become members of the community or to participate in some other way in a larger European market. The Ministers undertook to consult each other in the event of proposals being submitted to them, individually or collectively."

tries it referred vaguely to the possibility of association or preferential agreements, but it cautioned in the same breath against the complications these might bring to the effective operation of the community's institutions and the customs union.

This is not to say that Britain's application of the EEC's CXT generally, and specifically, to the Commonwealth and to EFTA, poses no negotiating problems. But none of these three issues—which together occupied the bulk of the negotiator's attention in 1962— would now qualify as major obstacles to Britain's accession, provided there were no other serious problems.

Agriculture: A Shared Problem? A substantial change in the negotiating situation with respect to the extension of the CAP to Britain has also occurred since 1963, but whether the consequences of this are equally hopeful is more difficult to say.[21] In 1961–62 the negotiations were without definitive result because the CAP was then in the painful process of coming into being. In his opening statement in October 1961, Heath said that Britain fully accepted the aims of the EEC treaty regarding agriculture, that the U.K. would participate in the CAP and that it agreed the community must include agriculture and trade in agricultural products. Moreover, after the outline of the CAP was finally agreed to by the EEC in January 1962, Heath said that the U.K. would accept this, subject to the adjustments necessitated by its application to an enlarged community. Nonetheless, Heath cautioned that such acceptance would cause major difficulties for the U.K. because the British system of supporting the farmer (with direct subsidies and price guarantees) was basically different from the EEC's reliance on import levies, because producer prices were considerably lower in Britain than on the Continent, and because Britain imported substantial quantities of food items from the Commonwealth.[22]

Despite these difficulties, however, one of the main achievements of the negotiations before their suspension in January 1963, was the EEC's acquiescence in a compromise version of a British proposal that the community adopt the U.K. system of an annual agricultural

---

[21] The problems posed for Britain and the community by the CAP have been the subject of numerous studies. For a brief summary of the findings of some of these, see William E. Pearson and Brian D. Hedges, *Implications of Common Market Membership for British Agriculture* (Washington, D.C.: Economic Research Service, U.S. Department of Agriculture, May 1968).

[22] Also see, "What EEC Membership Would Mean to British Farm Trade," *Foreign Agriculture* (U.S. Department of Agriculture, October 2, 1967), pp. 3–6.

review. Under this compromise the Commission (independently of any member-state reviews) would conduct an annual survey of agricultural profits, individual earnings, and CAP financing, and on this basis would make remedial proposals to the Council. In response to the British request to retain the deficiency payments system for certain products until adjustment to the CAP could be made, the EEC insisted that the CAP system be accepted immediately upon British entry. However, the community did offer to permit the British to pay out degressive consumer or producer subsidies in order to ease the transition, and toward the end of the negotiations, tentative agreement was reached that the U.K. would accept December 31, 1968 as the terminal date for its transitional period, the same deadline the community had set for the full institution of the CAP.[23]

In 1968, the CAP—such as it is—exists. The Commission in its September opinion on the British application declared that the policy was the product of long and difficult negotiation (and, it might have added, the declared condition of France's continuation in the market); hence, "any calling into question of the essential features of this policy . . . is therefore ruled out." Moreover, the Commission seemed to hold, there is no objective reason for questioning that policy since the accession of the four applicants would not materially change the community supply situation nor would the estimated 3 percent increase in Britain's living costs as a result of its acceptance of the CAP appear to be an unmanageable one.

The Commission's defense of the CAP "as is" is perhaps less categorical than it may seem on the face of it. Application of the community price patterns to the countries acceding to the EEC could, the Commission cautioned, produce shifts in production patterns which, while not necessitating a "revision" of the CAP, might require "changes" which "could be introduced in the course of future implementation and further development of this policy." "Certain natural, structural, or social difficulties which may exist in some border areas of the new member countries will make it more urgent to complete the structural side of the common agricultural policy." The Commission also recalled the 1962 agreement with the U.K. on the introduction of an annual review system, noting that inasmuch as the prices fixed by Council decision directly affect the economy of the EEC as a whole, any such procedure could not be restricted to consulation with the farmers' organizations alone.

[23] Commission *Report*, pp. 68–84.

In short, in light of the situation in the CAP in which excessive prices increasingly give rise to burdensome surpluses, may one not surmise that a more flexible pricing system, a greater emphasis on structural reforms, and a broader concept of agricultural policy generally are "concessions" to the British which the Commission and many of the member states might ultimately be eager to make?

If so, then this is another instance in which the difficulties posed by British entry would stem, not from London's rejection of the system, but from the weaknesses in the system itself. For its part, the Wilson government, once it had decided to undertake the fresh approach to the EEC, has made it perfectly clear that London would accept the CAP if necessary, along with the increase in the cost of living this would involve—provided only that there was a period of transition. As Wilson told the Parliamentary Labor Party in April 1967, "I doubt whether, given a fresh start, many countries of the Common Market would introduce this particular system. But we should be realistic in recognizing that it has come to stay as an integral part of the community, and in our decision we must recognize this."[24]

On the other hand, it would be unreasonable to expect the British to relinquish hope that the growing strains on the system and the prospect that Britain's entry would add to them would produce rational adjustments of the kind the Commission itself has called for. Commenting on the financial implications of the CAP, Wilson said in the April speech that the existing arrangements "would involve a British contribution to the fund in levies more or less equal to or greater than the contribution of all the six existing members, and a total contribution which might be twice as high as the next highest. . . . Such a system would, I think, be widely regarded here and in Europe as inequitable." While de Gaulle apparently believes that Britain, to prove its bona fides, must "really accept the system of levies laid down by the financial regulations, which would be crushing for it," it is in fact highly doubtful that community opinion in general would agree. In its September report, the Commission noted that FEOGA's expenditures would increase from an estimated $1.6 billion in 1970 to $1.8 billion if the community membership were increased from six to ten. However, if FEOGA's revenues at that time

[24] Wilson has used this formula on several occasions. For example, in the May 8, 1967 debate in Commons he said the CAP could not be "wished away"—"We have to come to terms with it."

were drawn predominantly from the levies on agricultural imports, income from this source would increase from $600 million in a community of six to $1.4 billion in a community of ten, while receipts from other sources (national contributions) would decline from $1.0 billion to $430 million. Most of the increase in revenue would thus come from the substantial rise in community imports of food resulting from Britain's accession—giving rise, as the Commission so gently puts it, "to a problem of balance in the sharing of financial burdens."[25]

DISEQUILIBRIUM IN COMMUNITY PERSPECTIVE

In 1968 the major objection to Britain's entrance is its questioned ability to function effectively within the community in light of its chronic disequilibrium and balance-of-payments difficulties, and in view of the responsibilities it has assumed as the manager of a money which is both a reserve currency and a widely used means of international payment. These are relevant considerations, but the discovery of the relevancy seems peculiarly belated given the persistence of Britain's economic ailments through the years, and the lack of community concern on this score five years ago.

On the fringes of the Brussels negotiations in 1962, it is true, there was speculation that British entry would likely be accompanied by a general realignment of exchange rates—by members and applicants alike. But this did not seem so extraordinary a prospect, and in view of the French devaluation in 1958, even a unilateral adjustment in the value of the pound would not have been taken as an unreasonable prelude to Britain's acceptance of the obligations of membership in the community. In light of the French precedent, it could in fact have been taken as evidence of London's determination to meet those obligations.

---

[25] Commission *Opinion*, pp. 39–41. Perhaps more important than Wilson's acceptance of the CAP as a fact of life, Britain's farmers—with whatever apprehensions and reservations—appear also resigned to the necessity of their having to adapt to the community method of agricultural regulation in the event of the U.K.'s accession. British farm spokesmen do continue to attach great importance to their system of annual review; they are dubious of some of the price relationships which have been established within the EEC; and they apparently expect—from their conversations on the continent —that the community farmers themselves will sooner or later wish adjustments in those relations. For the basic position of the National Farmers' Union, see its publication, *British Agriculture and the Common Market*, December 1966; and NFU News Press Release No. 20, January 25, 1967.

Moreover, insofar as Britain's ability to join with the community in the harmonization of economic and monetary policies was then a matter of concern, the EEC had at that point not advanced beyond the preparatory stage in its own efforts at harmonization and not until the Italian crisis of 1963 was there real awareness that coordination of cyclical policies is vital to stability in the community as a whole. Indicative of the state of community thinking at the time, the Commission's report on the talks with Britain merely noted that in response to a statement from a community spokesman Heath had "acknowledged the importance of the articles of the treaty dealing with economic union, and the importance of harmonizing national policies as foreshadowed in these articles."

Thus the preoccupation with the ramifications for the community of Britain's economic and financial woes is as much an unfolding of the essence of the community as it is a newfound awareness of the British malaise. As the Commission has put it, there has been a "recurrent conflict" in Britain over the past twenty years between its efforts to achieve and sustain a rate of growth comparable to that of other industrialized nations and its efforts to maintain a balance-of-payments equilibrium. Periodically the British have seen their growth rates improve only to incur the onset of deficits which have necessitated appeals for international support, followed by deflationary measures and restrictions on capital movements and imports of goods and services. Were this pattern to continue after Britain had become a member of the EEC, then the community might be faced with a new drag on its overall growth rate, an additional limitation on the further development of common policies (e.g., the further liberalization of capital movements), periodic appeals from London for exceptions or assistance, and ultimately, "the most serious danger to which a developing economic union could be exposed—the isolation of one of the national economies involved because of balance of payments difficulties."[26]

It is furthermore the Commission's opinion that the international functions of sterling are a source of special concern for the community. The Commission concedes that the total claims against sterling have fluctuated but little since World War II and, compared with Britain's gross national product and volume of exports, as well as

[26] One trusts that the community's perspective has been deepened by the difficulty since May 1968 in containing the damage which a crisis in one of the *present* members may cause.

with the external claims on the dollar, are declining in importance. Nevertheless, the ratio of assets to liabilities is a thin one, and in view of the more volatile political situations in some of the countries which are the principal holders of sterling, the risk of panic flights from sterling is a continuing one. The Commission likewise concedes the contribution which sterling and the London banking services might make to the commercial activities of an enlarged community, but it seems to question whether such a "privileged role" for London would be acceptable to the other member countries or compatible with the development of a community monetary system. "Management by the United Kingdom of a reserve currency would require an economic and financial policy geared at one and the same time to the Community's own objectives and to others extraneous to the Community."[27]

No one can say whether the community's estimates regarding the long-term outlook for economic equilibrium in Britain are well-grounded or not and whether the Wilson government has chosen the right policy-mix to remove the source of concern. What is more relevant is a sense of proportion and perspective in assessing the importance of equilibrium as a condition of Britain's entry into the Common Market—or even, as the French would have it, for negotiations to that end.

Regarding the *pertinence* of Britain's economic and monetary stability to the question of entry, there is, for example, no substantial difference of opinion either within the community or between it and London. All six members expressed the opinion at the December 19, 1967, Council meeting that reestablishment of equilibrium was of "essential importance," and Wilson himself has stated that this is a condition for British entry. Only France considers Britain's economic difficulties disqualifying. In the November 1967 press conference, de Gaulle alleged that the Commission had demonstrated a basic incompatibility between the community and British economies, that the adjustments required in the latter were too fundamental to be undertaken, and that its balance-of-payments deficit was not only chronic but indicative of a permanent disequilibrium. In fact, the Commission opinion demonstrated nothing of the kind. Although the Commission considers that the swings in British economic activity and the recurring disequilibriums would "put serious difficulties" in the way of Britain's fulfilling the obligations of community membership, it

[27] Commission *Opinion*, p. 55.

sees Britain's economic situation in a much less apocalyptic light than does de Gaulle. What is required, the Commission says, is the establishment of the necessary margin so that the British government could "shape its development policy not only with reference to considerations of domestic equilibrium, but also in the context of a vast, single market, *just as the six present members did in 1957.*"[28]

With the exception of de Gaulle, there is likewise a community consensus with Britain regarding the essential *relationship* between British economic recovery and accession. De Gaulle has declared that "everything depends . . . on the will and action of the British people" and that the British application cannot be "reconsidered" until recovery is complete. The Five, on the other hand, would wish negotiations and recovery to proceed in parallel, and some of them at least would accept the possibility that entry might even precede a total recovery. The difference here is not primarily one of timing, however. If entry were in prospect in the foreseeable future, London could adopt one set of recovery measures, but it must rely on other and less desirable ones if it is not. Whereas de Gaulle would compel the British to resort to the latter, the Commission and the Five would see mutual advantage in concerted action between London and Brussels.

It is worth noting as well that despite any other differences over the implications for the community of Britain's economic problems, France and the Five do not really differ on the remedial measures which are required. The community is of one mind in supporting the draconian measures to which the Wilson government has already resorted. This extends to and includes the November 1967 devaluation which Commissioner Barre advised the Council could constitute one of the necessary steps for the achievement of a lasting balance, provided the additional measures required to make exchange-rate manipulation a successful undertaking were put rapidly into effect.[29] Thus one cannot assume that British disequilibrium necessarily poses a problem of irreconcilable policy differences between London and the community which would make concerted action unattainable.

It is, finally, also apparent that the concern over Britain's ability to withstand Common Market competition is not unmixed with apprehension of the opposite sort: that individual British industries,

[28] *Ibid.*, pp. 50–51. (Italics supplied.)
[29] "Commart Told of Crisis without UK Bid Accord," *The Washington Post,* December 13, 1967.

and perhaps in the long-run the economy as a whole, might prove all too equal to the challenge. Commissioner Barre referred to the "powerful boost" to exports which should result from the November devaluation, and it is widely considered that London achieved the maximum export advantage it could from cheapening the pound without provoking defensive exchange-rate adjustments on the part of the EEC itself. British agriculture, described by the Commission as "run on relatively rational lines and noted for high productivity," would, it is expected, respond to the stimulus of the EEC's higher prices in ways not necessarily reassuring to the continental farmer. Likewise, the community's worries for the future of sterling are not lacking in sensitivity to the strength of London's commercial banking system—a product, in part, of the historic role of sterling, and continental opinion of Britain's capacities in the advanced technologies is on the whole an admiring one.

The economic difficulties of the Wilson government are real. But as an obstacle, and a newly found one at that, to Britain's admission to the community which exists in 1968, these difficulties deserve to be viewed with a sang froid which has too often been lacking even among those who profess to favor the community's enlargement. The weaker of the present members were not without apprehension for *their* ability to stand up to the competition of a larger market—a concern which proved for the most part exaggerated; all of them have seen their structural weaknesses—in coal, textiles, farming, etc.—revealed in a more glaring light by exposure to their community competitors; and all of them, at one time or another, have had to resort to retrenchment measures—not perhaps so severe, but similar in kind—to the ones which Britain as a nonmember has now been forced into with equal reluctance. The community may have an understandable hesitation to assume "responsibility" for Britain, but it cannot even now be indifferent to the future of the pound, nor is it entirely insulated from the consequences of Britain's current deflation and slow or even negative rate of growth. And finally, is it not perfectly clear that Britain's difficulties would be seen in a different light if the community which existed were strong, if its massive reserves were effectively pooled, if it had the instruments to conduct an effective anticyclical policy, and if the community authorities were confident they had the strength to find community alternatives to isolating a member in serious disequilibrium from the market?

156

IX BRITAIN AND THE DYNAMIC COMMUNITY

In the previous chapter we have treated Britain's incorporation into the customs union and the agricultural market as a problem of extending an existing system; in one context, that is the issue. The Rome and Paris treaties cannot be renegotiated, and if they do not reflect Britain's requirements, this is the penalty of London's refusal to participate in the enterprise from the beginning. Now it is a question of determining whether existing formulas can be made to apply to a new set of data with adjustments which, if necessary, are acceptable in the first instance to the members and to the applicants in the second. These formulas resulted from a meticulous balancing of interests, often achieved through agonized negotiation, and a simple extension might produce such ludicrous results as those we have cited in connection with Law 25. In any new negotiations with Britain, the achievement of a new equilibrium is unlikely to be painless, and the consequence of failure would be a loss of community cohesion.

Once the Common Market began functioning in 1958, the possibility of a simple lateral entry was closed off. The implementation of the economic union even within the precise limits set out in the Rome treaties remains incomplete. But even if it were completed its operation would still be a matter of constant reformulation of policy to deal with new data. During a period of negotiation with Britain and the other applicants, especially were it a long one, the developmental process could not be halted without serious risk to the community and to the national economies. Nor could the community remain static during a prolonged ratification process or transitional period.

That any accession negotiations aim ahead of the target was and is fully appreciated. In its "final observations" on the earlier round, the Commission noted in its 1963 report that the number and novelty of the problems raised and "the need to reconcile two sets of commitments as vast as those of the United Kingdom and those of the Treaty of Rome obviously posed extremely delicate problems for both . . .," i.e., the problems of cohesion. But, the Commission added, the "real difficulties" originated in the community's dynamic character. "The question was not only one of reconciling British systems and commitments with the letter of the Treaty of Rome: it was rather one of reconciling them with a Community in the full surge of development. The British application for membership involved an obligation to accept not only the Treaty but the substantial advances made since the treaty was signed. It was on these advances that discussion was sometimes most difficult. But the fact that in certain fields *the content* of the treaty was still in a preliminary stage, and that, broadly speaking, the implementation of its various aspects was in the *intermediary phase*, may also be considered as having made matters more difficult for the negotiators."[1]

The situation of the community in 1968 is substantially the same. "Where economic union is concerned," the Commission wrote in its 1967 opinion, "the work of implementing the EEC treaty is less advanced than it is with respect to the common agricultural and industrial markets. For this reason, the first condition for entry—i.e., acceptance by the new members of the rules and objectives already decided upon by the community, subject to minor adjustments that might have to be made—is not sufficient to ensure that the tasks remaining to be accomplished will be carried to a successful conclusion. It therefore remains to be seen whether the commitments provided for in the treaties or already undertaken by the present members [themselves] are sufficient to guarantee the efficiency of the enlarged communities or whether, on the contrary, *more precise commitments* are necessary, at least in certain sectors, with respect to *the aims to be achieved*."[2]

If this is true, then the time span in which the question of Britain's entry must be considered extends from the present (which in the measure of things is the least important) to a future some five to ten years hence (which is of far greater moment). The essential

[1] Commission *Report*, p. 111. (Italics supplied.)

[2] Commission *Opinion*, p. 6. (Italics supplied.)

conditions of an advantageous extension of the community are therefore clear: The accession negotiations and Britain's subsequent entry
must not prevent the achievement of agreement on those policies
which are more or less explicitly required by the treaties, but which
have yet to emerge from the negotiative or legislative mill. And
Britain's entry must not prevent the extension of the community
into those areas of comprehensive economic and political union which
were the objectives of the whole European movement, but which
still lie an unknown distance in the future.

The community could, of course, simply decline to run the risks
entailed by its enlargement. This is clearly what de Gaulle means
when he intones that to agree to negotiate is to give an advance
consent to "artifices" which would conceal the destruction of the
temple. Another easy answer—easier no doubt to give than to implement—is the concept of parallel development, under whatever
guise it may parade. The community and its prospective adherents
would proceed separately and independently toward a common future, for which the candidates would prepare by unilaterally adopting
as their own the policies and objectives of the community. At some
moment in time, then, a lateral entry *would* become possible. The
attractions of this approach are superficial. No applicant would find
it easy actually to adapt to a market of which it was not already a
member, nor could it readily relinquish a voice in determining the
character of the market to which its perparatory steps would increasingly commit it to join.[3] Nor for that matter would there be
any real assurance that the *community* would pursue in the interim
the policies required of *it* to prepare for the problems and the potential advantages of its later extension. The end result might be an
even greater divergence, rather than a convergence, as the target
date for enlargement arrived.

COMMUNITY RESPONSE TO PRESSURE

The question of whether a dynamic community and an enlarging
one are compatible deserves an answer in its own context. One of
these answers lies in the allegation that negotiations with outsiders

[3] "In our view, no British Government or Parliament could commit themselves to
accept and operate—at some date in the future when we become full members—far-
reaching economic and even political decisions which we cannot possibly foresee now,
and which we could not have the power to shape at the time when they were made."
Foreign Secretary Brown commenting on proposals for alternatives to full membership,
Weekly Hansard, January 24, 1968, p. 436.

159

are of necessity distracting, debilitating, divisive, and conducive to delay in the community's construction. From the uncritical acceptance of this allegation comes the frequent advice that the members get on with "community business," holding the applications for admission in abeyance until such time as the community is completed. Yet the whole weight of the community's experience to date is precisely to the contrary of this advice. The pressures generated by the necessity of facing the negotiating table have tended again and again to produce a unity of purpose and policy and a sense of common responsibility without which the community might not have "moved" at all.

This was surely the impact of the first round of negotiations with Britain. The derogations London proposed from the CXT seemed on the whole only to deepen the community's attachment to it. After the talks had begun in October 1961, the EEC members concluded the basic agreement on the CAP the following January. The British accepted the CAP in principle, and the acceptability of the transitional devices they proposed were thereafter judged by the EEC by their compatibility with the CAP; had the negotiations continued, the EEC would almost certainly have had to complete the CAP much sooner than it did. As the Commission saw it, the bargaining with the British was on the whole a blessing in disguise: "In many cases the right solutions could only be solutions which anticipated the future progress of the community . . . which had . . . the effect of leading the enlarged community, probably sooner than originally intended, to start working out common policies. The negotiations with the United Kingdom, because they brought these problems to the fore and in some cases considerably increased their scale, compelled the Community, then, to come to grips with them sooner than it otherwise would have done."[4]

Community authorities cite one exception to this—the impact which the negotiations with Britain had on the dispute over Law 25. The law was, as will be recalled, part of the original CAP agreement. It was poorly drafted, and in view of its great importance, its interpretation became almost immediately an issue of considerable proportions among the members. In these circumstances, Britain's acceptance of the regulation as community policy—an acceptance which was slow in coming and conditional on a definitive interpretation at some

[4] Commission *Report*, p. 112.

future date—was bound to have the effect of widening the existing differences. Those who liked the law—the French—wished for its earliest confirmation, while those who had reservations—the Germans and the Dutch—were quite happy to leave the interpretation open in the expectation of later British support.

The interesting point of the exception, however, is not that the negotiations with Britain were aggravating in this instance, but that the main attempt to find a solution—by looking to the future—had insufficient time and support to succeed. In the Commission view, a way out of the impasse lay, not in retreat from the ground the community had secured by its passage of Law 25, but in proceeding from there to a settlement of the much broader question of the community's own sources of revenue. A specific proposal to this effect—covering a good part of the ground covered by the Commission's financing proposals of April 1965—was in fact submitted by the Commission only a month before the talks with the British were suspended. The members, however, could not summon the courage to take a long view, and the issue was left to be dealt with (and to be left again basically unsettled) in the 1965–66 crisis when Britain's membership was no "distraction!"[5]

In any case, if Law 25 is an isolated case, Britain's proposals for a free trade area only made the community more aware of the essential elements of its own cohesion. EFTA has exerted little or no attractive pull on the EEC—quite the reverse. The Kennedy Round generated a good part of the steam which carried the CAP to its present state of completion, necessitated and therefore produced a far greater unity of view on trade and tariff policy than had previously existed, and bequeathed to the community a pressing requirement to get on with its common commercial policy. Nor is it unfair to say that EURATOM "discovered" the full significance of its safeguards program only when the negotiations on the nonproliferation treaty "threatened" to superimpose upon it the controls of the IAEA.

Thus, however great the psychological pressure to keep a corporation a closed one, there is every reason to believe that the community could withstand the "strains" of another round of bargaining with the U.K. and might indeed profit from it. If this is so, then the alleged threat to the community's continued advancement would

[5] Commission *Report*, Chap. 4, has text of Commission's proposed regulation.

arise, if at all, only when enlargement had become accomplished fact. Here, unfortunately, there is no relevant experience, and if de Gaulle wishes to contend that Britain's admission must mean the "tearing asunder, the breaking-up of what exists already," the only refutation is a conjectural one based on the considerations which are really germane. The two most important of these would be: (1) the *new data* Britain would bring into the market—not merely the state of its economy, but in the broadest sense, the economic, political, and social achievements and aspirations of its people; and (2) the *institutional structure of* the enlarged community, which would determine how effectively and to what degree the new data would be applied to the community's present and future problems.

The vital question is not what Britain will contribute to or detract from the present, but what it may add to or substract from the future. In this perspective—i.e., the dynamic development of the community—the only valid criterion for judging Britain's candidacy is whether the essential next steps required of the movement toward union loom larger with the British or smaller. In some cases, the British impact would be a negative, or at best, a neutral one. But for the most part, it is our conclusion that, *because* of the new data which Britain would contribute, the increased urgency which stalemated issues would take on, the positive assets which the British would bring with them, and the new political climate which would emerge, Britain's entry would produce that very momentum without which the community might linger—for a fatally long time—in its state of suspension.

BRITAIN AND THE MISSING COMMUNITY POLICIES
Among the great issues confronting the community in 1968 there are, as we have seen, the "missing policies"—areas in which community action or the conduct of a common policy was called for by the Rome treaties, but which, for one reason or another, remain largely within the purview of the national states. Notable among these are the common transport, commercial, and energy policies. The community has been bogged down with regard to transport for years, and despite the increased urgency which the mid-1968 opening of the customs union lent to a further attack on transport obstacles to competitive trade, the prospects are at best for a very long period of negotiation. Britain's entry would almost certainly not increase the obstacles to eventual agreement, and because of the increased role sea and air

transport would have in the enlarged community, there would arise in these particular sectors a considerably greater need for action than heretofore. Moreover, because of the greater scope which a bigger community would provide the transport industries of all the member states, one might well see a weakening of the protectionist-nationalist outlook which has been one of the chief stumbling blocks to a transport agreement.

Regarding the common commercial policy, the important consideration is the enormous impact which the accession of Britain and the other three applicants would have on the basic data with which the community has thus far been dealing. According to the Commission's estimates based on the 1965 figures, an enlargement to ten members would increase the EEC's exports to nonmembers by some 27 percent and would increase its imports from nonmembers by 39 percent. The community would then account for some 22 percent of all international trade and would clearly qualify as the world's "foremost commercial power." The four additional members would increase the EEC's share in the total exports of the United States from roughly 18 to 25 percent; of eastern Europe, from 8 to 12 percent; of the developing countries, from 28 to 32 percent; and the Middle East, from 39 to 54 percent.[6]

It is risky to assume that power ultimately breeds a sense of responsibility, but it is clear that Britain would give the community a new commercial dimension and give rise to new pressures for a rounding out of the community's authority in the field of trade policy. The internal as well as the external equilibrium of the market would simply require it. Competition within the enlarged market would likely be sufficiently keen that the members would be more disposed than ever to look with favor on community policing or administration to assure that no member obtained unfair advantage in the application of the CXT, community or national quotas, or the antidumping or antisubsidy rules. The members would not be likely to permit the *community's* enormous commercial leverage to be exploited for *national* advantage by the indefinite prolongation of existing bilateral trade agreements, unfair competition in the award of contracts by associated countries, or, for example, uncontrolled rivalry in offers of commercial credits to state-trading countries. As the Commission has cautioned with respect to trade with eastern Europe, "if each of the old or new member states tried to obtain individual

[6] Commission *Opinion*, pp. 23, 89–90.

advantages, the consequences would be damaging for the community," and for this reason there could be no delay in the development of a common trade policy toward that area.

In the energy sector, the important consideration in Britain's role in the dynamic development of the community would again be the magnitude of the new data its entry would bring into consideration. Among this data is the nationalized coal industry which produces almost as much as the CSC countries combined and which, like its community counterpart, has an excess capacity; the international petroleum and natural gas industry which has impressive but politically vulnerable resources in the Middle East and which is already largely integrated at the company level in its trade relations with the community; and finally, the British nuclear program with its assets which are at least as large as those now under the purview of EURATOM.

Leaving aside for the moment what it could do for EURATOM, Britain's accession would contribute a critical new requirement for the community to conclude its long-standing effort to contrive an effective energy policy. So far as coal is concerned, nothing like a free market for coal now exists in the CSC, and, since the late 1950s, the High Authority's role in the subsidized rationalization of the industry has been largely restricted to a policing one. Britain's accession would not add to the existing coal problem, if indeed the two markets could for the foreseeable future be linked at all, nor would its presence per se alter the fact that the present members are still pursuing national energy policies On the other hand, if the community's enlargement is accompanied by the increased competition one might reasonably expect, the resulting sensitivity to costs might give added fillip to the community effort to bring the coal problem within the framework of an energy policy which puts greater emphasis on the needs of the energy consumer.[7]

BRITAIN AND THE ECONOMIC UNION

In judging whether a community containing Britain would more likely move forward than backward, it is also instructive to look at the impact which London might have on several areas of the eco-

[7] The critical requirement for an energy policy is in any case the fusion of the EEC, CSC, and EURATOM treaties in a manner which will leave the community *generally* more effective. In our view, prospects are unfavorable that the fusion negotiations will produce this result if they are undertaken before the community faces up to the question of its extension.

nomic union, such as the development of an effective industrial policy, the strengthening of the existing means for maintaining economic equilibrium within the community, and the further extension of the elements of monetary union which have already emerged. The Commission ascribed the greatest difficulties to those aspects in the 1961–63 negotiations, noting that the two sides were trying to adjust a British system "to a community system which itself lay largely in the future." And in its 1967 opinion the Commission continued to stress "the importance for the development of the community . . . of the completion of the economic union."

To the extent that a coherent industrial policy is an important element of the economic union, it is evident that the Commission sees British entry in a distinctly favorable light. Although conditioning its expectations with references to the hazards of enlarging the market without taking the required organizational measures at the same time, the Commission believes that Britain and the other applicants would provide the requisite "scope" for a much more rational development of the community economy. "Extension of the Common Market to include countries whose level of development is comparable with that of the six would permit a better division of labor, greater economies of scale and further possibilities of mass production. It would also have the effect of increasing the extent to which the national economies depended on the community as a whole. . . . As a result of the extension, the community's economic potential would . . . be close to that of the world's leading economic power. . . . The entry of [the four applicants] would have the effect of bringing the Common Market's GNP up to about 60 percent of that of the United States."[8]

In considering the specific ingredients of an industrial policy which would make it possible for the community to reap the benefits of scale, the Commission is remarkably sanguine as well that Britain would contribute rather than detract. It notes that a larger market would permit a greater degree of industrial concentration without destroying competition, and from this point of view, Britain's accession "would make it easier to define and implement a competition policy compatible with the development of large-scale enterprises." The adoption of a European patent law, delayed by "political difficulties" in the Council would in all probability, the Commission

---

[8] Commission *Opinion*, pp. 19–20.

believes, be helped by British membership. While observing the importance of regional problems in the United Kingdom, the Commission also comments on the long experience the British government has had in dealing with them and suggests that some of its techniques might be adopted by the community. And while noting the substantial differences between EEC and British practice in such matters as industrial standards, foreign investment policy, and company law, the Commission nonetheless feels these differences are not insuperable obstacles.

When it comes to Britain's participation in the machinery for the conduct of countercyclical policy, the Commission's reservations are more prominent. In the absence of truly effective community machinery, the principle that national equilibrium is essential to community equilibrium becomes a fetish, and the Commission could not but be alarmed at the potentially disruptive effect which a continuation into the future of Britain's stop-and-go cycle of the past would have in an enlarged community. The Commission is acutely sensitive to the specific corrective devices to which Britain has had to resort in repeated balance-of-payments crises: Exchange controls and other restrictions on freedom of capital movements are precisely what the community must strive to eliminate if it is to move toward de facto monetary union.

Yet, here too, the understandable reservations occasioned by Britain's economic problems need to be tempered by perspective. In the first place, to the extent that these problems are not symptomatic of a deeper malaise, it is the objective of both London and Brussels to solve them at an early stage of the game. As the Commission puts it, the difficulties which "stem from cyclical swings in economic activity" could be "eliminated by following a more effective policy for the establishment of equilibrium," and while this is primarily Britain's responsibility, consultations with the community would be geared to the development of a program of adaptation to be carried out during Britain's transitional period. Where Britain's difficulties are structural—and the Commission seems to think this is "mainly" the case—then membership in the community would of itself constitute an important part of the remedy.

In the second place, the Commission's reservations reflect less concern that Britain would be unwilling or unable to hold up its end in the further development of the economic and monetary union than they reflect apprehension that the instruments presently available to the community are adequate—even to their present tasks. To be sure, the Commission advises seeking additional assurances from the applicants that they are aware they would be "joining communities in the process of development" and that their obligations go beyond the general objective of community economic policy to include "the priorities which advancing community coordination has made it possible to establish both internally and at the international level."

But throughout the Commission's opinion, the weight of the emphasis is that the community can cope with the economic problems which enlargement would raise if that extension is the opportunity for a leap forward into the realms of true economic and political union. After observing in a general way that it "remains to be seen whether the commitments provided for in the treaties or already undertaken by the present members are sufficient to guarantee the efficiency of the enlarged communities," the Commission quickly answers its own question: "The need to maintain and if possible to increase the efficiency and the role of the institutional machinery in an enlarged community is all the more obvious because it is more difficult to build an economic union than to eliminate obstacles to trade in accordance with hard and fast rules fixed in advance. On the contrary, economic union calls for a host of harmonization operations, adjustments and decisions that must be spaced out over a period of time and could hardly be brought about without adequate institutional machinery."[9]

The Commission is vigorous in its rejection of the once-stated British preference for dealing with the problems of sterling by unilaterally renouncing resort to some of the remedies the Rome treaties might provide or by seeking solutions in a framework broader than the community's.[10]

Nor does the Commission leave any doubt what it has in mind by way of a *community* approach. Although it considers useful the bilateral cooperation arrangements which the Bank of England negotiated with the various continental banks during the 1967 crisis, the Commission states that these "do not seem to constitute a solid enough base upon which to build up the monetary relations that seem to be required by an enlarged community in which one of the members had a currency with the present characteristics of the pound sterling and a financial center such as London." What is needed is

[9] *Ibid.*, pp. 7–10.
[10] *Ibid.*, p. 53.

"action of a wider scope," designed not only "to settle the situation arising from the complex of claims and liabilities constituted in the past between the United Kingdom and countries of the sterling area," but also to deal with the problems which would arise for an enlarged community if sterling were to retain its function as a reserve currency and if London were to retain the "privileged role" which sterling has given it. "No national currency could possibly assume the role of a *community monetary system*, which would have to result from gradual coordination of member states' policies and strengthening of the common economic, monetary, and financial policies."[11]

Thus, even in the vexing problem of the future of the pound, it is possible to see an opportunity to carry Europe forward toward the real union that a "community monetary system" would imply. Dozens of schemes have been suggested for community funding of the claims against sterling, for the pooling of the community's external reserves, for acceleration of the steps toward liberalizing of exchange controls, for creating a community capital market, and for undertaking the coordination of national policies required for monetary unification. Such proposals could be given the serious consideration they deserve if the monetary issue were to be lifted from the realm of nationalism and realpolitik in which de Gaulle has insisted on approaching them. Indeed, some of the most promising proposals have come from France. Pierre Mendes-France has long advocated that the EEC assist Great Britain in consolidating the claims on sterling. The former finance minister, Giscard d'Estaing, has urged that—in anticipation of Britain's eventual entry and the emergence of common political institutions—France take the lead in proposing a monetary community with a common currency as the ultimate objective. As preliminary steps to that end, the minister has suggested that community members might agree to fuse their present national quotas in the IMF and create a European central bank to which the members would commit a part of their reserves.[12]

[11] This $2 billion in stand-by credits which were negotiated by the Bank of England in July 1968 to "offset fluctuations in the sterling balances of sterling-area countries" is, of course, not a "community solution"—nor even a solution—to the sterling problem. Several of the community countries made credits available, however, and the Commission will no doubt welcome any stabilization of the pound—as a stop-gap measure, as another step toward equilibrium in Britain, and as a diminution in the reserve currency role of sterling—if not as a direct advance toward an enlarged community having a common currency which would assume the functions of sterling.

[12] Interview with a group of journalists, January 18, 1967. Private French comment has often been skeptical of the merits of the government's sterling argument against

168

BROADENING THE COMMUNITY'S PERSPECTIVES

Without the pressures, however, which the accommodation of sterling, for example, would generate, the situation in the community in 1968 is not propitious to ready agreement on solutions to problems of even the most pressing moment. In the case of the CAP, for example, the creakings and groanings clearly indicate that an unadjusted projection of the system into the indefinite future will result in burdens and inequities which the community members will ultimately reject. While the review of the CAP which has been under way since October 1967 may in fact bring forth some changes in emphasis, a major reorientation faces great obstacles. The program is enshrined in community policy by the years of painful negotiation which went into it, by the political importance which France attaches to it, and by the data to which the policy is addressed. But, how healthy a community will the EEC be in the 1970s if some 90 percent of its revenues are earmarked for the support of a program which is increasingly at odds with the majority interest?

The Wilson government has said, as we have noted, that the CAP is an essential feature of the community, and there is no reason to believe that the Commission or any of the members would permit Britain to renege on its commitment to accept it in any future negotiations. The British presence would inevitably make a difference. The CAP could not be extended to four new members without regard for its impact on prices, production, consumption, distribution, etc. And while the Commission believes that the change in the basic data would not make the CAP unworkable, it anticipates—and probably welcomes—the changes which would be necessary in its application. In this sense, the CAP would be "reopened" and the reassessment which is already in process might be advanced. In short, contrary to French fears that Britain's accession would destroy the CAP, it could provide the basis for a new balance which in the long run could save it.

Nor is this the only instance in which Britain's admission might create the opportunity for advance. In July 1966, it will be recalled,

---

British entry, holding variously that sterling's international role is an irrelevant technicality, no inconvenience to the community, or—in conjunction with the facilities of the city of London—a positive advantage. See, e.g., Raymond Aron, "Can the Pound Become a Currency Like the Others?," *Le Figaro*, November 3 and 6, 1967; and Robert Mosse, "The Pound Sterling and the City, Future Pillars of the Common Market," *Combat*, November 3, 1967.

the Council approved new legislation to finance the CAP for another interim period—the issue which precipitated the crisis. In general, it provided that FEOGA's expenditures be met by budgetary contributions allocated to the member countries in part according to a fixed scale and in part in proportion to the variable levies the members collect on their imports of agricultural items. The member states are required to transfer to the community's exchequer funds, equal to a progressively increasing proportion of the levies collected, and in 1970, these levies in their entirety will go directly to the community.

There are two major difficulties with the arrangement: First, unless the CAP is drastically revised, imports from outside the community will fall, the import levies collected will be a declining source of revenue, and the increasingly expensive farm program will put a rising burden on the national treasuries. Second, the formula is open-ended. As the July decision reads: "The Council will so initiate the procedure provided for under the provisions of Article 201 of the treaty that the provisions of Article 2 of Law 25 will become effective upon the expiration of the interim period spelled out in Article 8 of the treaty."[13]

Thus, before 1970, the community will have to take up again all the issues which nearly tore it asunder in 1965—not merely the question of agricultural financing, but the broader and far more important questions of the community's financial sovereignty and the exercise over it of democratic control. What impact would Britain's full participation in the community and its institutions have in a second confrontation on these issues? Britain's accession would exaggerate the existing imbalance in contributions based on levies; this would appear to dictate changes in the community's revenue system, putting it on a broader and more equitable basis. As the Commission has delicately put it, the principle that the import levies should accrue to the community should not go "by the board," but "the search for a suitable balance between the financial burdens borne by old and new members must not, of course, be limited to the agricultural sector."[14]

As for the political issue, there is one certainty: There is no reason to suppose that de Gaulle will be more charitable in 1969 toward parliamentary control over community expenditures than he was

---

[13] See p. 76 of Chapter V. Article 8 establishes December 31, 1969, as the end of the transitional (interim) period.

[14] Commission *Opinion*, p. 41.

in 1965. Will the countries which believed it essential in 1965 to strengthen the representative foundations of the community change their opinion in the future? If not, and if the Bonn government then attaches the same importance to its ties with Paris that it does now, where will the allies of a democratic Europe be found?[15]

Consider also the future of EURATOM and the prospect that it is only Britain's eventual membership which offers any real hope that the nuclear community can avert a major retreat. EURATOM's problems originate in part from France's minimalist and often hostile attitude toward the community and the poor leadership which the last French president of the Commission provided—and in part, from genuine disagreements among the members about priorities and from the growing competition among them in the industrial-commercial applications of nuclear energy. The culmination of these difficulties was the inability of the Council to agree in 1967 on the third five-year research program, the adoption in December of a standby budget, and the 1968 debate on what future, if any, EURATOM may have.

The outcome of that debate seems likely to be a further, overall, and possibly drastic retrenchment of EURATOM's role. France's approach and its example, if not its specific ideas, have simply gained widespread acceptance, and to the extent that a consensus exists in 1968 it is that EURATOM's future research activities should be narrowed and restricted to scientific "infrastructure," that the community should withdraw from further research in areas which have already entered into the commercial realm, and that the association agreements by which EURATOM has in the past helped finance developmental projects in the member countries should be reduced in number or abandoned altogether. While there has been talk of establishing within EURATOM a promotion fund to support industrial ventures for such purposes as the improvement of reactor design and fuel management, this undertaking would be unlikely to attain a

[15] It cannot, of course, be ruled out that—with a further increase in the costs of the CAP and a further exaggeration in the imbalance of advantage which it bestows on the various members—the previous agreement on community acquisition of the levies could not in fact be sustained and that the agricultural program would have to rely after 1970 on national contributions more or less commensurate with national benefits. This would put in jeopardy not only the principle of community financing and administration, but also the logic of the proposals to strengthen the European Parliament which derive in considerable part from those principles. In this lies one of the real and palpable threats of a reversion from the community system.

sufficient scope to reverse the retrenchment trend. On the other hand, under the banner of "increased flexibility," several quarters are advocating that fewer than the full membership be permitted to launch joint nuclear projects. While such bilateral or multilateral endeavors are being euphemistically referred to as "additional programs," they would of course be intergovernmentally organized, financed, and controlled, and they would in no real sense be a community responsibility.[16]

It is healthy that its members have accepted that EURATOM is too narrowly focused, but despite all the talk about the "technology gap," the narrowing of it will depend in the first instance on the further development of the economic community. It may still be a long time before a more meaningful common effort in the scientific field materializes, and when it does, there is no guarantee that that effort will be of a community nature. While the French have often taken the lead in advocating cooperation in this area, they have always acted to keep the supranational role to a minimum in the development of specific proposals, and as they do in the case of EURATOM, they favor "projects" in which the member states—or selected ones among them—get together under the community's imprimatur, but without its control. Those projects are the ones of primary national interest to France.

European opinion acknowledges that Britain's accession would put the community's consideration of the technology issue on a different plane. In September 1967 the Commission stated that Britain's basic nuclear facilities "give it a power which is . . . as great as that of the whole European community," and that its developmental and research work of the past twenty years has left the British with an "overall potential . . . today unequalled in Western Europe." With this potential added, the community could not hope to narrow the gap between Europe and the U.S., but without it, the European disadvantage would inevitably grow wider. Moreover, the Commission noted, British science and industry is in some cases "well-off . . . to

---

[16] As of this writing it is unclear whether EURATOM is moving toward a decision to build the isotope separation plant which has been considered for many years. A decision to do so could of course increase the "size" of the community effort, but it would still leave a question whether this was its most profitable direction. If it is considered necessary for reasons of security of supply to have another isotope separation plant within community borders, the cheapest way to do this would be to admit Britain. See *Agence Europe*, May 20, 1968, pp. 3–4, for a brief summary of the EURATOM negotiations.

meet the need for continuous innovation," Britain's accession would make it easier for Europe to "establish strong points and pioneering units," and the British contribution "often appears necessary" to any ambitious European program in such fields as molecular biology, solid state physics, electronics, aeronautics, and space technology.[17]

The modest goal of preventing the gap from widening cannot be attained, however, if it is the community's intention merely to tie into or to tap Britain's superior achievements—as Wilson made clear in his statement to the Parliamentary Labor Party in April 1967. He said:

In many technological sectors, we lead Europe and in some we lead the world. But we have no hope whatever of exploiting that lead as it should be exploited . . . without a far bigger market than that represented by 50 million souls within Britain or even 90 million in EFTA or the uncertain access to markets abroad. . . . Some argued in our debates that it is possible to get this technological cooperation in a market divided by trade barriers. . . . [But] it is no good hoping to produce the technological equipment of the 1970s if we are going to be faced with an 18 percent tariff on our exports—exactly the same tariff as the Americans face, confident in the knowledge that their R and D will have been written off in a vastly greater internal market, and one indeed where defense orders provide the solid foundation for so much of its R and D expenditure. Of course, technological cooperation across tariff barriers is better than no cooperation at all. . . . But it can succeed in the sense of a technological community *only if it operates within a single industrial and trading market.* . . . Without this . . . I believe that Europe, including Britain . . . might well be condemning ourselves to a second class role in which we shall be producing the conventional equipment of the 1960s, while becoming increasingly dependent on America—and possibly the Soviet Union—for the advanced technological equipment of the 1970s and 80s.[18]

In addition to a market of sufficient scope, however, there is also the prerequisite of effective organizational technique and control in the common undertaking. One may state the requirement as modestly as does the Commission which, after chiding the member states for the lack of direction in their existing bilateral and multilateral scientific endeavors, declares that "it would be illusory to think that the broadly complementary characters of the United

[17] Commission *Opinion*, pp. 76–86.
[18] See also Wilson's seven-point program on technological collaboration set forth in the Guildhall speech of November 13, 1967, reported in *The Times* (London), November 14, 1967.

Kingdom and the community . . . could *automatically* result in a division of labor that would be both economically and politically satisfactory. . . . The hope of [reversing the process by which Europe has more and more fallen behind] will . . . remain a hope unless the member states of the enlarged community are willing to pool their efforts unreservedly."[19]

The essential conditions for a successful attack on Europe's developmental lag may also be stated as extravagantly as Jean-Jacques Servan-Schreiber has put them in that European best-seller, *The American Challenge*. Europe will become competitive in "big science" and escape from the industrial-technological backwashes of the U.S. and the U.S.S.R. only with massive, coordinated aid. This cannot be achieved, however, by international cooperation—it requires an enlarged Europe and an integrated one. "Britain would be the *best possible ally* for France within the Common Market . . ." in the achievement of an economic union of sufficient scope, with an integrated capital market, and with industrial groups of a size to compete on a world scale. There must be a public authority within that union capable of giving the enterprise direction and therefore independent of the national states and disposing of its own financial resources. This state can only be a federal one. Thus, according to Servan-Schreiber, "Neither Europe nor France can escape American colonization until our present political structure is replaced by a European federation, which obviously must rest on a foundation of democracy and universal suffrage."[20]

BRITAIN AND THE PREREQUISITES OF POLITICAL UNITY

In whatever terms the requirement is stated, we return inevitably to the same issue: whether any common European undertaking can function within the limitations which are imposed upon it by de Gaulle. *This* is the real challenge to Europe today.

De Gaulle poses as the defender of the community's achievements and bids its members not be distracted by the disruptive myths of enlargement. But those achievements remain modest and in some respects dubious; the obstacles of an economic or technical nature to the community's extension are not insuperable; and in many instances it is Britain's accession which offers the best possibility of

[19] *Ibid.*, p. 85.
[20] Jean-Jacques Servan-Schreiber, *The American Challenge* (New York: Atheneum, 1968), pp. 162 and 175.

174

a further advance. The very problems it would pose would create the conditions for new solutions—as the Commission has said, by "impelling the community to tackle at one and the same time the problems involved in its development and those involved in its extension." De Gaulle also poses as the defender of the community's political integrity. But it is also possible to show that Britain's accession offers the best possibility of liberating the community from the stultifying impact which de Gaulle's organizational precepts have had on the community's institutional development.[21]

The Wilson government, as did the Macmillan one before it, has repeatedly stated that it accepted the political objectives of the Rome treaties, the institutions provided for therein, and the obligations which are thereby entailed. Indeed, Wilson, whose refusal to accept the political implications of the community has for years been a source of chagrin and disappointment to his socialist colleagues on the Continent, has lately insisted that those implications were the controlling and overriding reason for Britain's new candidacy. For example, in announcing on May 2, 1967, his government's decision to apply for accession, Wilson declared: "But whatever the economic arguments, the House will realize that, as I have repeatedly made clear, the government's purpose derives above all from our recognition that Europe is now faced with the opportunity of a great move

[21] "President de Gaulle has played an ironic role in the debate on American investment in Europe. The sharp knife of his nationalism has dissected and exposed latent problems which others have ignored. But, as in defense and politics, the logic of his own exposure [leads] inexorably to solutions sharply at variance with his own nationalist premise" (Christopher Layton, "European Pigmies, American Giant," *Encounter*, April 1967, pp. 74–82). Layton appears to have reached earlier the same general conclusions as Servan-Schreiber. "The industrial challenge from America, which President de Gaulle was the first to discern and diagnose, can thus be met only by the completion, in the industrial field, of the European union which the French President has been so reluctant to accept. . . . British participation is essential, above all in technology and science, where America's growing lead offers the biggest threat of all to the balance of the West's economy, and where Europe is so far merely on the threshold of a proper pooling of resources" (pp. 81–82). In the same article, Layton also diagnosed quite accurately the difficulties which overcame the European Launcher Development Organization (ELDO) a year later: "ELDO has shown that a space programme for Europe is absurd if it is conceived as a once-for-all project to be settled under a single agreement. Circumstances change; the costs of one scheme escalate; another suddenly becomes possible as technology advances. It is absurd for governments to be strait-jacketed by a choice between continuing an obsolete and expensive programme and ditching space cooperation altogether. What is needed is a much wider and more flexible programme, with some kind of central management institution capable of adjusting policy to events" (p. 82).

175

forward in political unity and that we can—and indeed must—play our full part in it."[22]

To be sure, neither on this nor on the other occasions when he has used this formulation did the Prime Minister state precisely how soon this move forward could be made (although he has mentioned the next ten or twenty years). He has suggested that "it is possible we may be able to get a much greater range of political unity in Europe without either advancing considerations of federal control of foreign policy or the creating of a European defense policy," and he has said that Britain's commitment to the community's institutions would be "neither more nor less" than that of the present members. Nevertheless, the fact remains that negotiations between Britain and the community could not be concluded without a decisive commitment from both parties as to the nature of that union. The extension of the communities would require the allocation of representation in the community institutions, presumably one commensurate with their respective national sizes and importance, to Britain and to the other applicants. As a *technical* matter, this should raise no substantial difficulty, although the necessary reshuffling would tend to accentuate the existing problem of overrepresentation of the smaller countries, confront some of them with the acceptance of only a rotating membership on the Commission (if the Commission were kept down to an efficient size), and perhaps reopen the long-stalemated question of popular election of the European Parliament.

However, these adjustments could not be effected without agreements of profound political significance. In a community more than a third again as large as now and more diverse, the Commission's power of initiative would appear more vital than ever, but the source

[22] For some of the more revealing remarks made in Commons on institutional questions, consult *Weekly Hansard*, 746, no. 723 (May 2, 1967), pp. 313, 314, 318, 326; and 746, no. 724 (May 8–10, 1967), pp. 1088–90, 1370, 1509, 1633. A passage from Wilson's address to the Parliamentary Labor Party on April 27, 1967, is also particularly revealing. After stating that it is the political arguments [for entry] which can be decisive," Wilson continued: "By political, I am not thinking primarily in institutional terms. The Foreign Secretary has said that the federal momentum towards a supranational Europe in which *all* issues of foreign and defense policy for example would be settled by majority voting has *for the moment at least* died away. Our decision must be based not so much on what might be, but on the *existing working of the community and of modern Europe*. I still believe that *for the immediately foreseeable future* this country would not—any more than would most of the community countries—contemplate a *rapid move* to a federal Europe. But it is also right to say—as the Foreign Secretary and I have said in Europe—that in all these matters we are prepared to accept the same obligations as our prospective Common Market colleagues—no more, no less."

of its mandate to speak for the community peoples would be all the more tenuous. As the head of an expanded bureaucracy disposing of even larger sums, would not democratic control of the Commission become even more imperative? Could a community with a GNP nearly two-thirds that of the United States continue to permit each of its ten members—four of them together accounting for less than 5 percent of the community's population—exercise a veto in such vital areas as the harmonization of legislation, initiation of new joint undertakings, or changing the arrangements by which the community is financed? If majority voting in the Council is essential to the exercise of effective presidential leadership by the Commission, what precise weight should be given the votes of each Council delegate, and how many votes should be required to constitute a qualified majority? On the other hand, if Council unanimity were still required to change a Commission proposal, might this not strengthen the Commission's hand too much?

If negotiations were undertaken, all these questions would be asked and answered in the context of the indecisive outcome of the 1965–66 crisis, and just as the Commission frequently sees British membership as the opportunity to consolidate the community on the economic front, so does it view that membership as the source of a categorical political imperative: that the member states restore and move beyond the institutional status quo ante of the Luxembourg settlement.

On the institutional requirements of an enlarged community the Commission said in its opinion of September 1967: "Any increase in the number of member states necessarily means that the institutional machinery of the communities may become more cumbersome. That is why the essential adaptation (of those institutions) must be brought about in such a way as to maintain the efficacy of the system and thus offset the mechanical effect of extension. . . . It would become even more necessary than in the present community for the institutional rules of the treaties to be applied *without being weakened in any way.*"[23]

On the necessity of executive leadership and majority voting in an enlarged community, the Commission stated: "The balance which has grown up between the community institutions and which entrusts the commission, in addition to its essential power of initiative, with responsibility for supervisory and administrative tasks in close

[23] Commission *Opinion*, p. 7.

liaison with the Council and the member states, *would have to be fully safeguarded.* . . . Where decisions are taken by the Council on a proposal from the Commission, the difficulties should not be unduly great if, on the one hand, the level of the qualified majority is so fixed that *it loses none of its power of dissuasion* should a member be tempted to prolong a debate indefinitely and if, on the other hand the Commission is able to play its full part in reconciling national interests *at the stage when* proposals are being drawn up."[24]

And on France's threat to withhold its vote in order to prevent a majority decision against a minority interest the Commission declared: "In a community consisting of a larger number of states, the community's dynamism would be more menaced by the tendency of the member states to refuse to assent to the majority point of view, even when their own interests were not seriously involved, or to make their acquiescence in decisions which did not affect their interests conditional on their obtaining concessions in other fields. This is a serious problem which would have to be solved during negotiations."[25]

Where in such negotiations would Britain stand? Wilson's more obvious hedging on the institutional issue since November 1966 has worried the proponents of British accession. In the context, however, of Wilson's tactical problems in negotiating accession, the evolution of British opinion toward Europe, and the situation as it exists in the community today, these concerns appear exaggerated. Even had Wilson's domestic political circumstances permitted him in early 1967 to endorse the concept of a strongly centralized Europe, it is doubtful that this would—*at that time*—have advanced his immediate objective of reopening the question of British admission to the EEC. A step-by-step approach, culminating in Britain's unequivocal acceptance of the community as it now exists, was probably the most and the best that could be hoped for.

The significance of that acceptance, however, should not be missed. Until the simple application for membership of May 10, 1967, the British approach could be construed to imply that basic features of the community might be reopened; in the course of such negotiations, the risk that Britain might seek to ease its entry with concessions to de Gaulle's views on political and institutional questions might therefore be a serious one. Obviously, one cannot say that

[24] *Ibid.*, p. 8. (Italics supplied.)
[25] *Ibid.*, p. 9.

this risk has now been eliminated entirely: Governments still do change in London, there are always those "statesmen" who are attracted to "deals," and how long the British can be expected to sustain a policy commitment which produces no results ought to be a question of greater moment to the community than it apparently is.

Nevertheless, *provided* Britain's admission is negotiated on the basis which London has now proposed, the fear of a Franco-British conspiracy against the community system does not seem a well-founded one. London accepted the community only after a fifteen-year search for alternatives to accepting it had failed; those now managing Britain's case have thus far proved immune to all the substitutes for full membership which have been proposed; they seem on the contrary wholly aware that the community's prime achievement is the creation of a pressing need for even greater unity; and there are few illusions in Britain or on the continent in 1968 that de Gaulle's Europe could somehow be converted into and managed as a triumvirate.

Unless therefore the community members themselves abandon their undertaking and reject the terms for admission which Britain has proposed—i.e., acceptance of the community—it is the requirements of efficiency and efficacy in an enlarged community which are likely in the end to seem more important than ideology or momentary tactical advantage. In a community of some 300 million people, with a GNP of some $500 billion a year, accounting for the largest proportion of world trade of any economic area, pursuing or beginning to pursue common agricultural, industrial, commercial, monetary, and cyclical policies, Britain—no less than the Commission, and no less than any of the present members save France—would recognize the need for central direction and a decision-making process which would work. The British would recognize that among the essential institutional features of such a community there would have to be an agency of sufficient independence and authority to represent the common interest and to propose policies in keeping with that interest, an agency or agencies to expose those policy proposals to the judgment of those affected by them, and an agency which without undue delay could eventually decide which policy proposals should become, in effect, community law.

In the new balance of power that would inevitably emerge in a new community of ten members, it is inconceivable that any one power, by itself or in combination with another, could achieve a

179

position of ascendancy from which it could determine the community's direction and decide its fate. The new equilibrium would permit the common institutional structure to resume exercise of its function of giving the community a policy which reflected the common interest rather than the prevailing interests of one or two of the members—including a foreign policy proportionate to the responsibilities of a great power and not the pretensions of a small one. These were, after all, the original objectives of the European movement, and they were the objectives which, after so many years of resisting, two British governments and both major parties finally accepted. If the community now rejects what Britain has accepted, it may find it has rejected as well the remaining opportunity to create the kind of European union with which the individual nations could at last identify their vital national interest.

As that indefatigable European, Lord Gladwyn, wrote in January 1967 on the eve of Wilson's tour of the EEC capitals: "No prospective British government could afford to acquiesce passively in an attempt to create either a 'Europe' without—that is to say against—our country, or one based on the admitted hegemony of any one European nation-state. . . . How, then, can 'Europe' be constituted at all unless it be by force, internally or externally applied? There is only one possible answer. Those European states which are now culturally, sociologically, economically, and indeed politically on much the same footing, and which are contiguous geographically, should come together in a 'community' in which decisions will, in all fields, increasingly be taken in common and in which, therefore, the general will, and not solely the will of the General, must in the long run prevail."[26]

[26] Lord Gladwyn, "Political Issues Must Dominate Coming EEC Talks," *The Times* (London), January 12, 1967.

Part IV: The Preservation of Europe

X

Writing in the spring of 1966 of the "compromise" which had just been effected at Luxembourg in February, Leon Lindberg suggested that the preceding clash between de Gaulle and the community did not necessarily contradict or invalidate the "spill-over" theories of integration.[1] Indeed, it might even have demonstrated "in a perverse sense . . . the 'tendency for economic and social decisions to spill over into the realm of the political, to arise from, and further influence the political aspirations of the major groupings and parties in democratic societies.' "[2]

Nevertheless, the crisis had, Lindberg believed, its unusual and disturbing aspects. It was a reminder of the extent to which *Grosspolitik* had not "lost its relevance." Unlike the community's previous crises, this was a dispute over institutions and rules, not economic policies, and it might be viewed "as a case of what can be a source of persistent tension in all political systems, and especially in incipient systems, i.e., the struggle over the form and content of the structures and procedures responsible for the making of authoritative decisions." Thus, for the first time, the European Movement seemed faced with the prospect that, despite the "infrastructure of integration" (i.e., the developing ties among community interests), the European community *system* (i.e., its institutions and rules) might not

[1] Lindberg, "Integration as a Source of Stress," p. 234.

[2] See Ernest B. Haas, *The Uniting of Europe: Political, Social, and Economic Forces, 1950–1957* (Stanford: Stanford University Press, 1958); and "International Integration: The European and the Universal Process," *International Organization*, 15 (1961), pp. 366–92.

be able to respond to the demands put on it and might collapse, "whether this took the form of a slow stagnation or a spectacular crash."[3]

In the concept of the European Community which we have set out heretofore—that its system involves, in addition to its institutions and operational code, a dedication to a common value and an equilibrium of power and influence among its participants—the possibility that the undertaking might not produce the anticipated results was similarly not excluded. In an evolutionary process such as the community envisages, the common goal is needed to assure that at each stage the political consequences of the progress made in the previous stages will be both known and accepted. The equilibrium is needed because the system must rely for its perpetuation on the absence of any rival power structure sufficiently strong to challenge it until such time as the process has produced its own power structure which, by itself or in alliance with existing power structures, is sufficient to assure that the process will continue to evolve.

From the inception of the community, de Gaulle has been at odds with this process. Since 1960 at least, it has been entirely clear that de Gaulle did not intend to accept *for France* the political implications of the advance toward economic integration. Since 1963, moreover, it has been equally evident that so long as the community system remained intact and therefore capable of resuming its development and so long as no other power structure developed within the community to rival France's advantageous position, de Gaulle has had no intention of admitting to the community an external power structure which would restore the preexisting equilibrium on which the community must be based.

For a variety of reasons, however, the contest between de Gaulle and the community system which seemed on the verge of producing a spectacular crash in 1965 has produced instead the slow stagnation which Lindberg foresaw as the other possibility. To effect a divorce between the infrastructure of integration and its logical consequences is possible, but it is not readily achieved. All the urgent tasks which confront the community point toward more integration and to the further political implications which these additional steps must have. No one could contend that, in the communal relationship of the Six, the Five have—in light of the French desertion—maintained

---

[3] Lindberg, "Integration as a Source of Stress," p. 236.

their own enthusiasm for the original contract. But commitments are less easily abandoned by responsive and responsible governments than by those who rule from Olympus, and even in the latter case, it is not always simple to convince a compliant electorate that what has been achieved should be risked—by desertion or incompletion—while political alternatives or chimeras are pursued.

To try to preserve the infrastructure of integration while discarding or permitting others to reject its implications, however, is not merely a matter of reconciling oneself to a drastic lowering of one's sights and the acceptance of second-best solutions. It may also involve a choice between abandoning the undertaking altogether and accepting—consciously or not—the alternative system. A Commission which is too cowed to lead, which does not act to preserve its independence, and which becomes merely the head of an administrative apparatus; a Council which has lost its collegial attributes, which has become merely the arena for finding the lowest common denominator among six national positions, and which cannot act even in extremis against the interest of a recalcitrant member; a Parliament which has no real influence over the community's decisions or its expenditures and which has no claim to a constituency; an atmosphere of suspicion, hostility, and supreme self-interest engendered by efforts of one member to preempt the right to speak for them all—this is not a pattern of relationships which the infrastructure of integration was intended to inspire. The European edifice becomes in these circumstances the foundation of a prison, and no wonder some of the Five hestitate now more than ever to proceed with the construction of the means to their own incarceration! "Real progress towards a really united Europe needs substantial concessions of national interest and national sovereignty—and who in Europe is going to concede anything to General de Gaulle?"[4]

On balance, one would be inclined to answer that no one will: The broad outlines of Gaullist foreign policy probably hold fewer attractions in western Europe in 1968 than at any time in the past ten years. Yet the record from the past is scarcely an unambiguous one. After the Luxembourg "compromise" in 1966, the community went on to conclude the Kennedy Round agreement, which on the whole was a monument to the Commission's initiative and ingenuity and to the determination of the Five to hold France to the bargain

[4] "Europe Desiccated," *The Times* (London), February 29, 1968.

which linked the trade negotiations schedule with the outstanding agricultural regulations. But, of course, France also got what it wanted. During the lengthy stalemate over the implementation of the treaty to fuse the community executives, France's attempts to purge the old Commission were beaten off for many months, but the new Commission—no doubt one of considerable competence—was appointed only after Hallstein had been sacrificed. For his part, de Gaulle was by no means shy about holding the future of the community in ransom in his campaign against the MLF. But no community country made any similar threat against France when it was disengaging itself from NATO—it was somehow thought more discreet to pretend that the community with all its political implications was a thing apart from the political maneuvers of its leading member.

These are the dimensions of the vacuum which exists in the center of Europe today and of the multiple dilemmas that emptiness has posed. The accomplishment of the community undertaking so far is the infrastructure of integration—economic and political—which has some of the attributes of a functioning economic-political system, superpower in scope. The void is the distance between the Common Market as it now exists and a truly regional economy; between the existing institutions, with the uncertain direction and guidance they are able to impart to the Common Market, and the institutions foreseen by the Rome treaties, which would be capable of taking the political decisions required to implement economic policies of community extent; and finally, it is the distance between a community operating in the economic sphere whose political impact is real but limited and unpredictable, and the political community to which it was intended to lead and to which there would ultimately accrue a jurisdiction commensurate with all the interests in common of the participants.

De Gaulle has amply demonstrated the possibility of preventing the transition from the present stage to the stages which lie an indefinite time in the future—in effect, of preventing the maturation of the political system on which the communiy is based. The possibility of such obstruction is one which remains open to *other* national powers which are of comparable size and which have freed themselves of the restraints normally associated with pluralistic societies. But de Gaulle has yet to demonstrate that he can fill the void with an alternative system—a French or a Franco-German imperium. Nor has he found it possible or yet seen it desirable to move decisively to break once and for all the ties which bind France to its community partners.

Europe's escape from this dilemma is contingent on the persistence and ultimate success of Britain's endeavor to assume its intended place within the community system. The decade of the sixties has fully established that the community *can* be made to work, and has amply recalled to London the magnitude of its mistake in declining to assume the proffered role when it was open. But the decade has also shown that Article 237 of the Common Market treaty, drafted with Britain in mind, was in fact an essential element in the whole community system. As many feared at the time, a community of six cut off from the rest of Europe is too small, lacking access not only to markets and irreplaceable technical skills, but also to the political genius of the most stable countries of Europe. And in particular because the balance of power contrived in the absence of Britain has been shown to be artificial and basically unstable, the community can no longer resolve the problems which its existence gives rise to and which, it was thought, would themselves contribute the necessary impetus.

To accept this is only the beginning of the search for a solution. Nothing that has transpired since December 19, 1967, has so far engendered the slightest hope that the second veto will be lifted during de Gaulle's term of office, nor has any movement of consequence suggested that time might ease the crisis of stagnation. But if the period of siege seems likely to be of some duration, this does not mean that those who wish the community to persist are without recourse. (1) *They ought to pursue every conceivable opportunity consistent with the community system which will contribute to the likelihood of Britain's accession at the earliest possible moment.* Since the crisis in the community is a fundamental one of balance this would be no less necessary, and conceivably more so, were the Gaullist regime expected to depart from France tomorrow.

(2) *They should diligently take every conceivable measure to sustain the British commitment to the European community at the level it reached in Wilson's offer to accept the Rome treaties virtually without condition.* Those who have been reluctant to push Britain's case to the limit on grounds that the community could not survive the withdrawal of France should ask themselves two questions: Can it survive the preponderance of any one power? Which country under

the present circumstances is the more likely to make a positive contribution to the further development of the community system— Gaullist France, which has committed itself to the overturning of that system, or the Britain in which the overwhelming parliamentary majority has now accepted it?

(3) *They must safeguard not only the infrastructure of integration, but the community system, until Britain's entry is achieved, while minimizing the risk of further entrapment in the competing system.*

For those who believe that Europe's future vocation is the construction of its own union, these injunctions are not so much a prescription for policy as a guideline or a test of policies which will in any case have to remain adventitious. The future is not foreseeable. The return of de Gaulle could not be anticipated by those who drafted the Rome treaties, nor can one know when and under what circumstances he will depart. The 1956 crisis in the Middle East contributed significantly to the conclusion of the Rome treaties, the 1967 crisis demonstrated the comparatively narrow confines within which something called "Europe" is operative, and no one could say when or if further turmoil in that or other areas of vital European interest would inspire another effort toward unity on the Continent or reveal its incapacity to act jointly for the protection of those interests. But, if there is agreement on the necessary conditions and objectives of unity, then it is possible to devise a policy of systematic exploitation of whatever opportunities arise, and even a period of stagnation might contribute in a negative way to movement toward the desired end. In fact, no movement might on occasion be far more profitable than an advance which accrued principally to the advantage of alternative or rival objectives.

A major factor in the community's failure has been the inability of the proponents of European unity to distinguish between the *requirements of the infrastructure* and the *demands of the system.* While de Gaulle, it is true, contributed to the negotiation of the main elements of the CAP which he later brought into crisis on systemic grounds, the absence within the community of a system-oriented policy is primarily the failure of the Five. France's Common Market "diplomacy" has achieved its objectives of the moment in return for vague promises to discuss the substantive and systemic objectives of the other members. All too often, in fact, some of the Five have lent themselves to the achievement of the Gaullist systemic goals.

Bonn's agreement to the unification of grain prices was a vital contribution to the infrastructure of the Common Market, but no government fully committed to the community system would have made its concession contingent on assurances that those prices would not be changed by subsequent majority vote. In 1967 when the community established a special committee—the so-called Marechal group—to consider technological cooperation, a policy of preserving and advancing the requirements of the community system would have led the Five to insist that this committee be subordinated to the Commission, not to the Council. In view of the majority voting provisions of the EEC treaty, the April 1968 offer of the Common Market to accelerate the Kennedy Round tariff reductions with the provision that *each* of the Six had satisfied itself that the United States in the meantime had introduced no measure of protection cannot be reconciled with any lively regard for the community as a political system. And since a system which is most likely to establish itself by accretion is most likely to suffer from slow attrition, it serves no great purpose to rush to the community's defense in times of obvious constitutional stress if, between times, the structure is simply permitted to erode.

To assure that any addition to the infrastructure of integration is tied into an advance in the community system, or at least involves no retreat, may not be enough, however, if the result is to reduce the possibilities for *future* defense of the system. In his article which followed the 1965–66 crisis, Professor Lindberg wrote that governments attempting to pursue a "business as usual" policy within the community might be incurring the "risks of subjecting themselves to unit-veto blackmail"—i.e., that France or Germany might take advantage of the "new opportunities made available by the system for influencing the behavior of partner countries and thus controlling the outcomes of the community system or for forcing policy preferences on extra-Community matters." In order to minimize these risks, Lindberg suggested that the weaker governments might seek "structural means" to prevent exploitation (upholding the Commission, limiting use of the veto), resort to "economic reprisals" against the offending country, or encourage procommunity political action within that country in order to inhibit its government's ability to have recourse to a blackmail policy. In addition, Professor Lindberg seemed to feel that these governments had the possibility of "holding back on future integrative commitments and accepting or promoting a weakening of central institutions and processes, either as a short-term strategy or as a long-term goal."[5]

To bring integration to a stop and to accept even a partial dismantling of the community's institutional structure *as a long-term goal* is tantamount to admission of defeat. It is to emulate de Gaulle's example and opt for freedom from the binding commitment which he himself has attempted to renounce. On the other hand, *as a short-term strategy* and particularly as a holding action until British entry is achieved, a refusal to make further commitments, *unless accompanied by parallel engagements to the community system*, might be an approach deserving consideration on a case by case basis. To agree to proceed with an additional undertaking in a Gaullist way may reduce the pressure to pursue the same objective in a truly integrative way, or it may mean that the appearance of a common undertaking conceals the reality that the objectives which will be achieved will be those primarily of France. No great prescience is required to see, for example, that this might well be the consequence of an acceptance of France's proposals for the future of EURATOM. There is, moreover, no impressive empirical evidence in Europe that cooperative enterprises evolve into integrated ones unless there are commitments to that objective in advance. If this is so, then there may in fact be instances in which, as we have said, a refusal to move to cope with recognized common problems on any other than an integrated basis would conserve the tension and stress in the system which would gradually improve the likelihood that this essential condition would in the long run be met.

Against these principles, how should one judge the various "initiatives" which have been launched since December 19, 1967, and which have as their reputed objective *the most expeditious possible movement toward Britain's entry, the preservation of Britain's pro-European stance, and the defense of the community as a system*? In the present situation of complete adamancy in Paris toward London's aspirations, whether any of the proposed substitutes for immediate negotiations on Britain's accession will long survive can only be surmised. In general, the proposals so far advanced—the Benelux, Italian, and German, as well as a Commission compilation of elements drawn from all three of them—have served to illumine the perils to the community of halfway measures and have demonstrated

---

[5] Lindberg, "Integration as a Source of Stress," pp. 263–64.

that, as *Agence Europe* has said, "between all or nothing, there is nothing."[6] They therefore deserve attention—not because they will necessarily lead to or away from Britain's accession—but because the consideration they receive is a further manifestation of the community's malaise.

German Proposals. The so-called German proposals stem from a view in Bonn—perhaps a transient one—that in light of the December 19 vote it is quixotic for London to hold out for full membership, and they reflect Chancellor Kiesinger's notion that patience and gradualism might prove more profitable. The proposals are also a product of Kiesinger's generous undertaking during his visit to Paris in February 1968 to spell out what de Gaulle might have had in mind with his repeated offers to Britain of "commercial arrangements." The main elements of this "spelling out" as they were discussed in a Council meeting in early March are: (1) a preferential trading area would be established between the community and the applicant countries, to consist in the industrial sector of a multilaterally agreed linear reduction in tariffs with a limited list of exceptions, and, in the agricultural sector, of bilaterally negotiated "long-term contracts" of purchase and supply; (2) while these arrangements would be intended to make Britain's membership easier, they would be negotiated under the EEC treaty provisions on trading policy, not Article 237; and (3) the community, having rapidly concluded its own consideration of its technological problem (the Marechal report), would then "study" with Britain the possibilities for "cooperation" in this area, a "special procedure" for cooperation between EURATOM and the United Kingdom might be laid down, and other forms of "cooperation" could be studied in matters of European company and patent law, and monetary and short-term economic policy.[7]

Apart from their vagueness, the main difficulties with the German proposals are that, though they "envisage" Britain's membership,

---

[6] *Agence Europe,* March 11, 1968.

[7] According to press reports, the German delegation to the May 30 meeting of the Council made certain "refinements" in the proposals submitted in March, stating in particular that the trade arrangement could be conceived only "in terms of and with a view to actual membership." After the arrangement was in operation for three years the Council would decide whether the necessary conditions for the opening of membership negotiations existed. These refinements reflect a sensitivity to the dilemma posed by French refusal to consider any approach to membership for the U.K., but they do not resolve it. A summary of the original German proposals and the reaction to them of the Commission and the other members of the Council was reported by the *Agence Europe,* March 9, 1968.

they do not necessarily lead toward it, nor do they lead toward a stronger and more integrated community—they point toward the reverse. By abandoning under French pressure its earlier suggestions for an automatic schedule negotiated within the context of Article 237, Bonn has denied Britain assurances that accession would occur even after the prescribed adjustments have been made. In effect, this is inviting Britain to attach itself as a kind of caboose to a train which is heading for an undisclosed destination to be determined by those in its cab.

That destination certainly would not be the integrated community with the functioning political system that the Rome treaties envisaged. Given the existence of the zone of free trade which is EFTA, the preferential arrangements linking Britain to the community would obviously have to be extended even beyond the other three applicants to those which have sought merely an association with the community or less. The prospect that the German proposals therefore hold out is not one which would be confined to some ten countries, but one involving some fifteen or more, several of which have not and would not accept any commitments to the principles of the treaties of Rome. Assuming that the offer to cooperate in non-trade fields—technology, monetary and economic policy—is a sincere one, can one possibly conceive that this would lead to or even facilitate agreement on the kind of integrated undertakings which have continued to elude the Six? On the contrary, in a Europe of inner and outer circles, the Gaullist-inspired centrifugal forces already so powerful at the center would be sustained and fortified by the attractive forces at the rim, and the community core would ultimately dissolve itself into the larger and more amorphous mass. Precisely for that reason the community has always rejected the ideas—often supported by Germany—for a simple European free trade zone, an EEC-EFTA trading arrangement, or Common Market "membership" in its trading rival.[8]

---

[8] In light of the self-serving assertions of some German leaders that London's insistence on full membership is a self-defeating, "all or nothing" attitude, London has responded gingerly to the proposals for some kind of interim commercial arrangement. There has thus far been no indication, however, that official circles have been intrigued by the possibility, and as long ago as last January, the then Foreign Secretary, George Brown, pointed out the difficulties very well. As reported by *Weekly Hansard* on January 24, 1968, Brown said: "The variety of possible forms of relationship with the Community which falls short of full membership is almost infinite, but one thing would be common to all: we should have a secondary, and, therefore, ineffective position in the institutions of the Community. We should have obligations with no corresponding powers. . . . As

192

Since France has made it clear that the German interpretation—even with the French-inspired amendments—goes beyond anything which de Gaulle has had in mind under the rubric of "association" for the U.K., and since it is also evident that a preferential agreement between Britain and the community would require negotiations no less protracted that those required by membership, one can only surmise what Bonn's purposes in undertaking the exercise might be. The charitable view is that, with the route to Britain's accession apparently blocked for the next few years at least, Bonn considers it useful to chip away at the roadblock in any way possible, to keep the issue alive, or to relegate it to an arena in which it is no longer an obstacle to the community's conduct of business as usual. At the same time the German "plan" enables the Kiesinger government to show at no great cost that it is pursuing a cause which it has repeatedly said was in Germany's national interest, while effectively precluding the other community countries from considering proposals which might cause Germany even greater difficulty with France.

But there is also the view that the plan reflects the policy of a government which no longer considers the preservation of the community system a desirable objective. These suspicions are loose in Europe today. "Germany has noted," the *Agence Europe* wrote in February 1968, "that it is impossible to make General de Gaulle change his mind on Britain and that the other alternative would be the destruction of the Community. In these circumstances, there is only one course open to Germany, which she must patiently follow: to improve her position in the Common Market . . . and to prepare herself to take over the first place now occupied by France in the Europe of the Six. But for this, Europe must remain the Europe of the Six, since Britain could successfully apply for this leadership. The

---

soon as the object of negotiations becomes something less than full membership all sorts of uncertainties about the object and areas of negotiation arise. We should certainly find the whole process of negotiations would take longer without there being any certainty that, at the end of our labors, the result would be immune from yet another French veto." It is true, of course, that so ardent a pro-European as Lord Gladwyn has speculated publicly about the possibility of a "delayed entry" for Britain—i.e., that Britain would sign the Rome treaties with a protocol which provided that, until the end of an agreed transitional period, the British would not be represented on the Council. It would, however, be consulted on all major decisions and would have observers on the Commission—the latter, so augmented, perhaps being authorized to consider matters connected with British membership and, as a last resort, to decide them by majority vote. (See "Europe—A Delayed Entry?," *Daily Telegraph* [London], June 15, 1967.) There is no reason at all to believe that de Gaulle would be interested in such a "compromise."

logical conclusion would be that Germany must now oppose British entry."[9]

Commission Proposals. In any case, Kiesinger's endorsement of the Gaullist formula for something less than full membership for Britain makes it difficult for the other principal parties to push for more. This is amply evident in the recommendations the Commission was prevailed upon to draft after the Council's abortive discussion of the German plan at the end of February.[10] The key proposal was an elaboration upon the possibilities of a commercial agreement between the community and the four applicants for membership. In industrial trade, there would be a limited linear reduction of tariffs, with more substantial cuts on items of technological significance and exceptions for sensitive products, and after this reduction had reached 30 percent, the applicant countries would begin aligning their tariffs on the community's CXT. Agricultural trade would be facilitated with "reciprocal preferences" at agreed prices approaching the community level. Once the Marechal group had completed its work—stymied since December 19 by a Dutch boycott—cooperation between Britain and the community in the technological field would be undertaken. The agreement would be valid for a predetermined period at the completion of which the Commission would submit an opinion on whether the applicants were ready for full membership. In the meantime, regular consultations between them and the community would have as their purpose the effecting of a gradual alignment of policies.

Were the Commission's plan acceptable to the French it would no doubt hold certain advantages over the German approach. It recognizes more clearly the relationship between commercial and economic policy and the need to accord the applicants a forum in which to present their views on community policy; it makes at least a limited tie-in between technological cooperation and the larger market which is an essential requirement of any significant undertaking in this field; and by involving the applicants in a gradual adoption of the Common Market's tariff structure and setting a specific date when the question of membership will again be considered, the Commission's proposals make an attempt to preserve some relationship between the commercial agreement and eventual accession. But no

[9] *Agence Europe*, February 20, 1968.

[10] The Commission's proposals are available in *Agence Europe*, April 4, 1968, Europe Document No. 471.

more than the German does the Commission's plan offer a guarantee of membership or say what would happen in the event of a third veto; while it insists that the further advance of the community ought not to be delayed, it does not say how the delaying impact of the continuing uncertainty over its future geographical and political dimensions could avert this; and it does not claim that it is something which could be negotiated so readily and advantageously that the British commitment to full membership will be conserved.

In any case, how could the Commission, the guardian of the community system, which in September 1967 saw Britain's accession as a potentially "decisive step forward towards the completion of the work for European unification," lend itself to a "compromise" which would hold no real promise of doing anything of the sort? Britain and the other applicants, still on the outside looking in, would not impel "the community to tackle at one and the same time the problems involved in its development and those involved in its extension": It would enable the community merely to delay. To offer the applicants an opportunity to "align" their policies with those of the community will contribute little or no assurance that those policies will befit a larger community with larger objectives. Nor will consultations between the community and the applicants in the Western European Union forum help the Commission to defend its power of initiative, to maintain the power of dissuasion implicit in the majority vote, and otherwise to assure that the institutional rules of the treaties will "be applied without being weakened in any way." For the Commission to have forgotten so soon that these were at one and the same time the rewards and the prerequisites of a successful accommodation with Britain bespeaks not only its timidity and lack of leadership, but a myopic view that to defend the present community is more important than to defend the system it represents.[11]

[11] The Commission has perhaps had second thoughts already about its April memorandum. In the July manifesto the Commission wrote: "The efforts to enlarge the community and unify the European continent must be resumed. The profound economic and social crisis in some of our countries, both within and without the community, has shown how far the destinies of the European states have become intermingled. The moment has come to face the implications of this fact." This was the the third of the four tasks which the Commission declared the community must accomplish in the next five years—the others being completion of the economic union, the enlistment of Europe's major economic and social forces in the construction of unity, *and* the revitalization of the community's institutions—the "reestablishment" of the Council "in its normal functioning as a body which can take majority decisions," the strengthening of the Commission's powers of initiative and management, and the popular election of a European Parliament with true budgetary and legislative functions.

Benelux Plan. It is in this context—the possibility that the community system may ultimately find its best defense in some parallel construction—that the plan which the Benelux countries submitted to their community partners and the four applicants in January 1968 has aroused an interest which its otherwise modest dimensions would have discouraged. Endorsed as "a basis for discussion" by the German and Italian foreign ministers[12] at a January WEU Council meeting but shunted aside by Bonn after Kiesinger's meeting with de Gaulle in mid-February,[13] the three-country memorandum is in the form of a statement of objectives and of proposals for action in the economic and political fields. The first part of the memorandum is a clear-cut reaffirmation of the desire of the Benelux countries to get on with the "European construction" in conformity with the letter and spirit of the Rome treaties. This, the memorandum states, implies *more than* the "development and the extension" of the European communities and the desirability of establishing (in the meantime) closer links between the members and the countries which have applied for membership. "When speaking of the European idea, it is necessary to go beyond words and the present situation of European economic construction within the framework of the treaty. In fact, Europe is not confined to the six countries which are united by the provisions of the Rome treaty. She must [also] continue her unification in *the fields which are not the subject of community decisions*." (Italics supplied.)

In the economic section, the memorandum renews the Benelux commitment to an active part in the development of the communities, but it also recommends the establishment of a "concrete procedure" to avoid "increased discrepancies" between them and the

---

[12] *Agence Europe*, January 30, 1968. The Italian endorsement was reportedly conditioned on the outcome of the Kiesinger-de Gaulle meeting. This caution as well as the subsequent decision of the Rome government to submit its own memorandum on the British question —rather than committing its all-out support to the Low Countries' initiative—is typical of the Italian performance in the community. The only significant contribution in the Italian memorandum was a proposal that the Commission be charged with a continuing examination of the problems of enlarging the community and how they might be resolved. Rome's proposals are available in *Agence Europe*, February 23, 1968, Europe Document No. 465.

[13] In an editorial on February 21, 1968, *Agence Europe* suggested that WEU consultations of the Five and the prospect that the Benelux plan might take on "considerable depth" accounted for de Gaulle's willingness to let the Germans explore the possibility of commercial arrangements for the British. From "the moment the Germans rallied to the French position," however, ". . . the Five no longer existed. . . ."

applicant countries. This should include, to begin with, a continued examination with the candidates of the problems involved in their accession, a task which might be entrusted to the Commission. Pending extension of the communities, however, two other steps should now be taken: (1) On matters within the community jurisdiction, a "well-defined procedure" for consultation should be instituted between the community and the applicants for membership to encourage a rapprochement among their respective policies and avert the adoption of measures which would make the communities' extension more difficult; and (2) in fields not covered by the treaties, "joint actions" should be undertaken by those countries wishing to participate, the number varying according to the project. These projects might include "development policy, joint production and purchase of military equipment, cooperation in the technological and scientific fields, and aid to developing countries."

In the political section, the memorandum simply states that "these proposals for European revival would not be complete without the strengthening of relations in the field of political unification." It thereupon notes that the three countries have for their part agreed to step up their political cooperation, and to that end have decided to consult with each other "before taking any decision or stand" on any major foreign policy problem, including those arising out of the North Atlantic, Rome, and Paris treaties, European political cooperation, relations with eastern Europe, and relations with the developing countries. "Without for the moment trying to set up a new institution," the Benelux countries therefore invite other European countries to "join in their experiment and thus give further proof of their will to achieve European political unification."[14]

The implications of the Benelux proposals have not on the whole been widely perceived except, perhaps, by those who saw in them the threat of a refusal to accept the December 19 veto as fait accompli. The renewal of de Gaulle's offer of a trade arrangement with Britain which Kiesinger helped to engineer during his visit to Paris in February 1968 and which the Commission was later drawn into has had the (intended?) effect of preventing the proposals from becoming the rallying point of the resistance to de Gaulle, and the events in France in May appear to have pushed them still further into the

[14] Text of Benelux proposals available in *Agence Europe*, January 29, 1968, Europe Document No. 462.

197

background. Nevertheless, the significance of what the three countries have proposed and offered to do ought not to be lost.

On the one hand, the Benelux plan accepts that the second veto may have brought to an end the line of development which began in 1955 with the foreign ministers conference in Messina. It suggests that the need to construct a line of defense against the Europe of the Fatherlands has perhaps become the stronger imperative of the moment than the need to proceed with the present community when to proceed might in fact weaken the community system. On the other hand, seeking to inspire the community undertaking with new life, the Benelux appeal to their partners to find the will and the courage to undertake a new "relaunching," equivalent in ingenuity and boldness to the one that began at Messina.

To elaborate, the Benelux plan is, from the first point of view, a proposed line of defense against Lindberg's "risk of unit-veto black-mail"—a risk too great to ignore, as the second rejection of Britain has shown. The proposed strategy is essentially to substitute a horizontal or lateral movement for the previous vertical movement or defense in depth. Since de Gaulle has called a halt to the intended institutional evolution of the community and since the Commission and majority voting can no longer be counted on as an effective guarantee against exploitation by dominant countries the Benelux countries propose to introduce into the community's policy-making machinery the views of the applicant countries. Any "well-defined consultative procedure" must, if it is meaningful, impose a certain restraint on the existing institutions, and the restoration of a political balance within them is purchased at the expense of abandoning for the time being at least any hope of restoring their intended method of operation. Moreover, since the extension of the community's jurisdiction into other fields of common endeavor can only be accomplished within the limits imposed by de Gaulle's preoccupation with the grandeur of France, and since of necessity any undertaking conforming to this condition must increase the risk of unit-veto blackmail, the Benelux countries in effect invite the other members and the applicants for membership to pursue the community's future in another context—one in which the Franco-German complex would no longer be the determining element.

The initially negative reaction to the Benelux plan on the part of President Rey, for example, is an understandable response to an implicit invitation to retreat from integration.[15] But fear of de Gaulle's threats is not, as Debre alleged, the beginning of wisdom: It begins in the realization by France's partners that Article 237 was an integral part of the Rome treaties and that the community's present difficulties stem in large part from the attempt to achieve its completion in the absence of its extension. The Benelux proposals offer the community a reasonable way of pursuing the examination of Britain's application for membership while assuring that the community and those who wish to join it do not in the meantime move in directions which would make membership more difficult. On the assumption that so long as de Gaulle is in power there is only the remotest possibility of Britain's entering the community *under conditions which would strengthen the community system*, the Benelux proposals also offer a chance to escape from the impasse to which the construction of European unity has been brought by the exclusive focus on a question which—it would appear—cannot now be resolved. As the *Agence Europe* wrote on January 29, 1968, "a dynamic policy and measures calculated to lead somewhere are vital if Europe is to emerge from a situation in which the acrimony and resurgent nationalism caused by acceptance of the vote can only lead to the community's being locked in a stranglehold." Comparing the Benelux memorandum to the note which the same three countries delivered to their community partners in the spring of 1955 and to the Messina Conference which followed, the paper added: "It [the initiative] is a headlong flight forwards—the only means of writing off what has gone, and thus of overcoming the difficulties."

Whether the Benelux proposals will in fact *provide* that means is beyond the range even of speculation, given the new variables which have entered the situation since the proposals were made. The peculiar talent of the regime in Paris is always to find allies in time, events, and inertia. As we have seen, to contain within the community the weakened France which emerged from the May "rebellion" is proving

[15] *Agence Europe* reported on January 23, 1968, that Rey told the European Parliament the Commission was categorically opposed to any moves intended to check the development of the community and to all "lateral moves outside the community whether they come from within or without." He apparently went on, however, to exclude the Benelux and German initiatives, *provided* they were based on the community. The Commission's responsibility is to defend the community and the threat posed by such initiatives as the Fouchet plan has no doubt made it sensitive to any suggestion that the community may no longer be the serviceable instrument of political unification. The defensive reflex may, however, serve only a limited purpose unless it is accompanied by positive action to re-create the conditions in which the advance towards unity can in fact be resumed.

no less preoccupying than to contain the strong France which before May was agressively exploiting its community ties to advance its own ends. A community under stronger pressure than ever to conserve what it has is not one given to proposing bold initiatives, and the kind of grinding crisis in which it now finds itself is one which produces manifestos like the Commission's but which does not necessarily produce the tensions from which there is no escape. The British question remains on the community agenda, and prospects are reasonably favorable that at least some of the bases for the objections to Britain's admission—e.g., the balance-of-payments deficit—will be removed. But, with a still further lapse of time, the British question can be made a burning issue only if London and its friends in the community act to make it so. And should this come about, the means at de Gaulle's disposal to prevent negotiations yet a third time, or to lead them into a blind alley, are surely not exhausted.

Moreover, there are other reasons—quite apart from the general situation which may prevail in the community—for fearing that the second Benelux initiative may lack the historical significance of the first one. The initiative has perhaps emanated from the wrong source because it is Britain which holds the key to the kind of community the Rome treaties aspired to build. The proposed line of action may be directed to the wrong purposes: To create more of the infrastructure of integration is a less urgent matter at the moment than to retrieve, preserve, and advance the community *system*—and new projects, functional ones, do not by themselves assure that. And, by foregoing "for the moment trying to set up an institution," the initiative may suffer from its excess of modesty: To translate the letter and spirit of the Rome treaties into the institutions of a political union of Europe, not to set those institutions aside, is, after all, the basic objective of the nearly two decades of effort.

If this is so, can one conceive the outlines and the opportunity for more promising approach? A bold strategist might wish to consider the circumstances in which a British government would decide conclusively to confirm that it has in fact drawn the full implications of its decision to seek to play its full part in the "opportunity of a great move forward in political unity" which Wilson said on May 2, 1967, is now facing Europe. In fact, as hopes have waned that any of the proposals advanced since the December veto will lead to the engagement of Britain in the task of retrieving the prospect of European unity, voices have been heard in Britain calling on the government to do just that. In the September 1968 issue of its journal, *Into Europe*, the pro-European organization Campaign for Europe urged Wilson to present proposals for a new community parallel to the EEC, open to all states wishing to join it, and having an agreed jurisdiction in such fields as technology, currency, foreign affairs, and defense. "The institutions of the new community," the journal suggested, "would be similar to the EEC but with stronger powers for a European Parliament, provisions for the transition to a directly elected assembly, and possibly a second chamber similar to the American Senate in which regional authorities would have equal representation. The community should be merged with the EEC as soon as this proved possible."[16]

Utopia? The foundations of Europe's unification are the product of monumental patience in the service of offers initially no less dramatic and courageous than this, and if those foundations threaten to rise no higher, it is because courage and patience seem to have failed. Since the inspired initiative which led to the Messina Conference and the Rome treaties, it is principally a dogged determination which first created and then preserved the working European structure that has now given way to stalemate in the elaboration and the extension of that structure. If patience and determination are lacking, may it not perhaps be a time when inspiration must suggest a means to leap over the impasse which has its source principally in the exclusion of Britain from the Common Market—a time for a "flight forward" which, while preserving the existing community, resolves the question of the institutions of the new Europe and its membership in a forum in which the deciding voice was not the present regime in France?

The Benelux proposals do in fact point in this direction—had they the courage of conviction. But, if a dialogue with Britain outside the existing community is to become the means of the community's preservation, that dialogue must *begin* as well as *end* with an acceptance of the community concept and its institutions. If the determination to do this were enunciated in the first instance by Britain, it would confirm beyond any remaining doubts the bona fides of its European aspirations, ensure itself against any backsliding from the commitment implied by its acceptance of the Rome

[16] "Britain Urged to Aim at a Europe Greater than EEC," *Manchester Guardian*, September 2, 1968.

treaties and make certain that a larger Europe will not be achieved at the price of one which is fatally weak.

To be sure, this is not the kind of undertaking in which a Gaullist France would joyfully join. But, assuredly, the Paris which has aspired to organize an exclusive Europe would not choose ultimately to exclude itself once that undertaking promised to become the focus of the new Europe.

XI   THE NECESSITY OF EUROPE

European unity will become a reality only if Britain is ultimately engaged in and fully committed to the system of unification which the European community has launched but cannot complete. The case for the community's extension, therefore, is the case for a European Union of a particular sort, achieved by a certain means. If we turn now briefly to the necessity of this Europe, we assume neither that union is ultimately inevitable and the counterarguments therefore irrelevant, nor that in the achievement of union, no costs are involved. But we do rely on what we have already set forth as a demonstration of the validity of the community as a concept of union and a technique for achieving it, on the historical fact that much of the controversy about European union is basically an argument about the feasibility of its attainment, and on the assumption that no European seriously argues for European disunity. Even de Gaulle professes himself a kind of European and propounds a system which would enable him to achieve objectives beyond his nation's capacities —a system in which the *other* participating nations must inevitably count for less.

It would be useless to deny that the skeptics are numerous who, attributing to the Europeans a naïveté and idealism which was never theirs, doubt not only that union is attainable but increasingly question that the objective is even desirable. Yet, the whole movement toward union was born of and addressed itself to the critical problems and questions which the European nations faced at the end of World War II—within their own boundaries, in their relations with each other, and in their need to create for themselves a new world role. In this sense the European movement was totally realistic and pragmatic—no less so than the motivations of those who supported the movement from outside and who saw in it a practical way of achieving their own goals in Europe. Many of those goals, problems, and questions are no less urgent in 1968 than in 1945, even though the skeptic and the weary may have come to feel the effort no longer worth the candle.

(1) In many quarters, it is the fashionable view that the political situation in western Europe is "stabilized" and that this stability has been achieved in a classical pattern. According to this view, the advance toward unity in postwar Europe is a less remarkable phenomenon than the restoration of the nations. These nations are no longer a threat to themselves or to others, it is thought, and if differences arise among them, they will be resolved by harmonious concert.

Yet even among the community members there is one country (Belgium) which is periodically on the brink of acrimonious disintegration along ethnic lines. The government of the leading community country came to power only ten years ago by coup de force, and twice since then, only by force or the threat of it have incipient rebellions been quelled. Its aging leader rules under a personalized constitution which has polarized the political forces between right and left, and while his tenure is obviously limited, one has yet to see the assured beginnings of a transitional regime. Germany, economically the most powerful of the community's members, though governed at the moment by coalition, still lacks the experience of peaceful alternation of parties; its primary foreign policy aspiration is territorial restitution; and the alienation between the generations is as deep as in any country in the world. Italy, the third of the "big three"—where modern totalitarianism had a quarter century incumbency—has had since then no effective democratic opposition; its social structure still belongs basically to an earlier century, and the effective restoration of the reformist coalition which collapsed early in 1968 is conjectural. On the fringes of the community, Greece and Turkey—associates of and candidates for membership—are periodically on the brink of domestic upheaval and war over an offshore island.

The community is the only indigenous regional stabilizing mechanism which holds any promise at all of permanence. In the past certainly, and if one may credit the polls, even now, the aspiration toward European union remains an outlet for and an alternative to the fulfillment of aspirations which are unattainable and therefore unsettling or which can be achieved only at great cost or at the risk of external controversy. Even in France, Europe is an ideal which continues to compete favorably with the attractions of national "grandeur." To the extent that aspirations are individual and material, the community is already a current reality—painful or profitable, as a worker who has lost a job in a marginal industry or as the entrepreneur who has found a new commercial outlet will testify. Although the Common Market is a single economic area only to a limited extent, the community exerts a certain restraint on the kind and magnitude of the national objectives which each of its members may pursue. It is not inconceivable that the community will produce— from the organizations of economic interests and the first stirrings in international labor—the European political action centers which would make the nation-states increasingly less relevant to the problems they share in common.

(2) Unless the conditions are reestablished in which such truly European political forces can develop and flourish, there is a real risk that the community's combination of resources will remain the target of the hegemonial aspirations of one power or another. Since the late 1950s we have come to recognize, if not necessarily to accept, that France has achieved a certain preponderance of influence in the western reaches of the Continent. De Gaulle has been able to achieve this for France principally because, relieved of any real concern for French security by the American commitment to Europe and freed by his prestige and the new constitution of the normal restraints of domestic political pressures, he could pursue a foreign policy of maximum flexibility and minimum commitment. And he has the bomb. But the very means by which France has achieved this preeminence are an indication that it will lose its lead, if indeed, it has not already begun its decline. A nuclear weapons system of modest and finite dimensions is probably a declining and, because of the resources it absorbs, possibly even a negative asset in the kind of competition one may reasonably expect in western Europe in the future; a foreign policy of unlimited maneuver and deception works only for a time and only against those who do not emulate it; de Gaulle will leave the scene and a return to political "normalcy" if not to utter confusion will follow in France. In the long run, other and more decisive ingredients of national power—national product, technology, discipline, etc.—will enter into the calculation of the

balance. In these circumstances, one might perhaps imagine a Sixth Republic returning to the strategies of the Fourth: to secure the maximum opportunity to intervene in and exercise restraint over the threatened ascendancy of another power by accepting such restraints itself. But will time and the opportunity always remain?

(3) The European powers have seen clearly the threat to their status as developed countries when the less-developed nations rapidly acquire the earlier attributes of industrialization and the Europeans have yet to discover the means to assure themselves of the later ones. The community offers the option of the "total" approach—i.e., the pooling of technical resources in combination with the economic infrastructure—a market of sufficient size, the right blend of concentration and competition, investment incentives, capital resources, and so on, which make up the essential underpinning of technological advancement. There are other options of course: Europe may choose to rely on imports of technological achievements engineered elsewhere; it may produce other Switzerlands and Swedens who have fully demonstrated their capacities to maintain the good life; or it may choose to claim whatever advantages there may be in bilateral or multilateral cooperation on specific projects. But to rely on others requires a political decision which has seemed increasingly unpalatable; small but prosperous countries usually operate in relation to favorable external circumstances—which may or may not include an entire Continent of similarly oriented neighbors; and while successful cooperative ventures in research and development are not unknown in Europe, the landscape is strewn with ones which were not. They fail because they do not spring from a political system which can establish priorities based on the common interest and secure the necessary allocation of resources as they are needed to guarantee that the projects will be completed.

(4) European and world peace requires the assurance that the most vital of political issues at the center of Europe, German reunification, will always be approached in a way which offers both the hope that the issue will be resolved and that European tranquillity will survive its achievement. There is the concept that German and European reunification are not two problems but one.[1] In one version of this view, the priority requirement is the creation in western Europe of conditions of unity which are sufficiently binding—and which are

[1] See, for example, Pierre Hassner, "German and European Reunification: Two Problems or One?," *Survey*, October 1966, pp. 14–35.

mutually acceptable because they are equally applicable—that the eastern third of Germany would rejoin the western two-thirds under a European, as opposed to a national or international, aegis. German national unity would be reestablished without restoration of the German Reich, without disruption to the intra-European equilibrium which the German "rebirth" would otherwise cause, and without a tipping of the balance in favor of East or West which would assure that German unity would not in either event occur. To the extent that a community defense system existed, the question of German national rearmament or disarmament would simply not arise.

Fantastic? Perhaps so for the immediate future, but much less so than the shortcuts which others have entertained. Kiesinger has publicly stated that he believes de Gaulle is in favor of German unity. Yet it is the advocacy of unification, not its achievement, which preserves the influence Paris now wields in Bonn. As Pierre Hassner has pointed out, it is the paradoxical effect of the liberalization in eastern Europe (which de Gaulle only belatedly espoused and which has shown its limitations in Czechoslovakia) that it must strengthen the political immobilism of East Germany (which is asked in the end to sacrifice its very existence) and confirm the Soviet military authorities in their belief in the necessity of retaining their western marches.[2] And in lieu of some organized community-security system, which de Gaulle would never accept, what inducements could France possibly offer to secure a Soviet military retreat? Disarmament and a Soviet-guaranteed neutralization of a greater Germany which the Germans themselves would never accept.

(5) Western Europe will profit from the liberating forces in eastern Europe only if those forces are channeled in directions which do not recreate and expand the historic tinderbox of the two world wars. However great the western advantage in gradual disintegration of the Soviet system in eastern Europe before the forceful reassertion of historic national identities, there is a point beyond which these trends are no longer benign. That point is reached when, in an area in which boundaries have been drawn and redrawn, the national self-assertions are no longer directed at the excess of Soviet predominance, but at each other; when national rivalries recreate the historic opportunities for meddling, intervention, or even expansionism from the west; and when the insistence on national independence prevents that modicum

---

[2] *Ibid.* Also Pierre Hassner, "Change and Security in Europe, Part I: The Background," Institute for Strategic Studies, Adelphi Papers No. 45, February 1968.

of cooperation and integration which the far more advanced western European countries have found essential to continued progress and prosperity.

It is alleged that a supranational organization of western Europe will hold few attractions for countries which, after nearly a quarter century of subordination to a foreign power, are rediscovering their nationhood. However, to retreat from the community undertaking for the sake of attracting nations whose economic and political structures make intimate cooperation with the west difficult in any case involves the risk (with no certain compensating gains) of extending balkanization from the east to the west. In fact, the community as it exists does hold some charm for eastern Europe and has more than a far distant implication. Poland, Yugoslavia, and Hungary have all recognized the advantage or necessity of at least limited contacts with the Common Market; Budapest has sought diplomatic relations; and since mid-1968, preparations have been under way in Brussels for the negotiating of a trade agreement with Belgrade. East European interest will surely increase when and if the community's common commercial policy—with regulations for exchanges with state-trading countries—comes fully into effect. Were Bonn willing to use it, the community might provide a useful means of contact with East Germany—and an *attracting* one. Even the Soviet Union, which has heretofore declined to accept the community as a reality, has had to accept that the price of a nonproliferation treaty is some kind of accommodation between the EURATOM and the IAEA's safeguards systems.

(6) Should U.S. military involvement in western Europe one day prove for foreign or domestic reasons no longer indefinitely extendable, an alternative means of assuring European stability and security must be found. The rock of necessity on which the present Alliance system rests is the absence of any generally acceptable alternative to it. France, on whose geography and air space the Alliance must depend, remains an ally in name only and a conditional one at that, and the Gaullist regime—prior to the May 1968 eruption—broadly hinted at its embarkation on an "all azimuth" defense strategy which implies its abandonment of even the bilateral type of arrangements it had held out as an alternative to an alliance policy. The nuclear forces of Britain and France are increasingly burdensome and decreasingly impressive except perhaps in the western European region. Neither has come to terms with the rapid advancements of missile

technology, and Paris may find its national priorities increasingly competitive. The will of the other members to maintain their conventional forces has for some years drifted downward, and great optimism is required to believe that the Soviet occupation of Czechoslovakia has reversed the trend. Nor does past experience encourage great hope that the endeavor to expand on NATO's nonmilitary role will produce significant results.

Yet, the Europeans are very short on alternatives to NATO. They are painfully aware that an American withdrawal, even were they to judge it feasible on security grounds, would bring back into significance the balance of military power *within* western Europe which has been rendered insignificant for some twenty years by the great American preponderance. Germany's aspirations have never been directed toward achieving a nuclear parity with the U.S.—but with France and Britain—and we have seen the destabilizing consequences of one attempt to redress its disadvantage. Bilateral security commitments among the key members of the old alliance must inevitably require a careful balancing of commitments—and incur the risk of competing "special relationships." And one must ponder what a system of bilateral commitments might lead to were *key* allies to become involved in the kind of competition which has prevailed in recent years between such lesser allies as Greece and Turkey.

In short, until the conditions of durable balance and unity are created within western Europe the alternatives to the military system in which the U.S. provides the balance and carries the principal burden appear unpromising. If this is so, then Europe was far closer to a viable alternative in the mid-1950s than it has been at any point since, and it is to some kind of a community defense arrangement that Europe must ultimately return.

(7) The formula is yet to be found which would assure the most fruitful cooperation generally between Europe and the U.S. Purportedly in the cause of European unity, much has been said and written in recent years about U.S.-European "equality" and the Atlantic "partnership," with rather indifferent results. Even if a Europe were wholly and efficiently united, the prospect that it would soon challenge the American superiority in economic, military, and political influence is on the whole a remote one. Nor is it more than mythological to believe that once Europe is united it will proceed hand-in-hand with the United States in doing good deeds around the world. The working together will be confined to those areas in

which common interests are established. Other interests may not be shared, and still others will diverge and compete. If there are those who conceive of partnership as an extension of the area of compliance, the disillusion with European unity will soon be complete; too many clashes have already occurred.

There is on the other hand an equally peculiar notion that in the uniting of several fractious small countries one can legitimately expect only an equally fractious—and more powerful—whole. Obviously, much will depend on *how* the unification was achieved and how the resulting entity is governed. If achieved through and governed by the exercise of force by its most disagreeable and most powerful member, then the union will serve the rebellious or peevish objectives of that member. If achieved by fair negotiation and common consent and directed by some kind of representative institution, it is entirely reasonable to expect that the competition of interests within and among the constituent parts will produce a measure of moderation. Just as it is a matter of world concern which candidate wins the U.S. presidency, just as the world would rest a bit easier if Soviet policy were determined in a free and open society, so is it a matter of world concern how Europe is united and how its policy is determined. The last war if not the ones before it should have made that clear. Moreover, those who have little faith that Europe, united in a pluralistic society, is more likely to be benign than otherwise may take some comfort from perspective. If you are small, you sometimes have to be more aggressive than if you are big.

In any case, the justifications for European Union are to be found in its consequences for Europe itself: the maximization of its potential and the responsible application of that potential—inward and outward—to the solution of problems which the Europeans themselves will recognize as their own. On balance, it has been the American experience with the community that where unity is greatest, the results have been most satisfying. The conversion of such historically high-tariff countries as France and Italy into countries of modest or low tariffs and the successful negotiation of a 35 percent average reduction in tariffs by the industrialized countries of the world might have been made more urgent by the Common Market, but it could scarcely have been achieved without it. EURATOM's safeguards system has appeared to many an annoying obstacle to the conclusion of the nonproliferation treaty, but it has also provided the means by which West Germany and Italy could accept controls which would have been politically unacceptable as unilateral commitments. And EURATOM is the means by which some form of international surveillance can be maintained in a France which has spurned the thought of any international control. Even in the international monetary sphere, where the community's powers are legally only hortatory, one could scarcely conceive of the present government of France having been dragged into the Rio accords and having merely abstained on their confirmation in Stockholm but for its reluctance to incur at that particular time another break with its community partners.

(8) And finally, all these questions are subsumed within the ultimate one, the kind of force one wishes Europe to exercise in the world in the remaining third of the twentieth century: a small force or a large one, an unpredictable one or a responsible and responsive one. To accept the permanence of the diminution of European influence in the world is to accept consequences which go far beyond the confines of Europe. It is not only a waste of resources potentially available to the Europeans, it is a waste of what a more prosperous Europe could contribute directly to those less fortunate. It is the even greater loss of the predictable advancements which follow when two, three, or more great civilizations come in friendly contact with, stimulate, support, and compete with each other.

To be content with little Europe is not only to be content with the continuation of the postulated advantages of coexistence—or, as it has become politically more acceptable to call it, bipolarism with varying degrees of ascendancy attributed to one pole or the other, but also to accept the risks inherent in preserving the model by relying on the ability of the two mightiest powers always to calculate in every situation the appropriate applications of force or restraint. What is needed is another element in the calculation: not an unpredictable, floating voter who acts to tip the balance to enhance his own advantage, but a force which by its very existence has reduced substantially the chances that an intra-European quarrel will ignite a great conflict. If the great need of the day is an increase in the areas of regional stability, where better to complete its achievement than in the third most powerful region of the world?.

But, if one aspires to see what Europe can still do for the world in a responsive and responsible way, having perhaps its own capacities to exercise a stabilizing and nonincendiary influence elsewhere, then the vital question is how that Europe comes into being and for what purpose. Anguished by the continental expressions of satisfaction that Britain, by abandoning her commitments east of Suez, terminating her world role, and preparing to give up part of her monetary and financial role, is providing "palpable, long-awaited proof" that she is finally becoming European, the *Agence Europe* wrote last January: "The Europeans' view of their own Continent must have sunk low indeed for such comments to be made. To be European, they are saying, a touch of poverty is essential. Ambition is out. Someone else must take thought for world affairs. Back to the fields, back to our little garden where we will cultivate the plant Modesty. . . . Exalting such withdrawal as an eminently European virtue strikes us as the blackest feature of our age. We wanted Britain in Europe just because she is a great country—because she has a past, but most of all, a future. Only insofar as France is strong, Germany, Italy, and the Benelux countries are strong, will Europe have her say."

To imagine how this might be done at this particular stage in history after so many stages have passed requires a certain concept which, while sui generis in its European application, derives nonetheless from a larger concept of human behavior. After all, it takes no great insight to recognize that de Gaulle's quarrel is not solely with the community; it is a dispute with a certain approach to the conduct of world affairs. His is an affinity for old realities, like the nation-state and its requirements, and for old forces, which, like gold, are not only immutable, impartial, and universal, but also irrational. The community perhaps belongs to that school which considers that the human condition requires the continuation of patient efforts to bring such realities and forces under human control.

INDEX

Adenauer, Konrad, 123, 124
Agricultural Guidance and Guarantee Fund (FEOGA): established, 14; functioning described, 75–76; impact of U.K. accession, 151–52
Agricultural policy, common (CAP): Commission objectives, 74, 77–78, 79, 80, 87, 88; Council decisions of December 1964, 82–83; dairy surpluses, 34, 35, 37; described, 14; early development, 73–83 *passim*; estimated costs, 15; federal character, 14; French interest in, 74, 78–79, 87; main characteristics, 74–75; price-fixing problems, 34; strains on system, 35; and U.K., 169.
—financing of: Britain and Law 25, 160–61; Commission's proposals of April 1965, 84–85; consequences for Britain, 82; expected member receipts and contributions—1963, 77–78; Law 25, 75–78; new decisions needed by 1970, 170; and parliamentary control, 170–71
Agriculture: in Britain, 149; percent of GNP in EEC, 30–31

Barre, Raymond, 155, 156
Belgium: insecurity of nationhood, 204; national priority for workers, 32; views on capital market, 18
Belgium-Luxembourg (BLEU): trade within EEC, 31
Benelux countries: plan for lateral ties with U.K., 196–99; unreliable "Europeans," 125, 126; weighted role in EC institutions, 60
Benelux Union, 57
Boyer de la Giroday, F.: on monetary integration, 47
British membership in the communities: agricultural financing, 151–52; agricultural policy, 169; agricultural questions in first application, 149–50; application form in 1961, 139–40; broader implications of, 137, 138; and commercial policy, 163–64; Commission opinion on first veto, 135, 135n, 136; Commission opinion on second application, summarized, 136, 138; and CAP review, 150–51; common external tariff, 145; Commonwealth problems, 146; community association policy, 148; and community solidarity, 160; and community trade patterns, 163; Council impasse, December

THE JOHNS HOPKINS PRESS

Designed by James Wageman

Composed in Primer, with Antique (Modern) No. 26
and Karnak Black display, by Monotype Composition Company, Inc.

Printed offset on 60 lb. P&S R by Universal Lithographers, Inc.

Bound in Columbia Riverside Vellum RV-3492 by L.H. Jenkins